Lecture Notes in Computer Science

Lecture Notes in Computer Science 5812

Commenced Publication in 1973
Founding and Former Series Editors:
Gerhard Goos, Juris Hartmanis, and Jan van Leeuwen

Ute Schmid Emanuel Kitzelmann
Rinus Plasmeijer (Eds.)

Approaches and Applications of Inductive Programming

Third International Workshop, AAIP 2009
Edinburgh, UK, September 4, 2009
Revised Papers

Volume Editors

Ute Schmid
Emanuel Kitzelmann
Otto-Friedrich-Universität Bamberg
Fakultät Wirtschaftsinformatik und Angewandte Informatik
96045 Bamberg, Germany
E-mail: {ute.schmid,emanuel.kitzelmann}@uni-bamberg.de

Rinus Plasmeijer
Radboud University Nijmegen
Institute for Computing and Information Sciences
6525AJ Nijmegen, The Netherlands
E-mail: rinus@cs.ru.nl

Library of Congress Control Number: 2010923416

CR Subject Classification (1998): I.2, D.2, F.3, H.3, D.3, F.4.1

LNCS Sublibrary: SL 2 – Programming and Software Engineering

ISSN 0302-9743
ISBN-10 3-642-11930-1 Springer Berlin Heidelberg New York
ISBN-13 978-3-642-11930-9 Springer Berlin Heidelberg New York

springer.com

Printed in Germany

Typesetting: Camera-ready by author, data conversion by Scientific Publishing Services, Chennai, India
Printed on acid-free paper 06/3180

To Phil Summers
who laid the foundation

Preface

Inductive programming is concerned with the automated construction of declarative – often functional – recursive programs from incomplete specifications such as input/output examples. The inferred program must be correct with respect to the provided examples in a generalizing sense: it should be neither equivalent to it, nor inconsistent. Inductive programming algorithms are guided explicitly or implicitly by a language bias (the class of programs that can be induced) and a search bias (determining which generalized program is constructed first). Induction strategies are either generate-and-test or example-driven. In generate-and-test approaches, hypotheses about candidate programs are generated independently from the given specifications. Program candidates are tested against the given specification and one or more of the best evaluated candidates are developed further. In analytical approaches, candidate programs are constructed in an example-driven way. While generate-and-test approaches can – in principle – construct any kind of program, analytical approaches have a more limited scope. On the other hand, efficiency of induction is much higher in analytical approaches.

Inductive programming is still mainly a topic of basic research, exploring how the intellectual ability of humans to infer generalized recursive procedures from incomplete evidence can be captured in the form of synthesis methods. Intended applications are mainly in the domain of programming assistance – either to relieve professional programmers from routine tasks or to enable non-programmers to some limited form of end-user programming. Furthermore, in future, inductive programming techniques might be applied to further areas such as support inference of lemmata in theorem proving or learning grammar rules.

Inductive automated program construction has been originally addressed by researchers in artificial intelligence and machine learning. During the last few years, some work on exploiting induction techniques has been started also in the functional programming community. Therefore, the third workshop on "Approaches and Applications of Inductive Programming" took place for the first time in conjunction with the ACM SIGPLAN International Conference on Functional Programming (ICFP 2009). The first and second workshop were associated with the International Conference on Machine Learning (ICML 2005) and the European Conference on Machine Learning (ECML 2007).

AAIP 2009 aimed to bring together researchers from the field of inductive functional programming from the functional programming and the artificial intelligence communities and advance fruitful interactions between these communities with respect to programming techniques for inductive programming algorithms, identification of challenge problems and potential applications. Accordingly, the organizers as well as the Program Committee and the reviewers consisted of members from both communities.

The workshop was enriched by three invited talks from members of the functional programming community and we want to thank Lennart Augustsson, Pieter Koopman and Neil Mitchell for their support. We are very grateful to Martin Hofmann, who invested much of his time to support the workshop organization. Furthermore, we want to thank all presenters for submitting their work to our workshop and all attendants for stimulating discussions.

We are proud that all authors of accepted workshop papers as well as two of the invited speakers provided revised papers for this proceedings publication. Thereby we can present a rather representative selection of current research in the field of inductive programming. For everybody interested in inductive programming, we recommend visiting the website www.inductive-programming.org.

December 2009

Ute Schmid
Emanuel Kitzelmann
Rinus Plasmeijer

Organization

Organizing Committee

Ute Schmid	University of Bamberg, Germany
Emanuel Kitzelmann	University of Bamberg, Germany
Rinus Plasmeijer	Radboud University Nijmegen, The Netherlands
Technical Support	Martin Hofmann, University of Bamberg, Germany

Program Committee

Pierre Flener	Uppsala University, Sweden
Lutz Hamel	University of Rhode Island, Kingston, USA
Jose Hernandez-Orallo	Technical University of Valencia, Spain
Johan Jeuring	University of Utrecht, The Netherlands
Susumu Katayama	University of Miyazaki, Japan
Pieter Koopman	Radboud University Nijmegen, The Netherlands
Oleg G. Monakhov	Russian Academy of Sciences, Siberian Branch, Russia
Ricardo Aler Mur	Universidad Carlos III de Madrid, Spain
Roland Olsson	Ostfold College, Norway
Maria José Ramírez Quintana	Technical University of Valencia, Spain

Board of Reviewers

All members of the Organizing Committee and of the Program Committee served as reviewers for the workshop and the proceeding submissions. In addition, we thank the following external reviewers:

Wolfgang Jeltsch	BTU Cottbus, Germany
Janis Voigtländer	University of Bonn, Germany

Table of Contents

Invited Papers

Regular Papers

Deriving a Relationship from a Single Example

Neil Mitchell

http://community.haskell.org/~ndm

Abstract. Given an appropriate domain specific language (DSL), it is possible to describe the relationship between Haskell data types and many generic functions, typically type-class instances. While describing the relationship is possible, it is not always an easy task. There is an alternative – simply give one example output for a carefully chosen input, and have the relationship derived.

When deriving a relationship from only one example, it is important that the derived relationship is the intended one. We identify general restrictions on the DSL, and on the provided example, to ensure a level of predictability. We then apply these restrictions in practice, to derive the relationship between Haskell data types and generic functions. We have used our scheme in the DERIVE tool, where over 60% of type classes are derived from a single example.

1 Introduction

In Haskell [22], *type classes* [29] are used to provide similar operations for many data types. For each data type of interest, a user must define an associated instance. The instance definitions usually follow a highly regular pattern. Many libraries define new type classes, for example Trinder et. al. [27] define the NFData type class, which reduces a value to normal form. As an example, we can define a data type to describe some computer programming languages, and provide an NFData instance:

```
data Language = Haskell [Extension] Compiler
              | Whitespace
              | Java Version

instance NFData Languge where
  rnf (Haskell x1 x2) = rnf x1 `seq` rnf x2 `seq` ()
  rnf (Whitespace   ) = ()
  rnf (Java x1      ) = rnf x1 `seq` ()
```

We also need to define NFData instances for lists, and each of the data types Extension, Compiler and Version. Any instance of NFData follows naturally from the structure of the data type: for each constructor, all fields have seq applied, before returning ().

Writing an NFData instance for a single simple data type is easy – but for multiple complex data types the effort can be substantial. The standard solution

U. Schmid, E. Kitzelmann, and R. Plasmeijer (Eds.): AAIP 2009, LNCS 5812, pp. 1–24, 2010.

is to express the *relationship* between a data type and it's instance. In standard tools, such as DrIFT [30], the person describing a relationship must be familiar with both the representation of a data type, and various code-generation functions. The result is that specifying a relationship is not as straightforward as one might hope.

Using the techniques described in this paper, these relationships can often be automatically inferred from a single example. To define the generation of *all* NFData instances, we require an example to be given for the Sample data type:

```
data Sample α = First
              | Second α α
              | Third α

instance NFData α ⇒ NFData (Sample α) where
  rnf (First        ) = ()
  rnf (Second x1 x2) = rnf x1 `seq` rnf x2 `seq` ()
  rnf (Third x1     ) = rnf x1 `seq` ()
```

The NFData instance for Sample follows the same pattern as for Language. From this example, we can infer the general relationship. However, there are many possible relationships between the Sample data type and the instance above – for example the relationship might always generate an instance for Sample, regardless of the input type. We overcome this problem by requiring the relationship to be written in a domain specific language (DSL), and that the example has certain properties (see §2). With these restrictions, we can regain predictability.

1.1 Contributions

This paper makes the following contributions:

- We describe a scheme which allows us to infer predictable and correct relationships (§2).
- We describe how this scheme is applicable to instance generation (§3).
- We outline a method for deriving a relationship in our DSL, without resorting to unguided search (§4).
- We give results (§5), including reasons why our inference fails (§5.1). In our experience, over 60% of Haskell type classes can be derived using our method.

2 Our Derivation Scheme

In this section we define a general scheme for deriving relationships, which we later use to derive type-class instance generators. In general terms, a function takes an input to an output. In our case, we restrict ourselves to functions that can be described by a value of a DSL (domain specific language). The person defining a derivation scheme is required to define suitable types named Input, Output and the DSL. To use a value of DSL, we need an apply function to serve as an interpreter, which takes a DSL value and an input and produces an output:

apply :: DSL → Input → Output

Now we turn to the derivation scheme. Given a single result of the Output type, for a particular sample Input, we wish to derive a suitable DSL. It may not be possible to derive a suitable DSL, so our derivation function must allow for the possibility of failure. Instead of producing at most one DSL, we instead produce a list of DSLs, following the lead of Wadler [28]:

sample :: Input
derive :: Output → [DSL]

We require instantiations of our scheme to have two properties – correctness (it works) and predictability (it is what the user intended). We now define both of these properties more formally, along with restrictions necessary to achieve them.

2.1 Correctness

The derivation of a particular output is correct if all derived DSLs, when applied to the sample input, produce the original output:

$\forall\, o \in \mathsf{Output} \bullet \forall\, d \in \mathsf{derive}\ o \bullet \mathsf{apply}\ d\ \mathsf{sample} \equiv o$

Note that given an incorrect derive function it is possible to create a correct derive function by simply filtering out the incorrect results – correctness can be tested inside the derive function.

2.2 Predictability

A derived relationship is predictable if the user can be confident that it matches their expectations. In particular, we don't want the user to have to understand the complex derive function to be confident the relationship matches their intuition. In this section we attempt to simplify the task of defining predictable derivation schemes.

Before defining predictability, it is useful to define congruence of DSLs. We define two DSLs to be congruent ($\cong$), if for every input they produce identical results – i.e. $\mathsf{apply}\ d_1 \equiv \mathsf{apply}\ d_2$.

$d_1 \cong d_2 \Longleftrightarrow \forall\, i \in \mathsf{Input} \bullet \mathsf{apply}\ d_1\ i \equiv \mathsf{apply}\ d_2\ i$

Our derive function returns a list of suitable DSLs. To ensure consistency, it is important that the DSLs are all congruent – allowing us to choose any DSL as the answer.

$\forall\, o \in \mathsf{Output} \bullet \forall\, d_1, d_2 \in \mathsf{derive}\ o \bullet d_1 \cong d_2$

This property is dependent on the implementation of the derive function, so is insufficient for ensuring predictability. To ensure predictability we require that *all* results which give the same answer on the sample input are congruent:

$\forall\, \mathsf{d_1, d_2 \in DSL \bullet apply\ d_1\ sample \equiv apply\ d_2\ sample \Rightarrow d_1 \cong d_2}$

The combination of this predictability property and the correctness property from §2.1 implies the consistency property. It is important to note that predictability does not impose conditions on the derive function, only on the DSL, the apply function and the sample input.

2.3 Scheme Roles

The creation and use of a derivation scheme can be split into separate roles, perhaps completed by different people, each focusing on only a few aspects of the scheme.

The scheme creator defines the Input, Output and DSL types, the apply function, and the sample value of type Input (§3). Their choice must satisfy the predictability property (§3.4).

The derivation function author defines the derive function (§4). They may choose to ensure the correctness property, or filter the results. They do not need to concern themselves with predictability.

The relationship creator gives an appropriate output based on the previously defined sample input (§1 and examples throughout). In order to ensure their relationship matches their intuition, they may wish to familiarise themselves with some details of the DSL, but hopefully these will not be too onerous.

The relationship user simply gives an input, and receives an output – the output will always be what the relationship creator intended.

3 Deriving Instances

In this section we apply the scheme from §2 to the problem of deriving type class instances. We let the output type be Haskell source code and the input type be a representation of algebraic data types. The DSL contains features such as list manipulation, constant values, folds and maps. We first describe each type in detail, then discuss the restrictions necessary to satisfy the predictability property.

3.1 Output

We wish to generate any sequence of Haskell declarations, where a declaration is typically a function definition or type class instance. There are several ways to represent a sequence of declarations:

String. A sequence of Haskell declarations can be represented as the string of the program text. However, the lack of structure in a string poses several problems. When constructing strings it is easy to generate invalid programs, particularly given the indentation and layout requirements of Haskell. It is also hard to recover structure from the program that is likely to be useful for deriving relationships.

Pretty printing combinators. Some tools such as DrIFT [30] generate Haskell code using pretty printing combinators. These combinators supply more structure than strings, but the structure is linked to the presentation, rather than the meaning of constructs.

Typed abstract syntax tree (AST). The standard representation of Haskell source code is a typed AST – an AST where different types of fragment (i.e. declarations, expressions and patterns) are restricted to different positions within the tree. The first version of DERIVE used a typed AST, specifically Template Haskell [24]. This approach preserves all the structure, and makes it reasonably easy to ensure the generated program is syntactically correct. By combining a typed AST with a parser and pretty printer we can convert between strings as necessary.

Untyped abstract syntax tree (AST). An untyped AST is an AST where all fragments have the same type, and types do not restrict where a fragment may be placed. The removal of types increases the number of invalid programs that can be represented – for example a declaration could occur where an expression was expected. However, by removing types we make it easier to express some operations that operate on the tree in a uniform manner.

For our purposes, it is clear that both strings and pretty printing combinators are unsuitable – they lack sufficient structure to implement the derive operation. The choice between a typed and untyped AST is one of safety vs simplicity. The use of a typed AST in the first version of DERIVE caused many complexities – notably the DSL was hard to represent in a well-typed manner and some functions had to be duplicated for each type. The loss of safety from using an untyped AST is not too serious, as both DSLs and ASTs are automatically generated, rather than being written by hand. Therefore, we chose to use untyped ASTs for the current version of DERIVE. We discuss possible changes to regain type safety in §7.

While we work internally with an untyped AST, existing Haskell libraries for working with ASTs use types. To allow the use of existing libraries we start from a typed AST and collapse it to a single type, using the Scrap Your Boilerplate generic programming library [16,17].

The use of Template Haskell in the first version of DERIVE provided a number of advantages – it is built in to GHC and can represent a large range of Haskell programs. Unfortunately, there were also a number of problems:

- Being integrated in to GHC ensures Template Haskell is available everywhere GHC is, but also means that Template Haskell cannot be upgraded separately. Users of older versions of GHC cannot take advantage of improvements to Template Haskell, and every GHC upgrade requires modifications to DERIVE.

- Template Haskell does not support new GHC extensions – they are often implemented several years later. For example, Template Haskell does not yet support view patterns.
- Template Haskell allows generated instances to be used easily by GHC compiled programs, but it makes the construction of a standalone preprocessor harder.
- If Template Haskell is also used to read the input data type (as it was in the first version of DERIVE) then only data types contained in compilable modules can be used. In particular, all necessary libraries must be compiled before an instance could be generated.
- The API of Template Haskell is relatively complex, and has some inconsistencies. In particular the Q monad caused much frustration.

We have implemented the current version of DERIVE using the haskell-src-exts library [2]. The haskell-src-exts library is well maintained, supports most Haskell extensions[1] and operates purely as a library. We convert the typed AST of haskell-src-exts to a universal data type:

```
data Output = OString String
            | OInt Int
            | OList [Output]
            | OApp String [Output]
```

OString and OInt represent strings and integers. The OList constructor generates a list from a sequence of Output values. The expression OApp c xs represents the constructor c with fields xs. For example Just [1, 2] would be represented by the expression OApp "Just" [OList [OInt 1, OInt 2]]. These constructed values represent the AST defined by haskell-src-exts, so can represent all of Haskell – e.g. a case expression would be OApp "Case" [on, alts].

Our Output type can represent many impossible values, for example the expression OApp "Just" [] (wrong number of fields) or OApp "Maybe" [] (not a constructor). We consider any Output value that does not represent a haskell-src-exts value to be an error. The root Output value must represent a value of type [Decl]. We can translate between our Output type and the haskell-src-exts type [Decl]:

```
toOutput   :: [Decl] → Output
fromOutput :: Output → [Decl]
```

We have implemented these functions using the SYB generics library [17], specifically we have implemented the more general:

```
toOut   :: Data α ⇒ α → Output
fromOut :: Data α ⇒ Output → α
```

These functions are partial – they only succeed if the Output value represents a well-typed haskell-src-exts value. When operating on the Output type, we are

[1] Haskell-src-exts supports even more extensions than GHC!

```
data DSL
      -- Constants
   = String String
   | Int Int
   | List [DSL]
   | App String DSL  {-[α] -}
      -- Operations
   | Concat DSL  {-[[α]] -}
   | Reverse DSL  {-[α] -}
   | ShowInt DSL  {-Int -}
      -- Fold
   | Fold DSL DSL
   | Head
   | Tail
      -- Constructors
   | MapCtor DSL
   | CtorIndex
   | CtorArity
   | CtorName
      -- Fields
   | MapField DSL
   | FieldIndex
      -- Custom
   | DataName
   | Application DSL  {-[Exp] -}
   | Instance [String] String DSL  {-[InstDecl] -}
```

Fig. 1. DSL data type

working without type safety. However, provided all DSL values are constructed by derive, and that derive only constructs well-formed DSL values, our fromOutput function will be safe.

3.2 Input

While the output type is largely dictated by the need to generate Haskell, we have more freedom with the input type. The input type represents Haskell data types, but we can choose which details to include, and thus which relationships we can represent. For example, we can include the module name in which the data type is defined, or we can omit this detail. We choose not to include the module name, which eliminates some derivations, for example the Typeable type class [16].

```
apply :: DSL → Input → Output
apply dsl input = applyEnv dsl Env {envInput = input}

data Env = Env {envInput :: Input, envCtor :: Ctor,
                envField :: Int,     envFold :: (Output, Output)}

applyEnv :: DSL → Env → Output
applyEnv dsl env@(Env input ctor field fold) = f dsl
  where
  vars = take (dataVars input) $ map (:[]) ['a' ..]

  f (Instance ctx hd body) = OApp "InstDecl"
    [toOut [ClassA (UnQual $ Ident c) [TyVar $ Ident v] | v ← vars, c ← ctx]
    , toOut $ UnQual $ Ident hd
    , toOut [foldl TyApp (TyCon $ UnQual $ Ident $ dataName input)
      [TyVar $ Ident v | v ← vars]]
    , f body]
  f (Application (f → OList xs)) = foldl1 (λa b → OApp "App" [a, b]) xs
  f (MapCtor dsl) = OList [applyEnv dsl env {envCtor = c}
    | c ← dataCtors input]
  f (MapField dsl) = OList [applyEnv dsl env {envField = i}
    | i ← [1 .. ctorArity ctor]]

  f DataName     = OString $ dataName input
  f CtorName     = OString $ ctorName ctor
  f CtorArity    = OInt    $ ctorArity ctor
  f CtorIndex    = OInt    $ ctorIndex ctor
  f FieldIndex   = OInt    $ field

  f Head = fst fold
  f Tail = snd fold
  f (Fold cons (f → OList xs)) =
    foldr1 (λa b → applyEnv cons env {envFold = (a, b)}) xs

  f (List xs) = OList $ map f xs
  f (Reverse (f → OList xs           )) = OList $ reverse xs
  f (Concat  (f → OList []           )) = OList []
  f (Concat  (f → OList xs           )) = foldr1 g xs
      where g (OList   x) (OList   y) = OList   (x ++ y)
            g (OString x) (OString y) = OString (x ++ y)
  f (String x) = OString x
  f (Int x) = OInt x
  f (ShowInt (f → OInt x)) = OString $ show x
  f (App x (f → OList ys)) = OApp x ys
```

Fig. 2. The apply function

Our Input type represents algebraic data types. We include details such as the arity of each constructor (ctorArity), the 0-based index of each constructor (ctorIndex) and the number of type variables (dataVars), but omit details such as types and record field names. Our Input type is:

```
data Input = Input {dataName :: String, dataVars :: Int, dataCtors :: [Ctor]}
data Ctor  = Ctor {ctorName :: String, ctorIndex :: Int, ctorArity :: Int}
```

Values of Input for the Sample data type and the Language data type (both defined in §1) are:

```
sampleType :: Input
sampleType = Input "Sample" 1
  [Ctor "First"  0 0
  ,Ctor "Second" 1 2
  ,Ctor "Third"  2 1]

languageType :: Input
languageType = Input "Language" 0
  [Ctor "Haskell"    0 2
  ,Ctor "Whitespace" 1 0
  ,Ctor "Java"       2 1]
```

The Input constructor contains the name of the data type, and the number of type variables the data type takes. For each constructor we record the name, 0-based index, and arity. These choices allow derivations to depend on the arity or index of a constructor, but not the types of a constructors arguments. In §5 we consider possible extensions to the Input type.

3.3 DSL

Our DSL type is given in Figure 1, and our apply function is given in Figure 2. The operations in the DSL are split in to six groups – we first give a high-level overview of the DSL, then return to each group in detail. The apply function is written in terms of applyEnv, where an environment is passed including the input data type, and other optional fields. Some functions in the DSL add to the environment (i.e. MapCtor), while others read from the environment (i.e. CtorName). Any operation reading a value from the environment must be nested within an operation placing that value in the environment.

Some operations require particular types – for example Reverse requires it's argument to evaluate to OList. Where possible we have annotated these restrictions in the DSL definition using comments. We have used view patterns, as implemented in GHC 6.10 [25], to perform matches on the evaluated argument DSLs. Our use of view patterns can be understood with the simple translation[2]:

[2] View-patterns and pattern-guards in GHC have different scoping behaviour, but this difference does not effect our apply function.

f (Reverse (f → OList xs)) = ...
 ≡
f (Reverse v_1) | OList xs ← f v_1 = ...
 ≡
f (Reverse v_1) | **case** v_2 **of** OList { } → True; _ → False = ...
 where v_2 = f v_1; OList xs = v_2

Some operations have restrictions on what their arguments must evaluate to, and what environment values must be available. It would be possible to capture many of these invariants using either phantom types [4] or GADTs [23]. However, for simplicity, we choose not to.

Constants. We include constants in our DSL, so we can lift values of Output to values of DSL. The String, Int, List operations are directly equivalent to the corresponding Output values. The App constructor is similar to OApp, but instead of taking a *list* of arguments, App takes a single argument, which must evaluate to an OList. Requiring an OList rather than an explicit list allows the arguments to App to be constructed by operations such as Reverse or Concat.

Operations. The operations group consists of useful functions for manipulating lists, strings and integers. The operations have been added as required, based on functions in the Haskell Prelude. The Concat operation corresponds to concat, and concatenates either a list of lists, or a list of strings. The Reverse operation performs reverse on a list. The ShowInt operation performs show, converting an integer to a string. We do not provide an append or (++) operation, but one can be created from a combination of List and Concat.

Some examples of these operations in use are:

Concat (List [String "hello ", String "world"]) ≡ OString "hello world"
Reverse (List [Int 1, Int 2, Int 3]) ≡ OList [OInt 3, OInt 2, OInt 1]
ShowInt (Int 42) ≡ OString "42"

Fold. The Fold operation corresponds to foldr1, but can be combined with Reverse to simulate foldl1. The first argument of Fold is a function – a DSL containing Head and Tail operations. The second argument must evaluate to a list containing at least one element. If the list has exactly one element, that is the result. If there is more than one element, then Head is replaced by the first element, and Tail is replaced by a fold over the remaining elements. This can be described by:

Fold fn [x] = x
Fold fn (x : xs) = fn [x / Head, Fold fn xs / Tail]

For example, to implement concat in terms of an Append operation would be Fold (Append Head Tail) (ignoring the case of the empty list). The fold operation is more complicated than the previous operations, but may still be useful to other DSLs.

Constructors. To insert information from the constructors we provide MapCtor. This operation generates a list, with the argument DSL evaluated once with each different constructor in the environment. The argument to MapCtor may contain CtorName, CtorIndex and CtorArity operations, which retrieve the information associated with the constructor. CtorName produces a string, while the others produce integers. An example of MapCtor on the Sample data type is:

```
MapCtor CtorName ≡ OList
  [OString "First", OString "Second", OString "Third"]
```

Fields. The MapField operation is similar to MapCtor, but maps over each field within a constructor. MapField is only valid within MapCtor. Within MapField, the FieldIndex operation returns the 1-based index of the current field. While most indexing in Haskell is 0-based, fields usually correspond to variable indices (i.e. x_1), which tend to be 1-based. As an example of MapField, using Second as the constructor in the environment:

```
Concat (List [List [CtorName],
  MapField (Concat (List [String "v", ShowInt FieldIndex]))])
  ≡ ["Second", "v1", "v2"]
```

Custom. The final set of operations are all specific to our particular problem. The simplest operation in this group is DataName, which returns the string corresponding to the name of the data type.

The second operation is Application. The haskell-src-exts library uses binary application, where multiple applications are often nested – we provide Application to represent vector application. Vector application is often used to call constructors with arguments resulting from MapField.

The final operation is Instance, and is used to represent a common pattern of instance declaration. For example, given the type Either α β, a typical instance declaration might be:

instance (Show α, Ord α, Show β, Ord β) $\Rightarrow$ ShowOrd (Either α β) **where** ...

This pattern requires each type variable to be a member of a set of type classes. The resulting instance construction is:

```
Instance ["Show", "Ord"] "ShowOrd" ...
```

The Instance fields describe which classes are required for each type variable (i.e. Show and Ord in this example), what the main class is (i.e. ShowOrd), and a DSL to generate the body. To specify this pattern without a specific Instance operation would require operations over type variables – something we do not support.

3.4 Restrictions for Predictability

To ensure predictability there must be no non-congruent DSL values which give equal results when applied to the sample input (see §2.2). Currently this invariant is violated – consider the counterexample DataName vs String "Sample". When applied to the sample input, both will generate OString "Sample", but when applied to other data types they generate different values. To regain predictability we impose three additional restrictions on the DSL:

1. The strings Sample, First, Second and Third cannot be contained in any String construction. Therefore, in the above example, String "Sample" is invalid.
2. All instances must be constructed with Instance.
3. Within MapCtor we require that the argument DSL *must* include CtorName.

We have already seen an example of the first restriction in practice, and the second restriction has similar motivation – to avoid making something constant when it should not be. Now let us examine the third restriction, with a practical example:

```
instance Arities (Sample α) where
  arities _ = [0, 2, 1]
```

Given this instance, we could either infer the arities function always returns [0, 2, 1], or it returns the arity of each constructor. While a human can spot the intention, there is a potential ambiguity. Using the third restriction, we conclude that this must represent the constant operation. To derive a version returning the arities we can write:

```
instance Arities (Sample α) where
  arities _ = [const 0 First{}, const 2 Second{}, const 1 Third{}]
```

While this code is more verbose, any good optimiser (e.g. GHC [25]) will generate identical code.

While our DSL has forms of iteration (i.e. MapCtor), it does not have any conditional constructs such as **if** or **case**. The lack of conditionals is deliberate – to maintain predictability every branch of every conditional would need to be exercised by a different constructor or field in the Sample type, thus increasing the size of Sample.

The restrictions in this section aim to ensure that no fragment of output can be represented by both a constant and be parameterised by the data type. The Sample type ensures no fragment can be parameterised in multiple ways, by having different arity/index values for some constructors – explaining why the Second constructor has arity 2, while the Third has arity 1. We believe that the restrictions in this section, along with the Sample data type, ensure predictability. We have not proved the predictability property, but we have checked it using QuickCheck [3]. We do not see any reason this property could not be proven more formally, but leave this task as future work.

4 Implementing derive

This section covers the implementation of a derive function, as described in §2. There are many ways to write a derive function, our approach is merely one option – we hope that the scheme we have described provides ample opportunity for experimentation.

Before implementing derive it is useful to think about which properties are desirable. It is easy to ensure correctness by filtering incorrect results (see §2.1), but our method chooses to only generate correct results. We follow all the restrictions in §3.4, which we believe ensure predictability. We want our derive function to terminate, and ideally terminate within a reasonable time bound. Finally, we would like the derive function to find an answer if one exists, i.e.:

$$\forall\, \mathsf{o} \in \mathsf{Output}, \mathsf{d} \in \mathsf{DSL} \bullet \mathsf{null}\ (\mathsf{derive}\ \mathsf{o}) \Rightarrow \mathsf{apply}\ \mathsf{d}\ \mathsf{sample} \not\equiv \mathsf{o}$$

We were unable to implement a derive function meeting this property for our problem which performed acceptably. Our method is a trade off between runtime and success rate, with a particular desire to succeed for real-world examples.

Our derive implementation is based around a parameterised guess. Each fragment of output is related to a guess – a DSL parameterised by some aspect of the environment. For example, OString "First" results in the guess CtorName parameterised by the first constructor. Concretely, our central Guess type is:

```
data Guess = Guess DSL
           | GuessCtr Int DSL   -- 0-based index
           | GuessFld Int DSL   -- 1-based index

derive :: Output → [DSL]
derive o = [d | Guess d ← guess o]

guess :: Output → [Guess]
```

Applying guess (OString "First") produces a guess of GuessCtr 0 CtorName. The GuessCtr and GuessFld guesses are parameterised by either constructors or fields, and can only occur within MapCtor or MapField respectively. The Guess guess is either parameterised by the entire data type, or is a constant which does not refer to the environment at all.

To generate a guess for the entire output, we start by generating guesses for each leaf node of the Output value, then work upwards combining them. If at any point we see an opportunity to apply one of our custom rules (i.e. Instance), we do so. The important considerations are how we create guesses for the leaves, how we combine guesses together, and where we apply our custom rules. We require that all generated guesses are correct, defined by:

$$\forall\, \mathsf{o} \in \mathsf{Output} \bullet \forall\, \mathsf{g} \in \mathsf{guess}\ \mathsf{o} \bullet \mathsf{applyGuess}\ \mathsf{g} \equiv \mathsf{o}$$

```
applyGuess :: Guess → Output
applyGuess (Guess      d) = applyEnv d Env {envInput = sample}
```

```
applyGuess (GuessCtr i d) = applyEnv d Env {envInput = sample, envCtor = c}
  where c = dataCtors sample !! i
applyGuess (GuessFld i d) = applyEnv d Env {envInput = sample, envField = i}
```

4.1 Guessing Constant Leafs

String To guess an OString value is simple – if it has a banned substring (i.e. Sample or one of the constructors) we generate an appropriately parameterised guess, otherwise we use the constant string. Some examples:

```
OString "hello" ≡ Guess (String "hello")
OString "Sample" ≡ Guess DataName
OString "First" ≡ GuessCtr 0 CtorName
OString "isThird" ≡ GuessCtr 2 (Concat (List [String "is", CtorName]))
```

Application. The guess for an OApp is composed of two parts – the name of the constructor to apply and the list of arguments. The name of the constructor in App always exactly matches that in OApp. The arguments to App are created by applying guess to the list, and wrapping the generated DSL in App op. The guess for OApp can be written as:

```
guess (OApp op xs) = map (lift (App op)) (guess (OList xs))

lift :: (DSL → DSL) → Guess → Guess
lift f (Guess      d) = Guess      (f d)
lift f (GuessCtr i d) = GuessCtr i (f d)
lift f (GuessFld i d) = GuessFld i (f d)
```

Integer. Given an integer there may be several suitable guesses. An integer could be a constant, a constructor index or arity, or a field index. We can guess an OInt as follows:

```
guess (OInt i) =
  [GuessFld i  FieldIndex | i ∈ [1, 2]] ++
  [GuessCtr 1 CtorIndex  | i ≡ 1] ++
  [GuessCtr 1 CtorArity  | i ≡ 2] ++
  [Guess (Int i)]
```

And some examples:

```
OInt 0 ≡ [Guess (Int 0)]
OInt 1 ≡ [GuessFld 1 FieldIndex, GuessCtr 1 CtorIndex, Guess (Int 1)]
OInt 2 ≡ [GuessFld 2 FieldIndex, GuessCtr 1 CtorArity, Guess (Int 2)]
OInt 3 ≡ [Guess (Int 3)]
```

When guessing an OInt, we never generate guesses for any constructors other than Second (represented by GuessCtr 1) – the reason is explained in §4.2.

4.2 Lists

Lists are the most complex values to guess. To guess a list requires a list of suitable guesses for each element, which can be collapsed into a single guess. Given a suitable collapse function we can write:

```
guess (OList xs) =
  mapMaybe (liftM fromLists ∘ collapse ∘ toLists) (mapM guess xs)

fromLists = lift Concat
toLists   = map (lift (λx → List [x]))

collapse :: [Guess] → Maybe Guess
```

The mapM function uses the list monad to generate all possible sequences of lists. The toLists function lifts each guess to a singleton list, and the fromLists function concatenates the results – allowing adjacent guesses to be collapsed without changing the result type. The function collapse applies the following three rules, returning a Just result if any possible sequence of rule applications reduces the list to a singleton element.

Promotion. The promotion rule adds a parameter to a guess. We can promote Guess to either GuessFld or GuessCtr, with any parameter value. The value Guess d, can be promoted to either of GuessCtr i d or GuessFld i d, for any index i. The promotion rule does not reduce the number of elements in the list, but allows other rules to apply, in particular the conjunction rule.

Conjunction. If two adjacent guesses have the same parameter value, they can be combined in to one guess. For example, given GuessCtr 2 d_1 and GuessCtr 2 d_2 we produce GuessCtr 2 (Concat (List $[d_1, d_2]$)). This rule shows the importance of each guess evaluating to a list.

Sequence. The sequence rule introduces either MapField or MapCtor from a list of guesses. Given two adjacent guesses we can apply the rule:

```
(GuessFld 1 d₁) (GuessFld 2 d₂)
  | applyGuess (GuessFld 2 d₁) ≡ applyGuess (GuessFld 2 d₂)
  = GuessCtr 1 (MapField d₁)
```

It is important that the fields are in the correct order, one of the DSL values (in this case d_1) is applicable to both problems, and the resultant guess is parameterised by the Second constructor (which has two fields). We also permit sequences in reverse order, which we generate by reversing the list before, and inserting a Reverse afterwards.

The sequence construction for fields can be extended to constructors by demanding three guesses parameterised by consecutive constructors. For constructors we only check using the DSL relating to the Second constructor, as this DSL is the only one that could have a MapField construct within it. Because we only test against the Second DSL, we can avoid generating CtorArity and CtorIndex guesses for the other constructors. We also require that when creating a MapCtor the guess contains a CtorName, to ensure the restrictions from §3.4 are met.

4.3 Folds

The addition of fold to our DSL is practically motivated – a number of real derivations require it. Currently we only attempt to find folds in a few special cases. We require folds to start with one of the following patterns:

```
OApp m [OApp m [x, op, y], op, z]
OApp m [x, op, OApp m [y, op, z]]
```

Given such a pattern, we continue down the tree finding all matching patterns of op and m. After constructing a fold we then apply guess to the residual list.

4.4 Application

As with fold, the introduction of Application is practically motivated. We replace any sequence of left-nested OApp "App" expressions with Application.

4.5 Instance

As per the restrictions given in §3.4, the only way of creating an Instance value as output is to use the Instance DSL operator – it is forbidden to use App "Instance". Given this restriction, we translate values to Instance where they follow the pattern set out in §3.3.

5 Results

This section discusses the results of using our automatic derivation scheme on real examples. We first categorise the instances we are unable to derive, then share some of the tricks we have developed to succeed with more examples. For each limitation we discuss possible modifications to our system to overcome it. Finally we give timing measurements for our implementation.

5.1 Limitations of Automatic Derivation

The instance generation scheme given is not complete – there exist instances whose generator cannot be determined. The DERIVE tool [21] generates instances for user defined data types. Of the 24 instances supported by DERIVE, 15 are derived from one example, while 9 require hand-written instance generators. All the examples which can't be derived are due to the choices of abstraction in our Input type. We now discuss each of the pieces of information lacking from Input that result in some instances being inexpressible.

Module Names. Some type classes require information about the module containing a type, for example Typeable instances [16] follow the pattern:

```
typename_Language = mkTyCon "ModuleName.Language"

instance Typeable Language where
  typeOf _ = mkTyConApp typename_Language []
```

The Typeable class performs runtime type comparison, so each distinct type needs a distinct string to compare, and the module name is used to disambiguate. Our Input type does not include the module name, so cannot be used to derive Typeable. It would be possible to define the string "Module.Name" as the module name of the sample, and treat it in a similar manner to the string "Sample". However, the only instance we are aware of that requires the module name is Typeable, so we do not provide module information.

Infix Constructors. Some instances treat infix constructors differently, for example the Show instance on a prefix constructor is:

```
instance Show PrefixConstructor where
  show (Prefix x y) = "Prefix " ++ show x ++ " " ++ show y
```

But using an infix constructor:

```
instance Show InfixConstructor where
  show (x :+: y) = show x ++ " :+: " ++ show y
```

Our Input type does not express whether a constructor is infix or prefix, so cannot choose the appropriate behaviour. The loss of infix information mainly effects instances which display information to the user, i.e. Show and pretty printing [10]. For most type classes, the infix information is not used, and infix constructors can be bracketed and treated as prefix (:+:). To deal with infix constructors would require an infix constructor added to the Sample data type, and modifications to the DSL to allow different results to be generated depending on infix information. These changes would pose difficulties to predictability and require all example instances to have at least one additional case defined – we do not consider this a worthwhile trade off for a small number of additional instances.

Record-based definitions. Haskell provides records, which allow some fields to be labelled. Some operations make use of the record fields within a data type, for example using the data type:

```
data Computer = Desktop {memory :: Int}
              | Laptop  {memory :: Int, weight :: Int}
```

It is easy to write the definition:

```
hasWeight Desktop{} = False
hasWeight Laptop{}  = True
```

Where hasWeight returns True if the weight selector is valid for that constructor, and False if weight $x \equiv \perp$. Unfortunately our Input type does not contain information about records, so cannot express this definition. There are only a few type classes which exhibit label specific behaviour, such as Show which outputs the field name if present.

Record fields are not present in our Sample type, but could be added. The difficulty is that Haskell allows for one field name to be shared by multiple constructors, and allows some constructors to have field names while others do not. This flexibility results in a massive number of possible combinations, and so a Sample type with sufficient generality would require many constructors. Allowing records would be more feasible for a language such as F#, where records contain only one constructor and all fields must be named.

Type-based definitions Our Sample data type has a simple type structure, and our DSL does not allow decisions to be made on the basis of type – these restrictions means some type classes can't be defined. For example, a Monoid instance processes items of the same type using mappend, but items of a different type using mempty. Several other type classes require type specific behaviour, including Functor, Traversable and Uniplate.

The lack of type information has other consequences. For example, we can write the definition:

```
fromFirst  (First        ) = const First{}  $ tuple0
fromSecond (Second x1 x2) = const Second{} $ tuple2 x1 x2
fromThird  (Third  x1    ) = const Third{}  $ tuple1 x1
```

This function returns the elements contained within a constructor, generalising operations such as fromJust, and has seen extensive use in the Yhc compiler [26]. When compiled with GHC this code generates a warning that no top-level type signatures have been given. These type signatures can be inferred, but the Haddock documentation tool [18] won't include functions lacking type signatures. Without type information in Input, we can't generate appropriate type signatures.

We see no easy way to include type information in our derivation scheme – types are varied, and different type classes make use of different type information. It may be possible to identify some restricted type information that could be used for a subset of type-based instances, but we have not done so.

5.2 Practical Experiences

This section describes our experiences with specifying instances in a form suitable for derivation. Ideally, we would write all instances in a natural way, but sometimes we need to make concessions to our derivation algorithm. Using the techniques given here, it seems possible to write most instances which are based on information included in the Input type.

Brackets Matter. The original DERIVE program used Template Haskell, which does not include brackets in the abstract syntax tree. For example, the expressions (First) and First are considered equal. However, using haskell-src-exts, brackets are explicit and care must be taken to ensure every constructor has the same level of bracketing. Examples of otherwise unnecessary brackets can be seen with fromFirst in §5.1, where the constructor First is bracketed. This restriction could be lifted if all brackets were removed before processing, then minimal brackets were added back afterwards.

Variable Naming. When naming variables it is important that a sequence of variables follow a pattern. For example, in §5.1 we use Second x_1 x_2, rather than Second x y. By naming variables with consecutive numbers we are able to derive the fields correctly.

Explicit Fold Base-Case. When performing a fold, it is important to explicitly include the base-case. In the introductory example of NFData the Second alternative is specified as rnf x_1 \`seq\` rnf x_2 \`seq\` (), however we can show that:

$\forall$ x $\bullet$ rnf x \`seq\` () $\equiv$ rnf x

Therefore we could write the Second alternative more compactly as the expression rnf x_1 \`seq\` rnf x_2. However, doing so would mean there was not one consistent pattern suitable for all constructors, and the derivation would fail. In general, when considering folds, the base-case should always be written explicitly.

Empty Record Construction. One useful feature of Haskell records is the empty record construction. The expression Second{} evaluates to Second $\perp$ $\perp$. This expression is useful for generating constructors to pass as the second argument to const[3], for some generic programming operations, and for values that are lazily evaluated. The pattern Second{} matches all Second constructors, regardless of their fields.

Constructor Count. Some instances aren't inductive – for example Binary instances require a tag indicating which constructor has been stored, but only if there is more than one constructor. This pattern can be written as:

```
instance Binary α ⇒ Binary (Sample α) where
  put x = case x of
    First         → do putTag 0
    Second x1 x2  → do putTag 1; put x1; put x2
    Third  x1     → do putTag 2; put x1
```

[3] "Second" would also work, but the use of a string feels too unpleasant.

```
    where
        useTag = length [First{}, Second{}, Third{}] > 1
        putTag = when useTag ∘ putWord8

  get = do
     i ← getTag
     case i of
        0 → do return (First)
        1 → do x₁ ← get; x₂ ← get; return (Second x₁ x₂)
        2 → do x₁ ← get; return (Third x₁)
        _ → error "Corrupted binary data for Sample"
     where
        useTag = length [First{}, Second{}, Third{}] > 1
        getTag = if useTag then getWord8 else return 0
```

The value length [First{}, Second{}, Third{}] is used to compute the number of constructors in the data type, which can be tested to get the correct behaviour. This pattern is used in other classes, for example Enum and Arbitrary. Using simplifications we can remove the test and produce code specialised to the number of constructors.

The pattern for the number of constructors is useful, but seems a little verbose. In the first version of DERIVE the constructor count was guessed from the number 3. Unfortunately, the inclusion of this guess breaks the restrictions we have imposed for predictability. Another way of simplifying this pattern would be to introduce a meta function ctorCount, which expanded to the number of constructors. This solution would mean inputs were not real example instances, and would require users to learn part of the DSL – something we have tried to avoid. In the end, we simply accept that the constructor count is slightly verbose.

5.3 Timing Properties

We have implemented the methods described in this paper, and have used them to guess all 15 examples referred to in §5.1, along with 2 additional test cases. For each example we perform the following steps:

1. We derive the DSL from an example.
2. We apply the DSL to the Sample data type and check it matches the input example.
3. We apply the DSL to three other data types, namely lists, the eight element tuple and the expression type from the Yhc Core library [7].

To perform all steps for 17 examples takes 0.3 seconds when compiled with GHC -O0 on a laptop with a 2GHz CPU and 1Gb of RAM. We consider these times to be more than adequate, so have not carried out further experiments or investigated additional optimisations.

6 Related Work

An earlier version of the DERIVE tool was presented in a previous paper [20]. The previous work described only the derivation algorithm. There was no intermediate DSL, and no predictability. Given a single example the tool could produce multiple different answers, and would always use the first generated – not always corresponding to the users intention. In practice the lack of predictability meant the scheme could only be used under careful supervision, and thus offered only minimal benefits over writing the relationship by hand. This paper presents a much more general scheme, along with many improvements to the previous work. Crucial improvements have been made to the derivation algorithm, particularly when dealing with lists.

6.1 Deriving Type Classes

Jeuring et. al. [11] generate Haskell type classes by using the Djinn tool [1] to automatically generate candidate instances, which were then checked using QuickCheck properties [3]. Their work takes a substantially different approach to ours – rather than generating relationships from implementations, they generate relationships from specifications (both types and properties). The tool based on their work is still a proof of concept, and has only been used to infer a handful of relationships (such as maps and zips), specifically it is limited to not calling other generic functions, and does not support recursive data types. Using properties to ensure both predictability and correctness is an interesting approach, but does require sufficient properties to completely capture the semantics of the type class.

6.2 Specifying Type Classes

From an end-user perspective, the DrIFT tool [30] is similar to DERIVE – both take data types and produce associated instances. To add a type-class to DrIFT the programmer manually writes a translation from input types to Haskell source code, using pretty-printing combinators. There is no automatic derivation of instance generators, and no underlying DSL. As a result, it is substantially easier to add generators which can be derived from one example to DERIVE.

Another mechanism for specifying type classes is to use generic type classes [9], a language extension supported by GHC. A programmer can write default instances for type classes in terms of the structure of a type, using unit, products and sums. There are many restrictions on such classes, including restrictions on the type of instance methods and the structure of the input type. Using the abstraction of products and sums, it is impossible to represent many instances such as those dealing with records or containing type specific behaviour.

6.3 Deriving Relationships

The purpose of our work is to find a pattern, which is generalised to other situations. Genetic algorithms [6] are often used to automatically find patterns in a data set. Genetic algorithms work by evolving a hypothesis (a gene sequence) which is tested against a sample problem. While genetic algorithms are good for search, they usually use a heuristic to measure closeness – so lack the exactness of our approach.

There is much research on learning relationships from a collection of input/output pairs, often using only positive examples [13]. Some work tackles this problem using exhaustive search [12], a technique that could possibly replace our derive function. Instead of using specific examples, some work generalises a set of non-recursive equations into a recursive form [15,14]. All these pieces of work require a set of input/output examples, in contrast to our method that requires only one output for a specific input.

The closest work we are aware of is that of the theorem proving community. Induction is a very common tactic for writing proofs, and well supported in systems such as HOL Light [8]. Typically the user must suggest the use of induction, which the system checks for validity. Automatic inference of an induction argument has been tried [19], but is rarely successful. However, these systems all work from one positive example, attempting to determine a reasonably restricted pattern.

7 Conclusions and Future Work

We have presented a scheme for deriving a DSL from one example, which we have used to automatically derive instance generators for Haskell type classes. Our technique has been implemented in the DERIVE tool, where 60% of instance generators are specified by example. The ease of creating new instances has enabled several users to contribute instance generators. The DERIVE tool can be downloaded from Hackage[4], and we encourage interested users to try it out.

One of the key strengths of our derivation scheme is that concerns of correctness and predictability are separated from the main derivation function. Correctness is easy to test for, so incorrect derivations can simply be discarded. Predictability is a property of the DSL and sample input, and can be determined in isolation from the derivation function. The derivation function merely needs to take a best guess at what derivation might work, allowing greater freedom to experiment.

We see several lines of future work:

- By deriving an explicit DSL, we can reuse the DSL for other purposes. A DSL could be used to prove properties, for example that all Eq instances are reflexive, or that put/get in Binary are inverses. Another use might be to generate human readable documentation of an instance. We suspect there are many other uses.
- The Sample data type (from §1) allows many instances to be inferred – but more would be desirable. We have discussed possible extensions in §5.1, but none seems to offer compelling benefits. An alternative approach would be

[4] `http://hackage.haskell.org/package/derive`

to introduce new sample data types with features specifically for certain types of definition. Care would have to be taken that these definitions still preserved predictability, and did not substantially increase the complexity of writing examples.
- While our scheme is implemented in a typed language, most of the actual DSL operations work upon a universal data type with runtime type checking – essentially a dynamically typed language. In order to preserve types throughout we could make use of GADTs [23].
- We have implemented our scheme specifically for instance generators in Haskell, but the same scheme could be applied to other computer languages and other situations. One possible target would be F#, where there are interfaces instead of type classes. Another target could be an object-orientated language, where design patterns [5] are popular.

Computers are ideally suited to applying a relationship using new parameters, but specifying these relationships can be complex and error prone. By specifying a single example, instead of the relationship, a user can focus on what they care about, rather than the mechanism by which it is implemented.

Acknowledgements

Thanks to Stefan O'Rear for help writing the first version of the DERIVE tool. Thanks to Niklas Broberg for the excellent haskell-src-exts library. Thanks to Hongseok Yang for fruitful discussions on the original instance generation work. Thanks to Mike Dodds and the anonymous referees for useful feedback on earlier drafts.

References

1. Augustsson, L.: Putting Curry-Howard to work. In: AAIP 2009: Proceedings of the ACM SIGPLAN Workshop on Approaches and Applications of Inductive Programming, p. 1 (2009)
2. Broberg, N.: Haskell-src-exts (2009), `http://www.cs.chalmers.se/~d00nibro/haskell-src-exts/`
3. Claessen, K., Hughes, J.: QuickCheck: A lightweight tool for random testing of Haskell programs. In: Proc. ICFP 2000, pp. 268–279. ACM Press, New York (2000)
4. Fluet, M., Pucella, R.: Phantom types and subtyping. In: Proc. TCS 2002, Deventer, The Netherlands, pp. 448–460 (2002)
5. Gamma, E., Helm, R., Johnson, R., Vlissides, J.: Design patterns: elements of reusable object-oriented software. Addison-Wesley Professional, Reading (1995)
6. Goldberg, D.E.: Genetic Algorithms in Search, Optimization, and Machine Learning. Addison-Wesley Professional, Reading (1989)
7. Golubovsky, D., Mitchell, N., Naylor, M.: Yhc.Core – from Haskell to Core. The Monad. Reader 1(7), 45–61 (2007)
8. Harrison, J.: HOL light: A tutorial introduction. In: Srivas, M., Camilleri, A. (eds.) FMCAD 1996. LNCS, vol. 1166, pp. 265–269. Springer, Heidelberg (1996)
9. Hinze, R., Peyton Jones, S.: Derivable type classes. In: Hutton, G. (ed.) Proc. Haskell Workshop 2000. Elsevier Science, Amsterdam (2000)

10. Hughes, J.: The design of a pretty-printing library. In: Jeuring, J., Meijer, E. (eds.) AFP 1995. LNCS, vol. 925, pp. 53–96. Springer, Heidelberg (1995)
11. Jeuring, J., Rodriguez, A., Smeding, G.: Generating generic functions. In: WGP 2006: Proceedings of the 2006 ACM SIGPLAN workshop on Generic programming, pp. 23–32. ACM, New York (2006)
12. Katayama, S.: Efficient exhaustive generation of functional programs using Monte-Carlo search with iterative deepening. In: Ho, T.-B., Zhou, Z.-H. (eds.) PRICAI 2008. LNCS (LNAI), vol. 5351, pp. 199–210. Springer, Heidelberg (2008)
13. Kitzelmann, E.: Data-driven induction of recursive functions from input/output-examples. In: Proceedings of the Workshop on Approaches and Applications of Inductive Progamming (AAIP 2007), pp. 15–26 (2007)
14. Kitzelmann, E.: Data-driven induction of functional programs. In: Proc. ECAI 2008. IOS Press, Amsterdam (2008)
15. Kitzelmann, E., Schmid, U.: Inductive synthesis of functional programs – An explanation based generalization approach. Journal of Machine Learning Research 7, 429–454 (2006)
16. Lämmel, R., Peyton Jones, S.: Scrap your boilerplate: a practical design pattern for generic programming. In: Proc. TLDI 2003, pp. 26–37. ACM Press, New York (2003)
17. Lämmel, R., Peyton Jones, S.: Scrap more boilerplate: reflection, zips, and generalised casts. In: Proc. ICFP 2004, pp. 244–255. ACM Press, New York (2004)
18. Marlow, S.: Haddock, a Haskell documentation tool. In: Proc. Haskell Workshop 2002, Pittsburgh Pennsylvania, USA. ACM Press, New York (2002)
19. Mintchev, S.: Mechanized reasoning about functional programs. In: Hammond, K., Turner, D.N., Sansom, P.M. (eds.) Functional Programming, pp. 151–166. Springer, Heidelberg (1994)
20. Mitchell, N.: Deriving generic functions by example. In: Mühlberg, J.T., Perna, J.I. (eds.) Proc. York Doctoral Symposium 2007, October 2007, pp. 55–62. Tech. Report YCS-2007-421, University of York (2007)
21. Mitchell, N., O'Rear, S.: Derive - project home page (2009), `http://community.haskell.org/~ndm/derive/`
22. Peyton Jones, S.: Haskell 98 Language and Libraries: The Revised Report. Cambridge University Press, Cambridge (2003)
23. Peyton Jones, S., Vytiniotis, D., Weirich, S., Washburn, G.: Simple unification-based type inference for GADTs. In: Proc. ICFP 2006, pp. 50–61. ACM Press, New York (2006)
24. Sheard, T., Peyton Jones, S.: Template meta-programming for Haskell. In: Proc. Haskell Workshop 2002, pp. 1–16. ACM Press, New York (2002)
25. The GHC Team. The GHC compiler, version 6.10.3 (May 2009), `http://www.haskell.org/ghc/`
26. The Yhc Team. The York Haskell Compiler – user manual (February 2007), `http://www.haskell.org/haskellwiki/Yhc`
27. Trinder, P., Hammond, K., Loidl, H.-W., Peyton Jones, S.: Algorithm + strategy = parallelism. JFP 8(1), 23–60 (1998)
28. Wadler, P.: How to replace failure by a list of successes. In: Proc. FPCA 1985, pp. 113–128. Springer-Verlag New York, Inc. (1985)
29. Wadler, P., Blott, S.: How to make ad-hoc polymorphism less ad hoc. In: Proc. POPL 1989, pp. 60–76. ACM Press, New York (1989)
30. Winstanley, N.: Reflections on instance derivation. In: 1997 Glasgow Workshop on Functional Programming. BCS Workshops in Computer Science (September 1997)

Synthesis of Functions Using Generic Programming

Pieter Koopman and Rinus Plasmeijer

Nijmegen Institute for Computing and Information Sciences,
Radboud University Nijmegen, The Netherlands
{pieter,rinus}@cs.ru.nl

Abstract. This paper describes a very flexible way to synthesize functions matching a given predicate. This can be used to find general recursive functions or λ-terms obeying an input–output behavior specified by a number of examples. Generating complex algorithms from just a small number of simple input-output pairs is the goal of inductive programming. This paper illustrates that our approach works well in some challenging examples.

1 Introduction

Inductive programming aims to synthesize functions or programs from a small number of input-output pairs. In general there will by many functions that have the desired behavior. From this family of solutions we are interested in the smallest or simplest solution. In some situations there are (often well-know) algorithms to construct such functions, for instance for fitting a linear function through a set of points in the $\mathbb{R}^2$. In general it is very hard to construct functions for arbitrary data types in this way. Instead of constructing a function that has the desired behavior we use a generate-and-test based approach. Our system generates a sequence of more and more complex candidate functions, the system verifies if these candidates have the desired behavior and yields the first candidate that passes this test.

Since there are enormous many candidate functions one has to guide this search process in one way or another to synthesize the desired function in reasonable time. In this paper we show how we can control the synthesis of candidate functions effectively by defining a tailor made data type for the grammar of the candidate functions. The instances of these data types represent the candidate functions, in fact the generated instance of the data type are the abstract syntax trees of the corresponding functions. In contrast with real functions, these syntax trees can be easily inspected and manipulated.

To reduce the manual effort in defining algorithms to generate candidate candidate functions we introduce a generic algorithm that enumerates the instances of any (recursive) data type from small to large. We show how we can use this to generate tailor-made candidate functions with very little effort. Usually we only have to specify the constants to be used explicitly, everything else is done by the generic algorithm and the type definitions.

U. Schmid, E. Kitzelmann, and R. Plasmeijer (Eds.): AAIP 2009, LNCS 5812, pp. 25–49, 2010.

It appears that the generic algorithm for generating instances of a data type that is used to generate test suites in the model-based test tool G∀st is very effective to synthesize candidate functions in inductive programming. In order to verify if a synthesized abstract syntax tree represents the correct function, the system needs to be able to execute it as a function. This is done by a user defined function that transforms the abstract syntax tree to the corresponding function.

Using a test system to generate candidate functions and check their suitability has additional advantages. Instead of specifying just input output pairs for the functions one can specify an arbitrary predicate in first order logic.

For a new application domain the user has to define the grammar of candidate functions as a data type and how instances of this data type are transformed to functions. Next the user specifies a predicate about the specific function wanted. The system synthesizes the instances and tests the candidates until one (or more) functions with the desired behavior are found.

This paper first gives an explanation of the generate and test approach to synthesize functions in section 2. In section 3 we explain how the candidate functions can be synthesized using generic programming. Section 4 shows how the desired functions can be selected from the candidates with the model-based test tool G∀st.Then we show some nontrivial examples of our approach. Keppler's third law relating the distance of planets and their period is rediscovered empirically in section 5. Next we show how one can synthesize primitive recursive function in section 6. Section 7 shows how to synthesize complex λ-terms. Finally we discuss related work, section 8, and conclude in section 9.

2 The Generate and Test Approach to Synthesis Functions

It is a challenging idea to create a computer system that is able to produce the function we have in mind based on just a few examples from input and output. On one hand it is obvious that such a system cannot exist for arbitrary functions, e.g. we cannot expect a function that solves the halting problem based on some examples of terminating and nonterminating functions. On the other hand there are couple of examples in the literature (e.g. [8,3,6,11,14]) that show that these kind of systems can be constructed and that these systems are capable to find solutions in a number of situations.

In this paper we are looking for a system that synthesizes a function based on some partial specification, usually a small number of typical input–output pairs. Since the specification given by these input–output pairs is partial (usually the given inputs are only a small fraction of the domain of the function) there are generally many functions that match this specification. A trivial one is the function that maps only the given inputs to the associated outputs. Such a function is not what we are looking for. Apart from mapping the given inputs to outputs we have the following constraints:

1. A function with a small body is considered to be better than a function with a big body. We will use the size of the abstract syntax tree as a measure for the size of the function body.
2. As a consequence of the previous point we generally prefer a nonrecursive definition over a recursive one and single recursion over double recursion.
3. The function should contain at most a few special case for specific arguments. A recursive function needs of course some stopping criterion, but we do not want many special cases. If there are special cases the should preferably handle the non-recursive alternatives of a recursive data type (e.g. empty list or empty tree), or common stop criteria for other functions (e.g. the numbers 0 or 1).

These additional properties are not added to the specification. In order to specify that one function is smaller or simpler than another solution we need both functions and compare them. Instead we will use a predicate to capture only the constraints like input–output pairs. The numbered constraints will be met by the kind and order in which candidate functions are generated. When we do not generate functions with excessive pattern matching on input arguments, such a function will never be found. By generating candidate functions from small to large the first function matching the constraints will be the smallest function we are looking for.

An example illustrates the preference of functions. Suppose we are looking for a function f that has the following behavior: $f(0) = 0$, $f(2) = 4$ and $f(3) = 9$. Some functions displaying the required input–output behavior are:

```
f1 0 = 0
f1 2 = 4
f1 3 = 9
f1 x = x

f2 x = x*x

f3 x = x^2

f4 x = g x
where
    g 0 = 0
    g y = x + g (y-1)
```

From these functions f1 is clearly undesirable, it contains too much specific patterns for the given input–output pairs. The functions f2 and f3 are equally good, they are small and meet the desired input–output relations with a general pattern. Function f4 implements the multiplication by repeated addition. Since its definition is larger than the definition of f2 and f3 we do not prefer the solution f4.

2.1 Partial Specification of the Functions

We prefer a richer specification language than just input–output pairs. We also want to be able to express properties like $f(1) \geq 0$, or even $\forall x \,.\, f(x) \geq (0)$ and $\forall x \,.\, f(x) \geq (0) \Rightarrow f(x+1) > f(x)$. To be able to specify this kind of properties we use first order logic as specification language for the functions we are looking for rather than only input–output pairs.

The predicate corresponding to the input–output pairs $f(0) = 0$, $f(2) = 4$ and $f(3) = 9$ becomes $p_1(f) = f(0) = 0 \wedge f(2) = 4 \wedge f(3) = 9$. In our implementation this is modeled by a Boolean–valued function in the functional programming language Clean [13].

```
p1 :: (Int→Int) → Bool
p1 f = f 0 == 0 && f 2 == 4 && f 3 == 9
```

Our test system G∀st provides a full range of logical operators. Using some of these logical operators the predicate $f(2) = 4 \wedge \forall x\,.\,f(x) \geq (0) \Rightarrow f(x+1) > f(x)$ can be written as

```
p2 :: (Int→Int) → Property
p2 f = f 2 == 4 ∧ ForAll λx . f x ≥ 0 ⟹ f (x+1) > f x
```

Each property that uses logical operators from G∀st yields `Property` instead of `Bool`. This is necessary in the implementation, but the user can consider this type as an equivalent for Booleans.

Since these predicates in general do not pinpoint the desired functions completely, the predicates are partial specifications.

2.2 Automatic Test Systems

Automatic test systems like G∀st [10] and QuickCheck [5] are designed to handle these kind of predicates. The test system is designed to falsify a property by finding a counterexample. A typical example of such a property for the functions `abs` that computes the absolute value of an integer is $\forall i \in \mathrm{Int}\,.\,\mathrm{abs}(i) \geq 0$. Expressed as a Boolean function that can be handled by G∀st this is:

```
pAbs :: Int → Bool
pAbs i = abs i ≥ 0
```

This property can be tested automatically by executing

```
Start = test pAbs
```

To test this property the system executes the following subtasks.

Test suite generation. The test suite is the collection of values that will be used in the test. For our test tool the test suite is a, potentially infinite, list of values.

In this example the function `test` detects that the property `pAbs` ranges over integer values. A test suite for the type integer and other predefined types is provided by G∀st.

If we want to deviate in a specific test from the predefined test suite we can use the operator `For`. The property `pAbs` can be tested for integers between −100 and 100 by executing

```
Start = test (pAbs For [−100..100])
```

Test execution. Since the property is generated and the test suite is given as a list of values, test execution is basically just a map of the property over the test suite.

Generating a verdict. The test system generates a verdict by inspecting the first N (by default 1000) Boolean values in the list generated by test execution. Basically the property passes the test is all Booleans have the value `True` and fails otherwise.

In reality the verdict is a little more detailed. Possible verdicts are:

Proof. The property holds for all elements of the test suite. Such a proof by exhaustive testing is only possible when the size of the test suite is smaller than the maximum number of tests to be done.

Executing the test `Start = test (pAbs For [-100..100])` yields Proof since there are only 201 test cases and they all succeed.

Pass. If all tests done are successful, but there are more values in the test suite than the maximum number of tests to be done, the test result is Pass.

Counterexample. If one of the test results is `False` the property obviously does not hold. The test system G∀st does not only yield the test result Counterexample, but also prints the test value that causes this counter example. Moreover, it is possible to indicate that one wants at most M, by default 1, counterexamples in the first N test cases.

Executing the test `Start = test pAbs` yields the counterexample -2147483648, which is the minimum integer number of the 32-bit integers. This counterexample is found almost immediately since integers that are known to be often good test values (like 0, 1, ,-1, maxint, and minint) are placed near the head of the test suite for integers.

Testing of properties is not restricted to properties with a single universal quantified variable, or predefined data types. Suppose we have a function `rev :: [x] → [x]` that reverses lists. A desirable property is given by the list law $\forall\, xs,\, ys\,.\, rev\ (xs{+}{+}ys) = rev\ ys \mathbin{+\!\!+} rev\ xs$. This law [4] can be directly used to formulate a property to be tested by G∀st. We only have to add a data type to be used in the test and make sure to use a defined instance for the equality.

```
pRev :: [Color] [Color] → Bool
pRev xs ys = rev (xs++ys) === rev ys ++ rev xs

:: Color = Red | Yellow | Blue
```

In the next section we show generic, also called polytypic, programming [2] removes the burden to define these things from the user of the test system. The test system has generic definitions for operations like generation of test suites, equality of elements and showing the elements. The desired operations can be derived by the compiler from the generic definitions. The user just has to write

```
derive ggen    Color    // generic generation of the list of all Colors
derive gEq     Color    // generic equality for Color
derive genShow Color    // generic show (transformation to strings) for Color
```

Now the property can be tested by executing `Start = test pRev`. For a correct function `rev` the test result will be Pass. For a correct function there will be no counterexamples, but the generated test suite is an infinite list of lists of colors. For an incorrect implementation a typical test result is: `Counterexample 1 found after 1 tests: [Yellow] [Blue]`. The generic algorithm generates test values from small to large. This implies that the counterexamples found are the smallest counterexample that exists. Having small counterexamples is beneficial since this makes it usually much easier to find the bug in the system under test (SUT, here the function rev).

Although the goal of these test systems is just opposite to inductive programming, we can reuse the automatic test machinery in inductive programming.

2.3 Selecting Functions with an Automatic Test System

Above we developed a property for G∀st that captures the desired input–output behavior. The goal of inductive programming is to find a function that satisfies this predicate, and hence posses the desired input–output relation. A test system is designed to find counterexamples, which is just the opposite of finding evidence that such a function exists. Instead of change the test system to an inductive programming system we will change the properties. Constructing a new system requires additional work to change the system. Moreover, we need to maintain two systems.

By a small change of the properties we obtain exactly the desired effect. Instead of specifying what properties the desired function has, we specify that all functions does not poses the desired properties. Counterexamples found by the test system are exactly the functions we are looking for.

For example we replace property p1 from section 2.1 by

```
p1‘ :: (Int→Int) → Bool
p1‘ f = ¬(f 0 = 0 && f 2 = 4 && f 3 = 9)
```

Using De Morgan's law this can also be written as:

```
p1‘‘ :: (Int→Int) → Bool
p1‘‘ f = f 0 ≠ 0 || f 2 ≠ 4 || f 3 ≠ 9
```

The generation of candidate functions is now the only missing part. This is handled in the next section.

3 Generic Synthesis of Functions

The crux of the synthesis of functions using generic programming is the systematic generation of candidate functions. In order to limit the search space we will use a data type that corresponds directly to the grammar of the candidate functions.

As an example we start with arithmetic expression with a single variable. The syntax is:

$$\begin{aligned} Expr &= IConst \mid Var \mid BinOp\ Expr \\ BinOp\ e &= e\ +\ e \mid e\ -\ e \mid e\ \times\ e \mid e\ \hat{}\ PConst \\ Var &= X \\ IConst &= 1..5 \\ PConst &= 2..4 \end{aligned}$$

We have used a higher order grammar rule for *BinOp* in order to reuse it later with a different argument.

Each grammar rule is directly mapped to an algebraic data type. In order to reduce the number of constructors needed we will use the data type OR to indicate a binary choice.

```
:: OR s t = L s | R t
```

The data types corresponding to the grammar rules above are:

```
:: Expr    = Expr (OR (OR Var IConst) (BinOp Expr))
:: BinOp e = OpPlus e e | OpMinus e e | OpTimes e e | OpPower e PConst
:: Var     = X
:: IConst  = IConst Int
:: PConst  = PConst Int
```

For the constants IConst and PConst we have added a constructor to make it a data type on its own instead of using the type synonym :: IConst := Int. These separate data types appear to be convenient in the generation of instances.

Using these data types the expression $(X + 1)\hat{}2$ is represented by a data type of the form OpPower (OpPlus (L X) (R (IConst 1))) (R (PConst 2)) of type BinOp (OR Var IConst.

The next step is generating instances of these data types that are going to be used as candidate function bodies. Rather than defining this for each and every data type over and over again we are going to define one generic algorithm that is able to enumerate the instances of any data type.

3.1 Generic Programming

The basic idea of generic programming is very simple. It is based on a uniform representation of arbitrary, user defined, data types. The language compiler can transform instances of an arbitrary data type to this uniform representation and from this representation back to the original data type. If we need a class of similar function we define the function on the generic representation instead of on all types individually. Famous examples are operations like equality and pretty printing etcetera. Generic programming is however by no means limited to these simple examples.

Generic Representation of Values. The uniform representation of data types is constructed with ordinary algebraic data types. These data type are used to construct binary trees representing the usual constructors. The basic types to construct these binary trees are:

```
:: UNIT       = UNIT                 // leaf
:: EITHER a b = LEFT a | RIGHT b     // choice
:: PAIR   a b = PAIR a b             // grouping
```

The type UNIT represents the leaves of the binary tree. The type EITHER is used to indicate a choice. Using these choices the representation indicates what constructors is actually used. This is very similar to the type OR introduced above[1]. The type PAIR is used to glue things together, typically arguments to constructors.

In addition to the basic types it appears to be convenient to have some additional types carrying information about objects and constructors. We only introduce the type CONS indicating explicitly that there is a constructor at this spot in the generic representation. In the Clean version of generic programming this constructor is able to provide information about the actual constructor (like name, arity, type it belong to etc.).

```
:: CONS a = CONS a
```

The generic representation of the type Color introduced in section 2.2 is

```
:: Color_g = EITHER (CONS UNIT) (EITHER (CONS UNIT) (CONS UNIT))
```

The generic representation of the constructors Red, Yellow, and Blue from this type become:

```
Red_g    = LEFT (CONS UNIT)
Yellow_g = RIGHT (LEFT (CONS UNIT))
Blue_g   = RIGHT (RIGHT (CONS UNIT))
```

If a constructor has an argument, this argument replaces the place holder UNIT in the generic representation. For example the generic representation of the type IConst is:

```
IConst_g = CONS Int
```

As an example of of grouping things together by PAIR we give the generic representation of x1. This value represents the expression $x + 1$ as an algebraic data type of type BinOp (OR Var IConst) (a binary operator expression over variables or constants).

```
x1 :: BinOp (OR Var IConst)
x1 = OpPlus (L X) (R (IConst 1))
```

The generic representation of this expression is:

```
LEFT (LEFT ((CONS (PAIR (LEFT (CONS (CONS UNIT)) (RIGHT (CONS (CONS 1))))))))
```

Here the PAIR glues both arguments of OpPlus together. This generic form of $x+1$ is huge and quite incomprehensible. Fortunately, those generic representations of expressions are usually generated. The transformation between the generic representation and the usual representation of data types can always be handled automatically by the compiler.

Generic functions. The power of generic programming is that an operation can be applied to an arbitrary data type by defining it only for the basic generic types (UINT, EITHER, PAIR, and CONS). Since the transformation of the data type to

[1] In fact there is no need to introduce the type OR, we can use EITHER equally well. We have introduced OR only to prevent confusion between the ordinary domain of data types and the domain of generic representation of these data types.

its generic representation is done by the language implementation all we have to do is to provide an instance for the four generic data types.

The classical example of generic programming is equality. First we define the general generic function, similar to a class definition.

```
generic gEq a  :: a a → Bool
```

Next we define instances for the generic types and the basic types used in our program.

The instant for UNIT is very simple, there is only one constructor in the data type (line 1 in the code block below). Without looking at the argument supplied we known that the elements must be equal.

The type EITHER indicates a choice. The given elements can only be equal if the make the same choice between LEFT and RIGHT. If they make the same choice we have to compare the arguments (line 2 and 3). In contrast with a class the comparison of the arguments of LEFT and RIGHT is not done by an overloaded recursive call of geq. In the generic programming variant implemented in Clean the functions to compare the type arguments of EITHER are supplied as additional arguments by the generic system. In the code below we call these functions fl and fr.

Since the type PAIR has also two type arguments the generic instance of geq for PAIR has also two additional functions as arguments. The type PAIR has only one alternative (line 5). Hence we can immediately start with comparing the arguments of the constructor PAIR using the given functions.

For the single argument type CONS we have only one additional function. Since there is again only one constructor in the type, the only task we have is to compare the function arguments using the given function f (line 6).

In this example the only basic type needed is Int. Integers are compared using the ordinary equality on integers (line 7).

All code for defined instances of geq together is:

```
1 geq{|UNIT|}               _             _             = True
2 geq{|EITHER|} fl fr (LEFT x)       (LEFT y)       = fl x y
3 geq{|EITHER|} fl fr (RIGHT x)      (RIGHT y)      = fr x y
4 geq{|EITHER|} fl fr _              _              = False
5 geq{|PAIR|}   fx fy (PAIR x1 y1) (PAIR x2 y2) = fx x1 x2 && fy y1 y2
6 geq{|CONS|}   f     (CONS x)       (CONS y)       = f x y
7 geq{|Int|}          x              y              = x == y
```

For any other data type we can define an instance like the instances shown above. The power of generic programming however is that we can *derive* these instances.

```
derive geq OR, BinOp, Var, IConst, PConst
```

Now you can use the operation geq for all types mentioned. The Clean system implements those operations by transforming the instances of the type to their generic representations and comparing those representations using the definitions given above.

Using those definitions we can compare the values IConst 5 and IConst 7 by executing

```
Start = geq{|*|} (IConst 5) (IConst 7)
```

As we might expect and hope the result is `False`.

One might wonder what the result of comparing `IConst 3` and `PConst 3` world be. These values have the same generic representation, but a different type. If one tries to compare them in an expression like `geq{|*|} (IConst 3) (PConst 3)`, this fails rather than yielding `True`. This expression contains a type error since the generic function definition `generic gEq a :: a a → Bool` requires that both arguments have the same type.

It is important to realize that generic programming is by no means limited to the simple classical examples like equality and pretty printing. In this paper we will use it to generate the instances of data types.

3.2 Generic Generation of Instances of a Data type

Now we consider the task of generating a list of values for all types. We approach this task by generic programming. Our algorithm will generate the generic instances of those values and the Clean system will convert those generic values to ordinary values whenever desired.

What we need is a generic function that yields a list of all values of a given type. This is:

```
generic gengen a :: [a]
```

Again we define the instances for the generic types and derive the instances of other types whenever possible.

The instance for `UNIT` is again very simple (line 1 in the numbered code block below). There is only one value of this type: the constructor `UNIT`. So, the list of values contains only this constructor.

For the type `CONS` we only have to apply the constructor `CONS` to all possible arguments (line 2). The list `l` of possible arguments is supplied by the generic system, just as the functions to compare arguments in `geq` above.

For the type `PAIR` we have to combine the elements from the given lists is all possible ways. We use the library function `diag2` to ensure that the elements are mixed in a 'fair' way. This prevents that we take the first element of one of the lists and pair it with all elements of the second list before we consider the second argument of the first list. To illustrate this mixing of list elements with some ordinary types we consider the unbounded lists of integers `[0..]` and the list of characters `['a'..]`. The expression `diag2 [0..] ['a'..]` yields

```
[(0,'a'),(1,'a'),(0,'b'),(2,'a'),(1,'b'),(0,'c'),(3,'a'),(2,'b'),(1,'c'),(0,'d'),..
```

An ordinary combination of list elements with `[(i,c) \\ i←[0..], c←['a'..]]` yields

```
[(0,'a'),(0,'b'),(0,'c'),(0,'d'),(0,'e'),(0,'f'),(0,'g'),(0,'h'),(0,'i'),(0,'j'),..
```

Here only the integer `0` is used.

For the choice between elements from two lists in the type `EITHER` we apply the combinators `LEFT` and `RIGHT` to the elements in the given lists (line 4). The function `merge` merges the resulting list by taking repeatedly one element from the first list and one element from the second list.

The instance of the generic generation of lists of values for integers is defined such that it yields the list `[0,1,−1,2,−2,3,−3,..` (line 9).

```
gengen{|UNIT|}       = [ UNIT ]
gengen{|CONS|}   l   = map CONS l
gengen{|PAIR|}   l m = [ PAIR a b \\ (a,b) ← diag2 l m ]
gengen{|EITHER|} l g = merge (map LEFT l) (map RIGHT m)
where
    merge []    m  = m
    merge l     [] = l
    merge [a:r] m  = [a:merge m r]
gengen{|Int|}        = [0:[j\\i←[1..],j←[i,−i]]]
```

After these preparations we can derive the generation of our data types by

```
derive gengen OR, BinOp, Var
```

From the syntax in section 3.2 we see that the values for `IConst` vary from 1 to 5 and the values for `PConst` range from 2 to 4. This implies that they cannot be derived. By deriving those values all integers would occur. Instead of deriving we use tailor made definitions for these types.

```
gengen{|IConst|} = map IConst [1..5]
gengen{|PConst|} = map PConst [2..4]
```

Using this we can generate a list of expressions of type `BinOp (OR Var IConst)` just by writing

```
l :: [BinOp (OR Var IConst)]
l = gengen{|*|}
```

The first 10 expressions generated are:

```
[OpPlus  (L X) (L X)                // x+x
,OpTimes (L X) (L X)                // x×x
,OpMinus (L X) (L X)                // x-x
,OpPower (L X) (PConst 2)           // x^2
,OpPlus  (R (IConst 1)) (L X)       // 1+x
,OpTimes (R (IConst 1)) (L X)       // 1×x
,OpMinus (R (IConst 1)) (L X)       // 1-x
,OpPower (R (IConst 1)) (PConst 2)  // 1^2
,OpPlus  (L X) (R (IConst 1))       // x+1
,OpTimes (L X) (R (IConst 1))       // x×1
]
```

The mechanism to produce instances of data types introduced here appears to be very general. If we want an abstract syntax tree for an other grammar, we just define a new data type that mimics this syntax. For the generation we derive whatever possible and use a tailor made definition for the other types. The pattern seen here appears to be common, everything except the constants represented by basic types can be derived. The required manual definitions are very simple.

For instance if we want recursive expression given by the syntax

$$Expr = Var \mid IConst \mid BinOp\ Expr$$

we define the recursive data type `Expr`.

```
:: Expr = Expr (OR (OR Var IConst) (BinOp Expr))
```

After deriving `gengen` for `Expr` we can generate those expressions. The first 10 expressions generated are:

```
[Expr (L (L X))                                           // x
,Expr (R (OpPlus (Expr (L (L X))) (Expr (L (L X)))))      // x+x
,Expr (L (R (IConst 1)))                                  // 1
,Expr (R (OpTimes (Expr (L (L X))) (Expr (L (L X)))))     // x×x
,Expr (L (R (IConst 2)))                                  // 2
,Expr (R (OpMinus (Expr (L (L X))) (Expr (L (L X)))))     // x-x
,Expr (L (R (IConst 3)))                                  // 3
,Expr (R (OpPower (Expr (L (L X))) (PConst 2)))           // x^2
,Expr (L (R (IConst 4)))                                  // 4
,Expr (R (OpPlus (Expr (R (OpPlus (Expr (L (L X)))        // (x+x)+x
                                  (Expr (L (L X))))))
                 (Expr (L (L X)))))]
```

The actual generic generation algorithm ggen used by G∀st uses a pseudo random choice between the list with LEFT elements and RIGHT elements instead of a strict interleaving. As a result the order of elements in the resulting lists has a slight pseudo random perturbation compared with the algorithm presented here. Testers are found of such randomness. Here it does not harm us, but neither is a big advantage. In the rest of the paper we will use the generic function ggen from G∀st instead of the somewhat simpler version gengen introduced here.

3.3 Transforming Syntax Trees to Functions

Now we are able to generate abstract syntax trees of candidate functions in a convenient and high level way. Just by changing the algebraic data types representing the syntax trees, we can change the candidate functions considered.

However, in order to evaluate a predicate over a candidate function we do need the function instead of its abstract syntax tree. In order to construct these functions we define the class apply. The functions in this class produce a value v given a data type instance d and an environment e. As usual in interpreters and semantically descriptions this environment is used to store bindings of variables to values.

```
class apply d e v :: d → e → v
```

The first instance is for the type OR. The type restriction apply x b c & apply y b c says the we need to be able to apply the types x and y for the given binding b and value v[2]. All this function apply does is removing the constructor LEFT or RIGHT and apply the appropriate function apply to the argument of the constructor.

```
instance apply (OR x y) b c | apply x b c & apply y b c
where
    apply (L x) = apply x
    apply (R y) = apply y
```

Slightly more interesting is the instance of apply for binary operations, BinOp x. The definition just transforms the arguments of the operator to a value of type v by apply x b v or apply PConst b v and applies the indicated operator to the result. The class restriction just requires that all the operations are available.

---

[2] In Haskell one write such a type restriction as

```
instance (apply x b c, apply y b c) => apply (OR x y) b c
  where ..
```

```
instance apply (BinOp x) b v | apply x b v & +, −, ∗, ^ v & apply PConst b v
where
    apply (OpPlus  x y) = λb.apply x b + apply y b
    apply (OpMinus x y) = λb.apply x b − apply y b
    apply (OpTimes x y) = λb.apply x b ∗ apply y b
    apply (OpPower x p) = λb.apply x b ^ apply p b
```

Our very simple expressions of type Expr from section 3.2 just have one variable X. The environment needed to evaluate these expressions can be accordingly simple, we just have to store the value of this single variable. If we assume that this variable is of type Int we have:

```
instance apply IConst b   Int where apply (IConst i) = λb.i
instance apply PConst b   Int where apply (PConst i) = λb.i
instance apply Var    Int Int where apply X          = λi.i
instance apply Expr   Int Int where apply (Expr f)   = apply f
```

For the constants IConst and PConst we just ignore the binding environment b and yield the stored value. For a variable, Var, we produce the value stored in the environment. For an expression, Expr, we just remove the combinator and continue recursively.

Here it pays off to use the type OR instead separate constructors for all alternatives. If we had used separate constructors for the alternatives we would need one alternative of apply for each constructor. In our current approach the instance of apply handles all choices in the syntax.

After all these preparations we can reformulate our predicate and start the test system. The difference between this version of the predicate, p1e, and the predicate p1' from section 3.2 is that p1e ranges over Expr while p1' ranges over functions of type Int→Int. The test system generates instance e of type Expr effectively by the given instance of ggen. The generated abstract syntax tree e is transformed to the desired function f by the appropriate instance of apply. In this example we execute at most 1000 test and stop after finding 10 counterexamples, hence we use testnm instead of test since test will produce only one counterexample.

```
p1e :: Expr → Bool
p1e e = ¬(f 0 == 0 && f 2 == 4 && f 3 == 9) where f = apply e

Start = testnm 1000 10 p1e
```

The result produced by G∀st in 0.4 seconds is:

```
Counterexample 1 found after 16 tests: (x*x)
Counterexample 2 found after 22 tests: ((1*x)*x)
Counterexample 3 found after 38 tests: (x^2)
Counterexample 4 found after 358 tests: ((x*1)^2)
Counterexample 5 found after 381 tests: ((x^2)+(1-1))
Counterexample 6 found after 453 tests: ((x+(x*x))-x)
Counterexample 7 found after 491 tests: ((x*x)-(x-x))
Counterexample 8 found after 582 tests: (((x^2)+x)-x)
Counterexample 9 found after 713 tests: ((1+(x*x))-1)
Counterexample 10 found after 762 tests: (1*(x*x))
```

These counterexamples of the predicate p1 are all functions matching the input–output patterns $f\ 0 = 0$, $f\ 2 = 4$, and $f\ 3 = 9$.

Obviously we used a tailor made instance of the generic show function rather than deriving an instance. Our instance removes all unnecessary constructors and prints the binary operations as infix operators. The pretty printer here gives only the body of the function found. The first solution found should be understood as `f x = x**x`.

4 Selecting Candidate Solutions

Looking at the solutions found at the end of the previous section we notice that a desired solution is found quickly and is the first solution found. However, many of the other solutions have a rather undesirable form. For instance, for a human it is obvious that the second solution `f x = (1**)**x` represents semantically exactly the same solution as the first one `f x = x**x`.

There are at least three ways to avoid those kind of undesirable solutions.

1. One can design a better syntax that excludes those undesirable solutions. It is obvious how this should be done. Since the undesirable candidates cannot be represented in the new data types, they will never be considered. The advantage is that we obtain a complex syntax, and hence data type, for simple expressions. We will not elaborate on this since it is obvious how it should be done and we prefer a simple syntax (and hence data types).
2. We can adapt the generation of instances such that the undesirable candidate functions are never considered. This is an unattractive solution since we now have to define a generation algorithm manually instead of reusing the generic algorithm.

   In section 7 however we will provide an elegant solution that combines a simple data structure, generic generation and tailor made instances.
3. Finally we can at runtime exclude undesirable candidate solutions. This is possible since the candidate function is available as an abstract syntax tree. We can easily write a predicate `fit` that inspects the syntax tree and yields a Boolean indicating if this candidate function should be used. We will illustrate this solution here.

We will illustrate the selection of candidate functions here. First we define a class `fit` that determines if the candidate is healthy.

```
class fit a :: a → Bool
```

The maximum penalty for making the predicate not advanced enough is that a candidate function is considered that actually has not the desired form. The instances of this class presented below are pretty straightforward, of course we can make these predicates as cleaver as desired.

For the choice type `Or` the instance of `fit` determines what alternative we have at hand and applies the appropriate version of `fit` recursively.

The real work happens in the instance of `fit` for binary operations. For $x - y$ we require that $x \neq y$, $y \neq 0$, x is fit, y is fit, and that x and y are not both constants. For the other alternatives we impose similar constraints.

An expression of the form `Expr e` is fit if `e` is fit.

```
instance fit (OR s t) | fit s & fit t
where
    fit (L x) = fit x
    fit (R y) = fit y

instance fit (BinOp x) | gEq{|*|} x & isConst , fit x
where
  fit (OpMinus x y) = x =!= y   && ¬(is0 y)  && fit x && fit y && ¬(isAny x && isAny y)
  fit (OpPlus x y)  = ¬(is0 x)  && ¬(is0 y)  && fit x && fit y && ¬(isAny x && isAny y)
  fit (OpTimes x y) = ¬(is01 x) && ¬(is01 y) && fit x && fit y && ¬(isAny x && isAny y)
  fit (OpPower x (PConst p)) = p>1 && fit x

instance fit Expr where fit (Expr e) = fit e
```

In the code above we used the following predicates to decide if some data type represents the constant 0 (`is0`), the constant 0 or 1 (`is01`), or any constant (`isAny`).

```
is0 x   = isConst (λi.i==0) x
is01 x  = isConst (λi.i==0 || i==1) x
isAny x = isConst (λi.True) x
```

These predicates are built on top of the class `isConst` defined as:

```
class isConst a :: (Int→Bool) a → Bool

instance isConst (OR s t) | isConst s & isConst t
where
    isConst p (L s) = isConst p s
    isConst p (R t) = isConst p t
instance isConst IConst where isConst p (IConst i) = p i
instance isConst Expr   where isConst p (Expr e)   = isConst p e
instance isConst a      where isConst p a          = False
```

Using this predicate we can update our predicate to find functions matching $f(0) = 0$, $f(2) = 4$ and $f(3) = 9$ to:

```
p2 :: Expr → Property
p2 d = fit d ⟹ ¬(f 0 == 0 && f 2 == 4 && f 3 == 9) where f = apply d
```

In order to test the first 1000 candidates, the test system rejects 738 candidates that are not `fit` and not counted as a test. Within one second the test system produces the following result:

```
Counterexample 1 found after 13 tests:  (x*x)
Counterexample 2 found after 24 tests:  (x^2)
Counterexample 3 found after 253 tests:  ((x+(x*x))-x)
Counterexample 4 found after 332 tests:  (((x^2)+x)-x)
Counterexample 5 found after 419 tests:  ((1+(x*x))-1)
Counterexample 6 found after 654 tests:  (((x^2)+(x+x))-(x+x))
```

This shows that a number of undesirable results are removed. One might argue that the solutions from 3 up to 6 are all undesirable. They can be excluded by improving the predicate `fit` as well.

This concludes the generation of candidates for this simple example. Perhaps the reader wonders that we needed quite a heavy equipment to find rather simple functions. There are two answers to this concern. First and foremost, the test tool G∀st including the generic generation of instances of data types is existing technology. It is treated here to make this paper self-contained, but only the application as inductive programming tool is new. Second, the approach introduced here can also be applied to many other and more complicated problem areas. We show a couple of those applications in the next sections.

5 Keppler's Third Law

Kepler (1571-1630) studied the motion of planets of the Sun. He is famous for formulating 3 laws about the motion of planets. His third law was formulated more than ten years after the first two laws. This third law quantitatively relates orbital period and distance of the planet to the Sun. Apparently it was hard for him to find this law. This may be partially caused by the kind of equipment and data available in those days.

In order to test the power of our approach we try to rediscover Kepler's third law from data about the planets found on Wikipedia [1]. The basis of our data is table 1 containing the diameter, mass, orbital radius, and orbital period of the planets of our Sun. These parameters are given in astronomical units (AU), which means that these parameters are relative to the parameter for the Earth.

Table 1. Parameters of the planets

Name	Equatorial diameter (AU)	Mass (AU)	Orbital radius (AU)	Orbital Period (years)
Mercury	0.382	0.06	0.39	0.24
Venus	0.949	0.82	0.72	0.62
Earth	1.00	1.00	1.00	1.00
Mars	0.532	0.11	1.52	1.88
Jupiter	11.209	317.8	5.20	11.86
Saturn	9.449	95.2	9.54	29.46
Uranus	4.007	14.6	19.22	84.01
Neptune	3.883	17.2	30.06	164.8

In our synthesis this table is represented as a list of 5-tuples. Each tuple represents one line in the table.

```
// [(name, diameter, mass, orbital radius, and orbital period)]
planetTable :: [(String, Real, Real, Real, Real)]
planetTable
  = [("Mercury" ,0.382  ,0.06  ,0.39  ,0.24)
    ,("Venus"   ,0.949  ,0.82  ,0.72  ,0.62)
    ,("Earth"   ,1.00   ,1.00  ,1.00  ,1.00)
    ,("Mars"    ,0.532  ,0.11  ,1.52  ,1.88)
    ,("Jupiter" ,11.209 ,317.8 ,5.20  ,11.86)
    ,("Saturn"  ,9.449  ,95.2  ,9.54  ,29.46)
    ,("Uranus"  ,4.007  ,14.6  ,19.22 ,84.01)
    ,("Neptune" ,3.883  ,17.2  ,30.06 ,164.8)
    ]
```

For Keppler's third law we are looking for a function giving the period as function of the mass and the distance, that is a function of type $f\,(mass,\ distance) = period$.

Clearly we need slightly different expressions as above. Here we have two real numbers as argument instead of one integer. Moreover, there might be other operators involved. Apart from the expressions $x_1 - x_2$, $x_1 + x_2$, $x_1 \times x - s$ and $x\hat{\ }p$ (power) considered above, we include $\sin x$, $\cos x$ and $\sqrt{x}$. This are the usual operations found in any handbook of physics. The corresponding data types are:

```
:: Op x
     = OpPlus x x | OpMinus x x | OpTimes x x | OpPower x PConst
     | OpDivide x x | OpRoot x PConst | Sin x | Cos x
:: Var = Var Int
:: Expr = Expr (OR (OR Var RConst) (Op Expr))

:: RConst = RConst Real
:: PConst = PConst Real
```

Exactly as above we derive generation of instances of these types for all complicated types. The only interesting cases are the generation of variables and constants. In this situation we know that the arity (number of arguments) of the desired function is two. So, only the variables `Var 0` and `Var 1` make sense.

```
ggen{|Var|} n r = map Var [0..arity-1]
arity = 2
ggen{|PConst|} n r = map PConst [2.0..3.0]
ggen{|RConst|} n r = map RConst [1.0, pi, pi4]
```

The environment should here not consider a single integer value as above, but a real value for each argument. This is represented by a list of reals. The only slightly interesting instance is the one that looks up a variable in the environment.

```
instance apply Var [Real] Real where apply (Var i) = λe.e!!i
```

All other instances of `apply` are exactly similar to the once shown above. The only difference is that the resulting value is of type `Real`. Whenever necessary the environment should be given the type `[Real]`.

After these preparations we can immediately state the property for functions implementing Keppler's third law: The function k_3 should be *fit* and $k_3\,(m, r) \approx\ p$.

```
pKepler :: Expr → Property
pKepler k3 = fit k3 ⟹ ¬((λ(name,d,m,r,p). apply k3 [m,r] ≈ p) For planetTable)
```

In order to compensate for small errors in real calculations and finite precision the the numbers in the planet table we use $\approx$ instead of $=$. The operator $\approx$ considers two numbers equal if their relative difference is less than some δ, e.g. 1%.

```
(≈) infix 4 :: Real Real → Bool
(≈) x y = x==y || (abs (x-y)/(abs x+abs y)) ≤ delta
```

Within 0.5 second this system generates the first version of Keppler's third law. The first 5 functions generated are:

```
Counterexample 1 found after 4838 tests: k3 x0 x1 = (x1^(1/2))^3
Counterexample 2 found after 6121 tests: k3 x0 x1 = (x1^(1/2))*x1
Counterexample 3 found after 12286 tests: k3 x0 x1 = (x1^3)^(1/2)
Counterexample 4 found after 54331 tests: k3 x0 x1 = (x1*x1)/(x1^(1/2))
Counterexample 5 found after 80598 tests: k3 x0 x1 = (x1^2)/(x1^(1/2))
```

Note that the mass, `x0`, of the planet does not occur in the body of these functions. Apparently it plays no rôle in the law. If we had known this before, we could have searched for a function obeying the predicate $k_3\,(r)\ \approx\ p$. We pretended that we had just like Keppler no idea of the relation to be found. The generated functions are all equivalent to the official versions of Kepplers third law:

$$K_3 : \; p = \sqrt{r}^{\,3}$$

Our system found this law within one second. Even if we include the time to construct our function synthesis system this is much faster than the ten years Keppler needed. This is of course by no means a fair comparision. For instance we can lookup the data of planets simply at Wikipedia and have quite powerful computers available. However, this example shows that our approach is capable to solve nontrivial problems.

Until know we have shown that it is possible to generate functions with a body that is some expression over containing variables, and predefined operators. In the next sections we try to find recursive functions and λ–expressions obeying some predicate.

6 Synthesizing Primitive Recursive Functions

The principle introduced above can also be applied to recursive functions. However, the presence of functions imposes one additional concern. Suppose we synthesize a nonterminating function and start evaluating the predicate. This will start a nonterminating computation. We can look for three kind of solutions:

1. At first glance extending the predicate `fit` to allow only terminating functions looks tempting. Unfortunately termination of computations is an undecidable problem. Of course we make a safe approximation and allow only functions that are known to terminate. In case of doubt, the function is considered to be not `fit`.
2. A better solution is to synthesize only functions that are known to terminate always. We will explore this approach in this section for primitive recursive functions.
3. Another approach is to reduce functions only a finite amount of reduction steps, say 1000 step. If the predicate is not reduced to `True` in these steps we reject this candidate function. Of course this includes the risk to reject matching functions, but we avoid nontermination. This approach is explored in the next section.

In order to generate primitive recursive functions that are guaranteed to terminate we extend the syntax for expression from section 3.2 with the following syntax for recursive functions.

$$\begin{aligned}
Fun &= \mathbf{f(x)} = \{\; Expr \mid RFun \;\} \\
RFun &= \mathbf{if}\ (\mathbf{x} \leq \; Termval\ )\ \mathbf{then}\ Expr\ \mathbf{else}\ PRex \\
PRex &= FunAp \mid Var \mid IConst \mid BinOp\ PRex \\
FunAp &= \mathbf{f}\,(\,\mathbf{x} - \; FConst\,) \\
TermVal &= 0\,..\,2 \\
FConst &= 1\,..\,2
\end{aligned}$$

Again we map this directly to a data type that includes all variable parts of the functions. There is no reason to store constant parts in the abstract syntax tree. For this reason FunAp only contains the constant subtracted from the argument x in the recursive call.

```
:: PRex    = PRex (OR (OR FunAp Var) (OR IConst (BinOp PRex)))
:: FunAp   = FunAp Int
:: TermVal = TermVal Int
:: RFun    = RFun TermVal Expr PRex
:: Fun     = Fun (OR Expr RFun)
```

Like usual we derive the generation of everything in the abstract syntax trees but the constants. The generation of constants has the familiar pattern:

```
gengen{|TermVal|} = map TermVal [0..2]
gengen{|FunAp|}   = map FunAp   [1..2]
```

In order to evaluate the application of such syntax trees we use an environment that contains the recursive function as well as the value of the current argument: (Int→Int,Int).
In the instance for variable we select the appropriate field from this environment:

```
instance apply Var (x,Int) Int where apply X = λ(_,i).i
```

The interesting instances of apply are the recursive function call FunAp, and the initial function definition by RFun. In the instance for RFun we transform the abstract syntax tree to a function of type Int→Int and put it in the initial environment together with the current argument.

```
instance apply FunAp (Int→Int,Int) Int where apply (FunAp d) = λ(f,i).f (i−d)
instance apply RFun Int Int
where apply rf=:(RFun (TermVal c) t e) = f
      where f i = if (i≤c) (apply t i) (apply e (f,i))
```

We can synthesize functions for the input–output patterns from above: $f(0) = 0$, $f(2) = 4$ and $f(3) = 9$ by:

```
p3 :: Fun → Property
p3 d = fit d ⟹ ¬(f 0 = 0 && f 2 = 4 && f 3 = 9) where f = apply d

Start = testnm 1000 5 p1
```

Note that compared to p2 only the type used in the predicate is changed from Expr to Fun, this is all we need to do to change the search space. The results are:

```
Counterexample 1 found after 25 tests: f x = x*x
Counterexample 2 found after 57 tests: f x = x^2
Counterexample 3 found after 6241 tests: f x = ((x+x)−x)^2
Counterexample 4 found after 7500 tests: f x = ((x*x)+x)−x
Counterexample 5 found after 8336 tests: f x = if (x≤1) (x+x) (f (x−2)+(f (x−1)+x))
```

As expected the first results are identical to synthesizing using the type Expr since this is the first option in the type Fun. The fifth function synthesized however is a recursive function.

In exactly the same way we can synthesize familiar primitive recursive functions from a few input–output pairs. For instance:

```
p4 :: Fun → Property
p4 d = fit d ⟹ ¬(f 1 = 1 && f 4 = 24) where f = apply d
```

yields the factorial function.

```
Counterexample 1 found after 2785 tests: f x = if (x≤0) 1 (x*f (x−1))
```

and

```
p5 :: Fun → Property
p5 d = fit d ⟹ ¬(f 5 = 8 && f 7 = 21) where f = apply d
```

yields the famous Fibonacci function

```
Counterexample 1 found after 1167 tests: f x = if (x≤1) 1 (f (x−2)+f (x−1))
```

The Ackermann function cannot be synthesized in this way since it is not primitive recursive.

This approach is not restricted to function having a single integer variable as argument. Above we have shown how multiple arguments can be handled. In exactly the same way as functions over integers we have also synthesized recursive functions over lists and other recursive data types.

7 Synthesizing Lambda Expressions

In this section we show how λ-expressions with specific properties can be synthesized. This imposes two problems. First it is not possible to use a data type that represents only terminating functions. If we need to generate λ-expressions, the abstract syntax tree to be used reflects the structure of those λ-expressions. The second problem is a consequence of using those λ-expressions: it is hard to determine an interesting class of λ-expressions that is known to terminate.

We solve these problems one by one. First we define a data type to represent λ-expressions. Apart from the well-known variables (Var V), abstractions (Abs V LExpr), and applications (Ap LExpr LExpr), we have integer constants (Const C), and binary operator constants (OpConst String). These binary operations are integer manipulations like "+" and "-".

```
:: LExpr = Var V | Abs V LExpr | Ap LExpr LExpr | Const C | OpConst String
:: V = V Int      // variable
:: C = C Int      // constant
```

We do not include a build-in conditional for our λ-expressions. The Booleans and the conditional are represented by the expressions $\lambda\ v_0 \,.\, \lambda\ v_1 \,.\, v_0$ for True, $\lambda\ v_0 \,.\, \lambda\ v_1 \,.\, v_1$ for False, and the identity function $\lambda\ v \,.\, v$ for if. Represented as syntax trees this is:

```
TRUE  = Abs v0 (Abs v1 (Var v0))
FALSE = Abs v0 (Abs v1 (Var v1))
If    = Abs v0 (Var v0)
```

It is completely standard to write a reducer for λ-expressions of the form LExpr. We omit the details here for brevity and assume that we have a reducer to head normal form according to the lazy (left-most, outer-most) strategy.

```
hnf :: LExpr → LExpr
```

The only thing special about this reduce is that it does at most N reduction steps in order to ensure termination. In our test we used 1000 as upper limit for the number of reduction steps.

As a first approach we generate instance of `LExpr` in the now familiar way: we manually generate some appropriate constants and variables and derive generation for the other types. We reformulate property `p1` from above to find λ-expression matching $f(0) = 0$, $f(2) = 4$ and $f(3) = 9$ as:

```
pL1 :: LExpr → Bool
pL1 f = ¬(p 0 0 && p 2 4 && p 3 9)
where p x y = hnf (Ap f (Const (C x))) === (Const (C y))
```

Unfortunately our synthesis technique does not find an answer in reasonable time. Our approach fails since the search space is too large. Most of the generated expressions are ill-formed, like $\lambda a\,.\,b$, $\lambda a\,.\,+$, and so on.

There are several solutions for this problem. For instance we can define the generation of instances of `LExpr` manually as we did in [12]. This works well, but this approach is not very elegant. Another solution is to keep track of the type of the generated expressions during generating and make sure to yield only well-typed expressions. Katayama [8] uses this approach quite successfully. We find it less appealing since it further complicates the generation algorithm.

In this paper we propose a new method to control the generation of λ-expressions: we introduce an additional data type that corresponds to a high level language that describes the functions we want to consider. We synthesize instances of these high level data type in the usual way; define the instances of constants manually and derive the generation of the rest. Next we convert the instances of these high level syntax trees to λ-expressions. For this purpose we can introduce the class `conv`.

```
class conv a :: a → LExpr
```

However, it is more interresting and convenient to define a generic conversion.

```
generic gconv a :: a → LExpr
```

The instances for `EITHER`, `PAIR` and `CONS` do nothing else than applying the given conversion function to the arguments.

```
gconv{|EITHER|} gf gg (LEFT x)   = gf x
gconv{|EITHER|} gf gg (RIGHT y)  = gg y
gconv{|PAIR|}   gf gg (PAIR x y) = Ap (gf x) (gg y)
gconv{|CONS|}   g     (CONS x)   = g x
```

For all leaves of the tree we have to think what should be done. For this reason we do not provide an instance of `UNIT`.

The conversion of high-level functions to λ-expressions can be found in any textbook on semantics or implementation of functional languages.

We use a data type very similar to the one for primitive recursive functions shown in the previous section.

```
:: Op     = Op String
:: Oper x = Oper Op x x
:: X      = X
:: RecAp  = RecAp Int
:: Ex     = Ex (OR (OR X C) (Oper Ex))
```

```
:: Pr     = Pr (OR (OR X C) (OR (Oper Pr) RecAp))
:: RFun   = RFun C Ex Pr
:: Fun    = Fun Ex
```

As usual we define the generation of constants manually and derive generation for all other data types.

```
gengen{|Op|}    = map Op ["+","*"]
gengen{|RecAp|} = map RecAp [1..2]
derive gengen Oper, X, Ex, Pr, RFun, Fun
```

Similar to the previous section we can define an instance of fit for those types. This contains no surprises at all.

The conversion of these types to the corresponding types for λ-expressions is very simple for most types. Some typical examples are:

```
gconv{|C|} c = Const c
gconv{|V|} v = Var v
```

The conversion of a given body to a function is rather simple. We only have to add an abstraction to the converted body.

```
gconv{|Fun|} (Fun b) = Abs v0 (gconv{|*|} b)
```

Only the conversion of recursive functions deserves some attention. First we need to decide how we handle the recursion. Usually this is done by a Y-combinator defined as Y $f = f$ (Y f). Here we unfold the Y-combinator at conversion time. This implies that every recursive call gets its own function as λ-term as its first argument. By convention the function argument is represented by v_0 and the recursive function by v_1. This implies that the recursive call $f\,(x - c)$ is represented by the term $v_1\ v_1\ (-\ v_0\ c)$. In terms of our data types this is:

```
gconv{|RecAp|} (RecAp c)
 = Ap (Ap (Var v1) (Var v1)) (Ap (Ap (OpConst "-") (Var v0)) (Const (C c)))
```

A recursive function definition rearranged the argument and the function such that it can be recursively applied. That is the function is represented by the λ-expression $(\lambda v_4 \,.\, \lambda v_3 \,.\, v_4\ v_4\ v_3)\ f$ where f is the λ-expression corresponding to the primitive recursive function. This function f as a λ-expression gets itself and the argument x as arguments $(\lambda v_1 \,.\, \lambda v_0 \ldots)$. In a conditional expression (see If defined as the identity function above) it checks wether x is less or equal to the given constant: $\leq\ v_0\ c$. Depending on this condition it either executes the converted then-part t, or else-part e.

```
gconv{|RFun|} (RFun c t e)
 = Ap (Abs v4 (Abs v3 (Ap (Ap (Var v4) (Var v4)) (Var v3)))) f
where f = Abs v1 (Abs v0 (Ap (Ap (Ap If (Ap (Ap (OpConst "≤") (Var v0)) (Const c)))
                                              (conv t)) (conv e)))
```

The conversion of Ex, Pr, and OR can be derived.

```
derive gconv Ex, Pr, OR
```

After all these preparations it is easy to generate high quality λ-expressions. We simply convert the fit instance of functions Fun and recursive functions RFun.

```
ggen{|LExpr|} n r = map gconv{|*|} (filter fit (es n r))

es :: [OR Fun RFun]
es = gengen{|*|}
```

With these generator for instance of LExpr the test system finds solutions for predicate pL1 quickly:

```
Counterexample 1 found after 4 tests: (λa.(∗ a) a)
Counterexample 2 found after 748 tests: (λa.(+ ((∗ −1) a)) ((∗ a) ((+ a) 1)))
Counterexample 3 found after 863 tests: (λa.(+ ((∗ a) −1)) ((∗ a) ((+ a) 1)))
Counterexample 4 found after 1294 tests: (λa.(+ ((+ 1) ((∗ a) a))) −1)
Counterexample 5 found after 1484 tests: (λe.e e)(λb.λa.(((λa.a)((≤ a) −1)) 1)((∗ a)a))
```

In a similar way we can state some input–output pairs of the Fibonacci function:

```
pL2 :: LExpr → Bool
pL2 f = ¬(p 3 3 && p 4 5 && p 5 8 && p 7 21)
where
    p x y = hnf (Ap f (Const (C x))) == (Const (C y))
```

The first Fibonacci function in λ-calculus found is:

```
(λe.e e) (λb.λa.(((λa.a) ((≤ a) 1)) 1) ((+ ((b b) ((− a) 2))) ((b b) ((− a) 1))))
```

This λ-term corresponds exactly to the most common double recursive definition.

Of course it is also possible to select the desired (primitive recursive) functions in a way similar to the previous section and transform the matching functions to λ-terms. We prefer the route outline here. The synthesized λ expressions are really used to determine if they obey the given predicate. This gives much more confidence that they really are the expressions we are looking for. In the alternative approach mistakes in compiling high-level functions to λ-terms will pass unnoticed.

8 Related and Future Work

Many attempts have been described to construct inductive programming systems. The synthesize candidates and test approach here is just one of the possibilities. See for instance [14] for an overview.

Closely related to our work is the approach of Katayama [8]. He generates λ-expressions using type information and a set of user-defined functions in the functional programming language Haskell. Recursion for a data type that is used as argument of the generated functions has to be defined as one of the primitives in Haskell. The actual generation of λ-terms is a black box. Since our approach is based on a general test system supporting first–order logic, our system is able to handle a wider range of predicates. We can control the generation of candidate functions very easily by changing the appropriate data types. this make our approach more flexible. In [9] Katayama proposes to use a test based approach to determine the equivalence of functions as alternative to our function fit. It is very easy to add this to our system, but unnecessary. The given definitions of fit removes equivalent candidate functions effectively. Since fit only has to look at the current candidate it is more efficient if the system has to generate large number of candidates. The amount of work needed to compare a new candidates with the candidates seen before will increase if the number of candidates seen increases. An even better approach is to use a more sophisticated grammar and associated data-types that exclude many of the redundant function candidates. Using such a grammar we can for instance ensure that constants for operations like addition and multiplication only occur in one of the branches, and try to avoid subexpressions that contain only arithmetic operations applied to constants.

Our approach works for any kind of functions. The user has to supply only a data type representing the abstract syntax trees, a function apply that assigns a meaning to those syntax trees, and the generation of the trees. We have show that generic programming can really help to reduce the amount of functions that has to be defined manually.

In the future we want to develop a generic version of apply. This function has now a lot of dull instances that should be derived from a generic definition.

The current examples do not need much constants. In many kind of functions there are a lot of constants involved. Determining these constants by a generate and test approach will not be very effective. We want to investigate if it is possible to determine the shape of the functions by the techniques outlined in this paper and select the appropriate constants by a conventional technique like hill climbing.

The real challenge is of course to generate more complex functions using inductive programming. Despite all our efforts the search space for complicated functions still grows rapidly. Hence it will take much time to find such a function by a generate and test approach. There are two directions of optimizations possible. First we can generate more appropriate candidate expressions by adding knowledge to our system. If we somehow know what suitable building blocks of good candidates are, we add these primitives as additional items to our data types representing the candidate functions. Second we can try to split the problem area in smaller pieces and find solutions to these pieces separately, see [7]. In a next phase try to find solutions for the full problem by combining these partial solutions.

9 Conclusions

In this paper we have shown a very general and flexible approach to do inductive programming by a generate and test approach. The user defines the syntax of the functions to be generated by a set of algebraic data types. Using generic programming support the user defines the semantic of these syntax trees in function apply. The generation of instances of the algebraic data type representing the syntax of the candidate functions is done by a generic algorithm. Only the generation of constants deserves manual definitions. Using the model-based test tool G∀st one can specify high level predicates about determining the functions wanted.

In this paper we have shown that this system works for nonrecursive function, primitive recursive functions and λ-expressions. We are convinced that there are many more application areas.

Acknowledgement

We thank the anonymous reviewers for their useful feedback.

References

1. http://en.wikipedia.org/wiki/planet
2. Alimarine, A., Smetsers, S.: Efficient generic functional programming. Technical report niii-r0425, Institute for Computing and Information Sciences, Radboud University Nijmegen, The Netherlands (2004)
3. Banerjee, D.: A methodology for synthesis of recursive functional programs. ACM Transactions on Programming Languages and Systems (TOPLAS) 9(3), 441–462 (1987)
4. Bird, R.: Introduction to functional programming using Haskell, 2nd edn. Prentice Hall, Englewood Cliffs (1998)
5. Claessen, K., Hughes, J.: QuickCheck: a lightweight tool for random testing of Haskell programs. In: Proceedings of the 5th ACM SIGPLAN International Conference on Functional Programming, Montreal, Canada, pp. 268–279. ACM Press, New York (2000)
6. Cypher, A.: Watch what I do: programming by demonstration. MIT Press, Cambridge (1993)
7. Henderson, R.: Incremental learning in inductive programming. In: Schmid, U., Kitzelmann, E., Plasmeijer, R. (eds.) AAIP 2009. LNCS, vol. 5812, pp. 74–92. Springer, Heidelberg (2010)
8. Katayama, S.: Systematic search for lambda expressions. In: Proceedings of the 6th Symposium on Trends in Functional Programming (TFP 2005), pp. 195–205 (2005)
9. Katayama, S.: Efficient exhaustive generation of functional programs using monte-carlo search with iterative deepening. In: Ho, T.-B., Zhou, Z.-H. (eds.) PRICAI 2008. LNCS (LNAI), vol. 5351, pp. 199–210. Springer, Heidelberg (2008)
10. Koopman, P., Plasmeijer, R.: Fully automatic testing with functions as specifications. In: Horváth, Z. (ed.) CEFP 2005. LNCS, vol. 4164, pp. 35–61. Springer, Heidelberg (2006)
11. Koopman, P., Plasmeijer, R.: Systematic synthesis of functions. In: Nilsson, H. (ed.) Selected Papers of the 7th Symposium on Trends in Functional Programming, TFP 2006, Nottingham, UK, April 19-21, pp. 68–83 (2006). Intellect Books, ISBN 978-1-84150-188-8
12. Koopman, P., Plasmeijer, R.: Systematic synthesis of λ-terms. In: Barendsen, E., Capretta, V., Geuvers, H., Niqui, M. (eds.) Reflections on Type Theory, λ-Calculus, and the Mind - Essays dedicated to Henk Barendregt on the Occasion of his 60th Birthday, December 17, pp. 211–222 (2007) ISBN 978-90-9022446-6
13. Plasmeijer, R., van Eekelen, M.: Concurrent Clean language report (version 2.0) (December 2001), http://www.cs.ru.nl/~clean/
14. Schmid, U. (ed.): Inductive Synthesis of Functional Programs. LNCS (LNAI), vol. 2654. Springer, Heidelberg (2003)

Inductive Programming: A Survey of Program Synthesis Techniques

Emanuel Kitzelmann

Cognitive Systems Group, University of Bamberg
emanuel.kitzelmann@uni-bamberg.de

Abstract. Inductive programming (IP)—the use of inductive reasoning methods for programming, algorithm design, and software development—is a currently emerging research field. A major subfield is inductive program synthesis, the (semi-)automatic construction of programs from exemplary behavior. Inductive program synthesis is not a unified research field until today but scattered over several different established research fields such as machine learning, inductive logic programming, genetic programming, and functional programming. This impedes an exchange of theory and techniques and, as a consequence, a progress of inductive programming. In this paper we survey theoretical results and methods of inductive program synthesis that have been developed in different research fields until today.

1 Introduction

Inductive programming (IP) is an emerging field, comprising research on inductive reasoning theory and methods for computer programming, algorithm design, and software development. In this sense, albeit with different accentuation, the term has been used by Partridge [1], by Flener and Partridge [2], within the workshops on "Approaches and Applications of Inductive Programming", and within the ICML'06 tutorial on "Automatic Inductive Programming".

IP has intersections with machine learning, artificial intelligence, programming, software engineering, and algorithms research. Nevertheless, it goes beyond each of these fields in one or the other aspect and therefore is a research field in its own right, intrinsically.

It goes beyond classical machine learning in that the focus lies on learning general programs including loops and recursion, instead of merely (mostly non-recursive) models or classifiers in restricted representational frameworks, such as decision trees or neural networks.

In classical software engineering and algorithm design, a *deductive*—reasoning from the general to the specific—view of software development is predominant. One aspires a general problem description as starting point from which a program or algorithm is developed as a particular solution. Methods based on deductive reasoning exist to partly automatize the programming and verification process—such as automatic code generation from UML diagrams, (deductive) program synthesis to generate algorithmic parts, program transformation and refactoring

U. Schmid, E. Kitzelmann, and R. Plasmeijer (Eds.): AAIP 2009, LNCS 5812, pp. 50–73, 2010.

to optimize programs, and theorem proving, model checking, and static analysis to verify programs. To emphasize this common deductive foundation one might speak of *deductive programming* to subsume established software development methods.

Inductive programming, on the other side, aims at developing methods based on *inductive*—from the specific to the general—reasoning (not to be confused with mathematical or structural induction) to assist in programming, algorithm design, and the development of software. Starting point for IP methods is specific data of a problem—use cases, test cases, desirable (and undesirable) behavior of a software, input/output examples (I/O-examples) of a function or a module interface, computation traces of a program for particular inputs and so forth. Such descriptions of a problem are known to be incomplete. Inductive methods produce a *generalization* of such an incomplete specification by identifying general patterns in the data. The result might be again a—more complete—specification or an actual implementation of a function, a module, or (other parts of) a program.

Inductive reasoning is per se unsound. Inductively obtained conclusions are *hypotheses* and incapable of proof regarding their premises. This is, perhaps, the most severe objection against IP. What is the use of methods whose results cannot be proven correct and possibly deviate from what was intended? However, if the data at hand is representative then it is likely that identified patterns actually hold in the general case and that, indeed, the induced result meets the general problem. On the other side, *all* software development necessarily makes a transition from a first *informal* and often incomplete problem description by the user or customer to a complete and ideally formal specification. This transition is (i) also incapable of formal proof and (ii) possibly based on—non-systematic, inexplicit—generalization. Also, IP should not be understood as a replacement for deductive methods but as an addition. IP may be used in different ways: to generate candidate solutions subject to further inspection, in combination with deductive methods to tackle a problem from the general description *as well as* from concrete (counter-)instances, to systematize occurring generalizations, or to check the representativeness of example cases provided by the user. Some problems, especially many problems in the field of artificial intelligence, elude a complete specification at all, e.g., face recognition. This factum is known as *knowledge-acquisition bottleneck*. Overall, there is no reason why systematically incorporating existing or easily formulated data by inductive methods should not improve efficiency and even validity of software development.

One important aspect of IP is the inductive synthesis of actual, executable *programs* including recursion or loops. Except to professional software development, possible application fields of the (semi-)automatic induction of programs from exemplary behavior are end-user programming and learning of recursive policies [3] in intelligent agents. Research on *inductive program synthesis (IPS)* started in the seventies. However, it has, since then, always been only a niche in several different research fields and communities such as artificial intelligence, machine learning, inductive logic programming (ILP), genetic programming, and functional programming. Until today, there is no uniform body of theory and methods. This fragmentation over different communities impedes exchange of results and may lead to redundancies. The problem is all the more profound as only few people and groups at all are working on IPS worldwide.

This paper surveys theoretical results and IPS methods that have been developed in different research fields until today. We grouped the work into three blocks: First the classical, analytic data-driven induction of LISP programs as invented by Summers [4] and its generalizations (Section 3), second ILP (Section 4), and third several generate-and-test based approaches to the induction of functional programs (Section 5). In Section 6 we state some conclusions and ideas of further research. As general preliminaries, we informally introduce some common IPS concepts in the following section.

This survey is quite comprehensive, yet not complete and covers functional generate-and-test methods less detailed than the other two areas. This is due to limited space in combination with the author's areas of expertise and shall not be interpreted as a measure of quality. We hope that it will be a useful resource for all people interested in IP.

2 Basic Inductive Programming Concepts

IPS aims at constructing a computer program or algorithm from a *(known-to-be-)incomplete specification* of a function to be implemented, called *target function*. Incomplete means, that the target function is not specified on its whole domain but only on (small) parts of it. Typically, an incomplete specification consists of a subset of the graph of the function: *input/output examples (I/O-examples)*. Variables may be allowed in I/O-examples and also more expressive formalisms have been used to specify the target function.

An induced program contains function *primitives*, predefined functions known to the IPS system. Primitives may be fixed within the IPS system or dynamically be given as an extra, problem-specific, input. Dynamically provided primitives are called *background knowledge*.

Example 1. Suppose the following I/O-examples on lists (whatever the list elements $A, x, y, z, 1, 2, 3, 5$ stand for; constants, variables, or compound objects), are provided: $(A) \mapsto ()$, $(x, y, z) \mapsto (x, y)$, $(3, 5, 2, 1) \mapsto (3, 5, 2)$. Given the common list constructors/destructors `nil`, `cons`, `head`, `tail`, the predicate `empty` to test for the empty list, and the `if-then-else`-conditional as primitives, an IPS system might return the following implementation of the *Init*-function returning the input list without its last element:

```
F(x) = if empty(tail(x)) then nil
          else cons(head(x), F(tail(x))) .
```

Given a particular set of primitives, some target function may not be representable by only one recursive function definition such that a non-specified recursive *subfunction* needs to be introduced; this is called *(necessary) predicate invention* in ILP.

IPS is commonly regarded as a *search problem*. In general, the problem space consists of the representable programs as nodes and instances of the operators of the IPS system to transform one program into another as arcs. Due to *under-specification* in IP, typically infinitely many (semantically) different programs meet the specification. Hence, one needs criteria to choose between them. Such criteria are called *inductive bias* [5]. Two kinds of inductive bias exist: If an IPS system can only generate a certain proper subset of all (computable) functions of some domain, either because its language is restricted or because its operators are not able to reach each program, this constitutes a *restriction bias*. The order in which the problem space is explored and hence the ordering of solutions is the *preference bias*; it can be modelled as probability distribution over the program space.

3 The Analytical Functional Approach

A first systematic attempt to IPS was made by Summers [4]. He noticed that under particular restrictions regarding allowed primitives, program schema, and choice of I/O-examples, a recursive LISP program can be computed from I/O-examples without search in program space. His insights originated some further research.

3.1 Summers' Pioneering Work

Summers' approach to induce recursive LISP functions from I/O-examples includes two steps: First, a so-called *program fragment*, an expression of one variable and the allowed primitives, is derived for each I/O-pair such that applied to the input, evaluates to the specified output. Furthermore, predicates are derived to distinguish between example inputs. Integrated into a McCarthy conditional, these predicate/fragment pairs build a non-recursive program computing the I/O-examples and is considered as a first approximation to the target function. In a second step, recurrent relations between predicates and fragments each are identified and a recursive program generalizing them is derived.

Example inputs and outputs are *S-expressions*, the fundamental data structure of the LISP language [6]. We define the set of *subexpressions* of an S-expression to consist of the S-expression itself and, if it is non-atomic, of all subexpressions of both its components.

The programs constructed by Summers' technique use the LISP primitives *cons*, *car*, *cdr*, *nil*, *atom*, and T, the last denoting the truth value *true*. Particularly, no other predicates than *atom* and T (e.g., *eq* for testing equality of S-expressions), and no atoms except for *nil* are used. This choice of primitives is not arbitrary but crucial for Summers' methodology of deriving programs from examples without search. The McCarthy conditional and recursion are used as control structure. Allowing *atom* and T as only predicates and *nil* as only atom in outputs means that the atoms in the I/O-examples, except for *nil*, are actually considered as *variables*. Renaming them does not change the meaning. This implies that any semantic information must be expressed by the *structure* of the S-expression.

1. Step: Initial Non-recursive Approximation. Given a set of k I/O-examples, $\{\langle i_1, o_1 \rangle, \ldots, \langle i_k, o_k \rangle\}$, a program fragment $f_j(x), j \in \{1, \ldots, k\}$, composed of *cons*, *car*, and *cdr* is derived for each I/O-pair, which evaluates to the output when applied to the input: $f_j(i_j) = o_j$.

S-expressions are uniquely constructed by *cons* and destructed by *car* and *cdr*. We call *car*-*cdr* compositions *basic functions* (cp. [7]). Together with the following two conditions, this allows for determining unique program fragments. (i) Each atom may occur only once in each input. (ii) Each atom, except for *nil*, occurring in an output must also occur in the corresponding input. Due to the first condition, each subexpression occurs exactly once in an S-expression such that subexpressions are denoted by unique basic functions.

Deriving a program fragment works as follows: All subexpressions of an input, together with their unique basic functions, are enumerated. Then the output is rewritten by composing the basic functions from the input subexpressions with *cons* and *nil*.

Example 2. Consider the I/O-pair $((a\,.\,b)\,.\,(c\,.\,d)) \mapsto ((d\,.\,c)\,.\,(a\,.\,b))$. The input contains the following subexpressions, paired with the corresponding unique basic functions:

$$\langle ((a\,.\,b)\,.\,(c\,.\,d)), I \rangle\,, \quad \langle (a\,.\,b), car \rangle\,, \quad \langle (c\,.\,d), cdr \rangle\,,$$
$$\langle a, caar \rangle\,, \quad \langle b, cdar \rangle\,, \quad \langle c, cadr \rangle\,, \quad \langle d, cddr \rangle\,.$$

Since the example output is neither a subexpression of the input nor *nil*, the program fragment becomes a *cons* of the fragments for the *car*- and the *cdr*-component, respectively, of the output. The *car*-part, $(d\,.\,c)$, again becomes a *cons*, namely of the basic functions for d: *cddr*, and c: *cadr*. The *cdr*-part, $(a\,.\,b)$, *is* a subexpression of the input, its basic function is *car*. With variable x denoting the input, the fragment for this I/O-example is thus:

$$cons(cons(cddr(x), cadr(x)), car(x))$$

Next, predicates $p_j(x), j = 1, \ldots, k$ must be determined. In order to get the correct program fragment f_j be evaluated for each input i_j, all predicates $p_{j'}(i_j), 1 \leq j' < j$ (positioned before p_j in the conditional) must evaluate to *false* and $p_j(i_j)$ to *true*. Predicates fulfilling this condition exist if the example inputs form a chain.

We do not describe the algorithm here. Both algorithms, for computing fragments and predicates, can be found in [7]. Figure 1 shows an example for the first step.

I/O-examples:

$$\begin{aligned}(a) &\mapsto nil,\\ (a,b) &\mapsto (a),\\ (a,b,c) &\mapsto (a,b),\\ (a,b,c,d) &\mapsto (a,b,c),\\ (a,b,c,d,e) &\mapsto (a,b,c,d)\,.\end{aligned}$$

First approximation:

$$\begin{aligned}F(x) = (atom(cdr(x)) &\to nil\\ atom(cddr(x)) &\to cons(car(x), nil)\\ atom(cdddr(x)) &\to cons(car(x), cons(cadr(x), nil))\\ atom(cddddr(x)) &\to cons(car(x), cons(cadr(x), cons(caddr(x), nil)))\\ T &\to cons(car(x), cons(cadr(x), cons(caddr(x),\\ &\qquad cons(cadddr(x), nil)))))\end{aligned}$$

Fig. 1. I/O-examples and the corresponding first approximation

2. Step: Recurrence Relations. The basic idea in Summers' generalization method is this: The fragments are assumed to be the actual computations carried out by a *recursive* program for the intended function. Hence fragments of greater inputs must comprise fragments of lesser inputs as subterms, with a suitable substitution of the variable x and in a recurrent form along the set of fragments. The same holds analogously for the predicates. Summers calls this relation between fragments and predicates *differences*.

As a preliminary for the following, we need to define the concept of a *context*. A *(one-hole) context* $C[\,]$ is a term including exactly one occurrence of the distinguished symbol $\Box$. $C[s]$ denotes the result of replacing the $\Box$ by the (sub)term s in $C[\,]$.

Definition 1. *A* difference *exists between two terms (fragments or predicates) t, t' iff $t' = C[t\sigma]$ for some context $C[\,]$ and substitution σ.*

If we have $k+1$ I/O-examples, we only consider the first k fragment/predicate pairs because the last predicate is always 'T', such that no sensible difference can be derived for it.

Example 3. The following differences, written as recurrence relations ($2 \le i \le 3$), can be identified in the first $k = 4$ fragments/predicates of the program of Figure 1.

$$\begin{aligned}p_1(x) &= atom(cdr(x)) & f_1(x) &= nil\\ p_2(x) &= atom(cddr(x)) & f_2(x) &= cons(car(x), nil)\\ p_{i+1}(x) &= p_i(cdr(x)) & f_{i+1}(x) &= cons(car(x), f_i(cdr(x)))\end{aligned}$$

In the general case, we have (for k fragments/predicates):

$$
\begin{array}{ll}
j-1 \text{ “constant” fragments (as derived from the examples):} & f_1, \ldots, f_{j-1}, \\
\text{further } n \text{ constant base cases:} \quad f_j, \ldots, f_{j+n-1}, & \\
\text{finally, remaining } k-(j+n-1) \text{ cases recurring to} & \\
\text{previous cases:} \quad f_{i+n} = C[f_i\sigma_1] \quad \text{for } i = j, \ldots, k-n\,; & \\
\text{analogously for predicates:} \quad p_1, \ldots, p_{j-1}, p_j, \ldots, p_{j+n-1}, p_{i+n} = p_i(\sigma_2)\,. &
\end{array}
\tag{1}
$$

Index j denotes the first predicate/fragment pair which recurs in some following predicate/fragment pair (the first base case). The precedent $j-1$ predicate/fragment pairs do not recur. n is the interval of the recurrence. For Example 3 we have $j=2$ and $n=1$.

Inductive Inference. If $k-j \geq 2n$ then we *inductively infer* that the recurrence relations hold for all $i \geq j$.

In Example 3 we have $k-j = 2 \geq 2 = 2n$ and hence induce that the relations hold for all $i \geq 2$.

The generalized recurrence relations may be used to compute new approximations of the assumed target function. The mth *approximating function*, $m \geq j$, is defined as

$$F_m(x) = (p_1(x) \to f_1(x), \ldots, p_m(x) \to f_m(x), T \to \omega)$$

where the p_i, f_i with $j < i \leq m$ are defined in terms of the generalized recurrence relations and where ω means *undefined.* Consider the following *complete partial order* over partial functions, which is well known from denotational semantics:

$$F(x) \leq_F G(x) \text{ iff } F(x) = G(x) \text{ for all } x \in Dom(F)\,.$$

Regarding this order, the set of approximating functions builds a chain. The assumed target function $\mathbf{F}$ is defined as the supremum of this chain.

Now the hypothesized target function is defined, in terms of recurrence relations. In his synthesis theorem and its corollaries, Summers shows how a function defined this way can be expressed by a recursive program.[1]

Theorem 1 ([4]). *If* $\mathbf{F}$ *is defined in terms of recurrence relations as in* (1) *for* $j \leq i \in \mathbb{N}$ *then the following recursive program is identical to* $\mathbf{F}$*:*

$$
\begin{aligned}
F(x) &= (p_1(x) \to f_1(x), \ldots, p_{j-1}(x) \to f_{j-1}(x), \\
&\qquad T \to G(x)) \\
G(x) &= (p_j(x) \to f_j(x), \ldots, p_{j+n-1}(x) \to f_{j+n-1}(x), \\
&\qquad T \to C[G(\sigma(x))])\,.
\end{aligned}
$$

[1] This works, in a sense, reverse to interpreting a recursively expressed function by the partial function given as the fixpoint of the functional of the recursive definition. In the latter case we have a recursive program and want to have the particular partial function computed by it—here we have a partial function and want to have a recursive program computing it.

Example 4. The recurrence relations from Example 3 with $i \geq 2$ define the function **F** to be the *Init*-function. According to the synthesis theorem, the resulting program is:

$$F(x) = (atom(cdr(x)) \rightarrow nil, T \rightarrow G(x))$$
$$G(x) = (atom(cddr(x)) \rightarrow cons(car(x), nil), T \rightarrow cons(car(x), G(cdr(x)))) .$$

Introducing Additional Variables. It may happen that no recurrent differences can be found between a chain of fragments and/or predicates. In this case, the fragments/predicates may be generalized by replacing some common subterm by an additional variable. In the generalized fragment/predicate chain recurrent differences possibly exist.

3.2 Early Variants and Extensions

Two early extensions are described. A broader survey of these and other early extensions can be found in [7].

BMWk—Extended Forms of Recurrences. In Summers' approach, the condition for deriving a recursive function from detected differences is that the differences hold—starting from an initial index j and for a particular interval n—recurrently along fragments and predicates with a constant context $C[\,]$ and a constant substitution σ for x. The BMWK[2] algorithm [8] generalizes these conditions by allowing for contexts and substitutions that are different in each difference. Then a found sequence of differences originates a sequence of contexts and substitutions each. Both sequences are considered as fragments of new *subfunctions*. The BMWK algorithm is then recursively applied to these new fragment sequences, hence features the automatic introduction of (necessary) subfunctions.

Furthermore, Summers' ad-hoc method to introduce additional variables is systematized by computing *least general generalization (lgg)* [9] of successive fragments.

Biermann et al—Pruning Enumerative Search Based on Recurrences within Single Traces. Summers objective was to avoid search and to justify the synthesis by an explicit inductive inference step and a subsequent proven-to-be-correct program construction step. This could be achieved by a restricted program schema and the requirement of a well chosen set of I/O-examples.

On the contrary, Biermann's approach [10] is to employ traces (fragments) to speed up an exhaustive enumeration of a well-defined program class, the so-called *regular* LISP *programs.* Biermann's objectives regarding the synthesis were

1. *convergence* to the class of regular LISP programs,
2. convergence on the basis of *minimal input information,*
3. robust behavior on different inputs.

[2] This abbreviates *Boyer-Moore-Wegbreit-Kodratoff.*

Particularly 2 and 3 are contradictory to the recurrence detection method—by 2 Biermann means that no synthesis method exists which is able to synthesize every regular LISP program from fewer examples and by 2 he means that examples may be chosen randomly.

3.3 From Lisp to Term Rewriting Systems

At the beginning of Section 3.1 we stated the LISP primitives as used in programs induced by Summers' method (as well as by BMWK and Biermann's method). This selection is crucial for the first step, the deterministic construction of first approximations, yet not for the generalization step. Indeed, the latter is independent from particular primitives, it rather relies on matching (sub)terms over arbitrary first-order signatures. Two recent systems inspired by Summers' recurrence detection method use *term rewriting systems* over first-order signatures to represent programs. Special types of TRSs can be regarded as (idealized) functional programs.

A *term rewriting system (TRS)* is a set of directed equations or *(rewrite) rules.* A rule is a pair of first-order terms $\langle l, r\rangle$, written $l \to r$. The term l is called *left-hand side (lhs)*, r is called *right-hand side (rhs)* of the rule.

We get an *instance* of a rule by applying a substitution σ to it: $l\sigma \to r\sigma$. The instantiated lhs $l\sigma$ is called *redex* (*red*ucible *ex*pression). *Contracting* a redex means replacing it by its rhs. A *rewrite step* consists of contracting a redex within an arbitrary context: $C[l\sigma] \to C[r\sigma]$. The *one-step rewrite relation* $\to$ of a rule is defined by the set of its rewrite steps. The *one-step rewrite relation* $\to_R$ of a TRS R is the union of the one-step rewrite relations of its single rules. The *rewrite relation* of a TRS R, $\xrightarrow{*}_R$, is the reflexive transitive closure of $\to_R$.

Igor1—Inducing Recursive Program Schemes. The system IGOR1 [11] induces *recursive program schemes (RPSs).* An RPS is a special form of TRS: The signature is divided into two disjoint subsets $\mathcal{F}$ and $\mathcal{G}$, called *unknown* and *basic* functions, respectively; rules have the form $F(x_1, \ldots, x_n) \to t$ where $F \in \mathcal{F}$ and the x_i are variables, and there is exactly one rule for each $F \in \mathcal{F}$.

IGOR1's program schema is more general than Summers' in that recursive subfunctions are found automatically with the restriction that (recursive) calls of defined functions may not be nested in the rhss of the equations. Furthermore, additional parameters are introduced systematically.

(Mutually) recursive RPSs do not terminate. Their standard interpretation is the infinite term defined as the limit $\lim_{n\to\infty, F(\boldsymbol{x})\xrightarrow{n} t} t$ where F denotes the main rule of the RPS. One gets finite approximations by replacing infinite subterms by the special symbol Ω, meaning *undefined.* Certainly, such an infinite tree and its approximations contain recurrent patterns because they are generated by *repeatedly* replacing instances of lhss of the rules by instances of rhss. IGOR1 takes a finite approximation of some (hypothetical) infinite tree as input, discovers the recurrent patterns in it, and builds, based on these recurrences, an RPS R such that the input is a finite approximation of the infinite tree of R.

Example 5. For a simple example without subfunctions (the *Init* function again), consider the finite approximation of some unknown infinite term:

$$\begin{aligned}&\textit{if}(atom(cdr(\ x\ )), nil,\\&\quad cons(car(\ x\ ),\\&\qquad \textit{if}(atom(cdr(\ cdr(x)\ )), nil,\\&\qquad\quad cons(car(\ cdr(x)\ ),\\&\qquad\qquad \textit{if}(atom(cdr(\ cdr(cdr(x))\ )), nil,\\&\qquad\qquad\quad cons(car(\ cdr(cdr(x))\ ),\\&\qquad\qquad\qquad \Omega))))))\,.\end{aligned}$$

At the path from the root to Ω, where the latter denotes the unknown infinite subterm of the infinite target term and hence, which has been generated by an unknown recursive RPS, we find a recurring sequence of *if*-*cons* pairs. This leads to the hypothesis that a replacement of the lhs of a recursive rule by its rhs has taken place at the *if*-positions. The term is divided at these positions leading to three segments (assume, the break-positions are replaced by Ω). An approximation of the assumed rhs is computed as the lgg of the segments: $\textit{if}(atom(cdr(x)), nil, cons(car(x), \Omega))$.

The Ω denotes the still unknown recursive call. The non-equal parts of the segments, which are replaced by the variable x in the lgg, are highlighted by extra horizontal space in the term. These parts must have been generated by the substitution $\{x \leftarrow cdr(x)\}$ in the recursive call. Denoting the induced function by F, it is now correctly defined as

$$F(x) \rightarrow \textit{if}(atom(cdr(x)), nil, cons(car(x), F(cdr(x))))\,.$$

Different methods to construct a finite approximation as first synthesis step have been proposed. In [11], an extension of Summers' first step is described. Examples need not be linearly ordered and nested `if-then-else`-conditionals are used instead of the McCarthy conditional. In [3], *universal planning* is proposed as first step.

3.4 Igor2—Combining Search and Analytical Techniques

All methods based on Summers' seminal work described so far suffer from strong restrictions regarding their general program schemas, the commitment to a small fixed set of primitives, and, at least the early methods, to the requirement of linearly ordered I/O-examples.

The system IGOR2 [12] aims to overcome these restrictions, but not at the price of falling back to generate-and-test search (cp. Section 5). IGOR2 conducts a search in program space, but the transformation operators are data-driven and use techniques such as matching and least generalizations, similar to the methods described so far. In contrast to generate-and-test search, only programs being correct with respect to the I/O-examples in a particular sense (but possibly unfinished) are generated. This narrows the search tree and makes testing of generated programs unnecessary.

Programs (as well as I/O-examples and background knowledge) are represented as *constructor (term rewriting) systems (CSs)*. CSs can be regarded as an extension of RPSs: The function sets $\mathcal{F}$ and $\mathcal{G}$ are called *defined functions* and *constructors*, respectively. The arguments of a defined function symbol in a lhs need not be variables but may be terms composed of constructors and variables and there may be several rules for one defined function. This extension corresponds to the concept of *pattern matching* in functional programming. One consequence of the CS representation is that I/O-examples themselves already constitute "programs", CSs. Hence, rewriting outputs into fragments to get a first approximation (Section 3.1) is not necessary anymore.

IGOR2 is able to construct complex recursive CSs containing several base- and (mutually) recursive rules, automatically identified and introduced recursive subfunctions, and complex compositions of function calls. Several interdependent functions can be induced in one run. In addition to I/O-examples, background knowledge may be provided.

3.5 Discussion

Summers' important insights were first, how the algebraic properties of data-structures can be exploited to construct program fragments and predicates without search and second, that fragments (and predicates) for different I/O-pairs belonging to one recursively defined function share recurrent patterns that can be used to identify the recursive definition. Obviously, it is necessary for recurrence detection that I/O-examples are not randomly chosen but that they consist of the first $k \in \mathbb{N}$ examples regarding the underlying order on S-expressions, i.e., that they are *complete* up to some level.

If the general schema of inducible functions becomes more complex, e.g., if subfunctions can be found automatically, and/or if background knowledge is allowed, then search is needed. IGOR2 shows that Summers' ideas for generalization can be integrated into search operators.

Search is also needed if the goal is to induce programs based on minimal sets of randomly chosen examples. In this case, the recurrence detection method cannot be applied. Biermann's method shows that it is possible for particular program classes to use fragments as generated in Summers' first step to constrain an exhaustive search in program space.

4 Inductive Logic Programming

Inductive Logic Programming (ILP) [13,14] is a branch of machine learning [5]—intensional concept descriptions are learned from (counter-)examples, called *positive and negative examples.* The specificity of ILP is its basis in computational logic: First-order clausal logic is used as uniform language for hypotheses, examples, and background knowledge, semantics of ILP is based on entailment, and inductive learning techniques are derived by inverting deduction.

Horn clause logic together with resolution constitutes the (Turing-complete) programming language PROLOG. Program synthesis is therefore principally within the scope of ILP and has been regarded as one application field of ILP [13]. One of the first ILP systems, MIS [15], is an automatic programming/debugging system. Today, ILP is concerned with (relational) data-mining and knowledge discovery and program synthesis does not play a role anymore.

4.1 Preliminaries

An *atom* is a predicate symbol applied to arguments, a literal is an atom or negated atom. A *clause* is a (possible empty) disjunction of literals, a *Horn clause* is a clause with at most one positive literal, a *definite clause* is a clause with exactly one positive literal. A *definite program* is a finite set of definite clauses. A definite clause C consisting of the positive literal A and the negative literals $\neg B_1, \ldots, \neg B_n$ is equivalent to $B_1 \wedge \ldots \wedge B_n \rightarrow A$, written $A \leftarrow B_1, \ldots, B_n$.

4.2 Overview

In the definite setting, hypotheses and background knowledge are definite programs, examples are ground atoms. The following two definitions state the ILP problem with respect to the so-called *normal semantics.*[3]

Definition 2. *Let Π be a definite program and E^+, E^- be positive and negative examples. Π is*

complete *with respect to E^+ iff $\Pi \models E^+$,*
consistent *with respect to E^- iff $\Pi \not\models e$ for every $e \in E^-$,*
correct *with respect to E^+ and E^- iff it is complete with respect to E^+ and consistent with respect to E^-.*

Definition 3. *Given*

- *a set of possible hypotheses (definite programs) $\mathcal{H}$,*
- *positive and negative examples E^+, E^-,*
- *consistent background knowledge B (i.e., $B \not\models e$ for every $e \in E^-$) such that $B \not\models E^+$,*

find a hypothesis $H \in \mathcal{H}$ such that $H \cup B$ is correct with respect to E^+ and E^-.

Entailment ($\models$) is undecidable in general and for Horn clauses, definite programs, and between definite programs and single atoms in particular. Thus, in practice, different decidable (and preferably also efficiently computable) relations, which

[3] There is also a *non-monotonic* setting in ILP where hypotheses need not entail positive examples but only state true properties. This is useful for *data mining* or *knowledge discovery* but not for program synthesis, so we do not consider it here.

are sound but more or less incomplete, are used. We say that a hypothesis *covers* an example if it can be proven true from the background knowledge and the hypothesis. That is, a hypothesis is regarded correct if it, together with the background knowledge, covers all positive and no negative examples. Two commonly used notions are:

Extensional coverage. Given a clause $C = A \leftarrow B_1, \ldots, B_n$, a finite set of ground atoms B as background knowledge, positive examples E^+, and an example e, C *extensionally covers* e iff there exists a substitution θ such that $A\theta = e$ and $\{B_1, \ldots, B_n\}\theta \subseteq B \cup E^+$.

Intensional coverage. Given a hypothesis H, background knowledge B, and an example e, $H \cup B$ *intensionally covers* e iff e can be proven true from $H \cup B$ by applying some terminating theorem proving technique, e.g., depth-bounded SLD-resolution.

Example 6. As an example for extensional coverage, suppose $B = \emptyset$ and $E^+ = \{\, Init([c],[\,]), Init([b,c],[b]), Init([a,b,c],[a,b]) \,\}$. The recursive clause $Init([X|Xs],[X|Ys]) \leftarrow Init[Xs, Ys]$ extensionally covers the positive example $Init([b,c],[b])$ with $\theta = \{X \leftarrow b, Xs \leftarrow [c], Ys \leftarrow [\,]\}$.

Both extensional and intensional coverage are sound. Extensional coverage is more efficient but less complete. As an example for the latter, suppose the positive example $Init([c],[\,])$ is missing in E^+ in Example 6. Then the stated recursive clause together with the base clause $Init([X],[\,])$ still intensionally covers $e = Init([b,c],[b])$ yet the recursive clause *does not* extensionally cover e anymore. Obviously, extensional coverage requires that examples (and background knowledge) are complete up to some complexity (cp Section 3.5). Another problem with extensional coverage is that if two clauses each do not cover a negative example, both together possibly do.

Extensional and intensional coverage are closely related to the general ILP algorithm (Algorithm 1) and the covering algorithm 2 as well as to the generality models θ-subsumption and entailment as described below (Section 4.3), respectively.

ILP is considered as a search problem. Typically, the search operators to compute new candidate programs are based on the dual notions of *generalization* and *specialization* of programs or clauses.

Definition 4. *A program Π is* more general than *a program Φ iff $\Pi \models \Phi$. Φ is said to be* more specific than *Π.*

This structure of the program space provides a way for pruning. If a program is not consistent then all generalizations are also not consistent and therefore need not be considered. This dually holds for non-completeness and specializations. Algorithm 1 shows a generic ILP algorithm. Most ILP systems are instances of it.

A common instance is the *covering algorithm* (Algorithm 2). The individual clauses of a program are generated independently one after the other. Hence, the problem space is not the program space (*sets* of clauses) but the clause space (*single* clauses). This leads to a more efficient search.

Algorithm 1. A generic ILP algorithm.

Input: B, E^+, E^-
Output: A definite program H such that $H \cup B$ is correct with respect to E^+ and E^-

Start with some initial (possibly empty) hypothesis H
repeat
  if *$H \cup B$ is not consistent* **then** specialize H
  if *$H \cup B$ is not complete* **then** generalize H
until *$H \cup B$ is correct with respect to E^+ and E^-*
return H

Algorithm 2. The covering (typically interpreted extensionally) algorithm.

Input and **Output** as in Algorithm 1
Start with the empty hypothesis $H = \emptyset$
repeat
  Add a clause C not covering any $e \in E^-$ to H
  Remove all $e \in E^+$ covered by C from E^+
until $E^+ = \emptyset$
return H

Entailment ($\models$) as well as θ-subsumption (Section 4.3) are *quasi-orders* on sets of definite programs and clauses, respectively. We associate "more general" with "greater". The operators carrying out specialization and generalization are called *refinement operators*. They map clauses to sets of (refined) clauses or programs to sets of (refined) programs. Most ILP systems explore the problem space mainly in one direction, either from general to specific (*top-down*) or the other way round (*bottom-up*). The three well-known systems FOIL [16] (top-down), GOLEM [17] (bottom-up), and PROGOL [18] (mixed) are instantiations of the covering algorithm.

Example 7. For an example of the covering algorithm, let B and E^+ be as in Example 6 and E^- all remaining instantiations for the "inputs" $[c]$, $[b, c]$, $[a, b, c]$, e.g., *Init*$([b, c], [c])$. Let us assume that a (base-)clause *Init*$([X], [\,])$ is already inferred and added and hence, the covered example *Init*$([c], [\,])$ is deleted from E^+. Assume, our instantiation of the covering algorithm is a top-down algorithm. This means, each clause is found by starting with a (too) general clause and successively specializing it until no negative examples are covered anymore. Let us start with the clause *Init*$([X|Xs], Ys) \leftarrow$. It covers all remaining positive but also all corresponding negative examples; it is too general. Applying the substitution $\{Ys \leftarrow [X|Ys]\}$ specializes it to *Init*$([X|Xs], [X|Ys]) \leftarrow$. This excludes some negative examples (e.g., *Init*$([b, c], [c])$). Adding the literal *Init*(Xs, Ys) to the body again specializes the clause to *Init*$([X|Xs], [X|Ys]) \leftarrow$ *Init*(Xs, Ys). All remaining positive examples are still covered but no negative example is covered anymore. Hence, the clause is added and the algorithm returns the two inferred clauses as solution.

Both specializations were refinements under θ-subsumption (Section 4.3, "Refinement Operators").

4.3 Generality Models and Refinement Operators

Instead of entailment ($\models$), θ-subsumption is often used in ILP as generality model. It is incomplete with respect to $\models$ but decidable, simple to implement, and efficiently computable. If we have background knowledge B, then we are not simply interested in whether a clause C is more general than a clause D but in whether C together with B is more general than D (together with B). This is captured by the notions of *relative* (to background knowledge) entailment respectively θ-subsumption.

Refinement under (Relative) θ-subsumption

Definition 5. *Let C and D be clauses and B a set of clauses.*

*C θ-*subsumes *D, written $C \succeq D$, iff there exists a substitution θ such that $C\theta \subseteq D$.*

*C θ-*subsumes *D* relative to *B, written $C \succeq_B D$, if $B \models C\theta \rightarrow D$ for a substitution θ.*

A Horn clause language quasi-ordered by θ-subsumption with an additional bottom element is a lattice. This does not generally hold for relative subsumption. Least upper bounds are called *least general generalizations (lgg)* [9]. Lggs and greatest lower bounds are computable and hence may be used for generalization and specialization, though they do not properly fit into our general notion of refinement operators because they neither map single clauses to sets of clauses nor single programs to sets of programs.

A useful restriction is to let background knowledge be a finite set of ground literals. In this case, lggs exist under subsumption relative to B and can be reduced to (non-relative) lggs. The bottom-up system GOLEM uses this scenario.

In general, (relative) θ-subsumption is sound but not complete. If $C \succeq D$ ($C \succeq_B D$) then $C \models D$ ($C \cup B \models D$) but not vice versa. For a counter-example of completeness let $C = P(f(X)) \leftarrow P(X)$ and $D = P(f(f(X))) \leftarrow P(X)$ then $C \models D$[4] but $C \not\succeq D$. As the example indicates, the incompleteness is due to *recursive* rules and therefore especially critical for *program synthesis.*

Refinement Operators. A specialization operator refines a clause by

- applying a substitution for a single variable or
- adding one most general literal.

A generalization operator uses inverse operations.

Application of these operators is quite common in ILP, e.g., in the systems MIS, FOIL, GOLEM, and PROGOL.

[4] D is simply the result of self-resolving C.

Refinement under (Relative) Entailment. Due to the incompleteness of θ-subsumption regarding recursive clauses, refinement under (relative) entailment has been studied. *Relative* entailment is defined as follows:

Definition 6. *Let C and D be clauses and B a finite set of clauses. Then C* entails *D* relative to *B, denoted $C \models_B D$, if $\{C\} \cup B \models D$.*

Neither lggs nor greatest specializations exist in general for Horn clause languages ordered by (relative) entailment.

Refinement Operators. Roughly speaking, entailment is equivalent to resolution plus θ-subsumption. This leads to specialization operators under (relative) entailment. Objects of refinement under entailment are not single clauses but *sets* of clauses, i.e., programs. A specialization operator under entailment refines a definite program by

- Adding a resolvent of two clauses or
- adding the result of applying the θ-subsumption specialization operator to a clause or
- deleting a clause.

4.4 Automatic Programming Systems

The three general-purpose systems FOIL, GOLEM, and PROGOL are successful in learning non-recursive concepts from large data sets, yet have problems to learn recursive programs: Due to their use of the covering approach (extensional coverage), they need complete example sets and background knowledge to induce recursive programs. Since they (at least FOIL and GOLEM) explore (i) only the θ-subsumption lattice of clauses and (ii) do this greedily, correct clauses may be passed. Finally, their objective functions in the search for clauses is to cover as many as possible positive examples. Yet base clauses typically cover only few examples such that these systems often fail to induce correct base cases.

Hence ILP systems especially designed to learn *recursive* programs have been developed. They address different issues: Handling of random examples, predicate invention, usage of general programming knowledge, and usage of problem-dependent knowledge of the user, which goes beyond examples. A comprehensive survey of automatic programming ILP systems can be found in [19].

Inverting entailment by structural analysis. Several systems—CRUSTACEAN [20], CLAM [21], TIM [22], MRI [23]—address the issue of inducing *recursive* programs from *random* examples by inverting entailment based on structural analysis, similar to Section 3, instead of searching in the θ-subsumption lattice. These systems also have similar restrictions regarding the general schema of learnable programs. However, some of them can use background knowledge; MRI can find more than one recursive clause.

Top-down induction of recursive programs. Top-down systems can principally—even if they explore the θ-subsumption clause-lattice only—generate arbitrary (in particular all recursive) Horn clauses.[5] Thus, if a top-down covering system would use intensional instead of extensional coverage, it could principally induce recursive programs from *random* examples. Certainly, this would require to find clauses in a particular order—base clauses first, then recursive clauses, only depending on base clauses and themselves, then recursive clauses, only depending on base clauses, the previously generated recursive clauses, and themselves, and so on. This excludes programs with mutually interdepending clauses. The system SMART [24] is based on these ideas. It induces programs consisting of one base clause and one recursive clause. Several techniques to sensibly prune the search space allows for a more exhaustive search than the greedy search applied by FOIL, such that the incompleteness issue of θ-subsumption-based search is weaken.

The system FILP [25] is a covering top-down system that induces *functional* predicates only, i.e., predicates with distinguished input- and output parameters, such that for each binding of the input parameters exactly one binding of the output parameters exists. This makes negative examples unnecessary. FILP can induce multiple interdependent predicates/functions where each may consist of several base- and recursive clauses. Hence, intensional coverage is not assured to work. FILP starts with a few randomly chosen examples and tries to use intensional covering as far as possible. If, during the intensional proof of some example, an instance of the input parameters of some predicate appears for which an output is neither given by an example nor can be derived intensionally, then FILP queries for this "missing" example and thereby completes the example set as far as needed.

Using programming knowledge. Flener argued, in several papers, for the use of program schemas that capture general program design knowledge like divide-and-conquer, generate-and-test, global-search etc., and has implemented this in several systems. He distinguishes between schema-*based* systems inducing programs of a system-inherent schema only and schema-*guided* systems, which take schemas as dynamic, problem-dependent, additional input and thus are more flexible. Flener's DIALOGS [26] system uses schemas and strong queries to restrict the search space and thereby is able to efficiently induce comparatively complex programs including predicate invention.

Jorge and Brazdil have—besides for *clause structure grammars* defining a program class and thus similar to schemas as dynamic language-bias—argued for so called *algorithm sketches.* An algorithm sketch is problem-dependent algorithm knowledge about the target function and provided by the user in addition to examples. This idea is implemented in their SKIL and SKILIT systems [27].

---

[5] Hence, although θ-subsumption is incomplete with respect to entailment due to recursive clauses, every clause, in particular the recursive clauses, can be generated by refinement based on θ-subsumption—if one searches top-down starting from the empty clause or some other clause general enough to θ-subsume the desired clauses.

4.5 Discussion

Compared to the classical approaches in Section3 (except for IGOR2), ILP has broadened the class of inducible relations by allowing for background knowledge, using particular search methods and other techniques (Section 4.4).

Shapiro [15] and Muggleton and De Raedt [13] argued for clausal logic as universal language in favor to other universal formalisms such as Turing machines or LISP. Their arguments are: (i) Syntax and semantics are closely and in a natural way related. Hence if a logic program makes errors, it is possible to identify the erroneous clause. Furthermore, there are simple and efficient operations to manipulate a logic program with predictable semantic effects (cp. Section 4.3). Both is not possible for, say, Turing machines. (ii) It suffices to focus on the logic of the program, control is left to the interpreter. In particular, logic programs (and clauses) are *sets* of clauses (and literals), order does not matter.

The first argument carries over to other declarative formalisms such as equational logic, term rewriting, and functional logic programming (FLIP [28] is an IPS system in this formalism). The second argument also carries over to some extent, declarative programming all in all shifts the focus off control and to logic. Yet in this generality it only holds for non-recursive programs or ideal, non-practical, interpreters. For the efficient interpretation of recursive programs however, order of clauses in a program and order of literals in a clause matters. Hence we think that declarative, (clausal- and/or equational-)logic-based formalisms are principally equally well suited for IPS.

Logic programs represent general relations. (Partial) functions are special relations—their domains are distinguished into source and target (or: a functional relation has input and output parameters) and they are single-valued (each instantiation of the input parameters implies a unique instantiation of the output parameters). Regarding functional- and logic programming, there is another difference: Functional programs are typically typed, i.e., their domain is partitioned and inputs and outputs of each function must belong to specified subsets, whereas logic programs are typically untyped. Interestingly, all three "restrictions" of functions compared to relations have been shown to be advantageous from a learnable point of view in ILP. The general reason is that they restrict the problem space such that search becomes more efficient and fewer examples are needed to describe the intended function. In particular, no negative examples are needed since they are implicitly given by the positive ones.

ILP is built around the natural generality structure of the problem space. Regarding *functional* relations, we observe an "oddity" of this structure. For definite programs, "more general", with respect to the minimal Herbrand model, means "more atoms". If the relation is a *function*, an additional ground atom must have a different instantiation of the input parameters compared to all other included atoms. Thus, "more general" in the case of definite programs representing functions reduces to "greater domain". In other words: *All functions with the same domain are incomparable with respect to generality.* Since most often one is interested in total functions, generality actually provides *no structure at all* of the space of possible solutions.

5 Functional Generate-and-Test Approaches

The functional IPS methods in this third block have in common that their search is generate-and-test based. I/O-examples are not used as a means to *construct* programs but only to *test* generated programs.

5.1 Genetic Programming

Genetic programming (GP) [29], like other forms of *evolutionary algorithms* is inspired by biological evolution. GP systems maintain *populations* of candidate solutions, get new ones by stochastical methods like *reproduction*, *mutation*, *recombination/crossover*, and *selection*, and thereby try to maximize *fitness*. Evolutionary search can be useful when the problem space is too broad to conduct an exhaustive search and simultaneously nothing or few is known about the *fitness landscape*, i.e., when it is not possible to construct sensible heuristics. The randomness of the search cares for a widespread exploration of the problem space which is guided by the fitness measure. On the other side, this "chaotic" search in a space with unknown properties makes it difficult to give any guaranties regarding solutions and leads to only approximated solutions. A GP problem is specified by *fitness cases* (e.g., example inputs of the target function), a fitness function, and primitives to be used in evolved expressions. There are no predefined goal criteria or preference biases in GP systems. The search is completely guided by the fitness function that is to be maximized.

Data structures and recursion do not play a predominant role in GP. A typical evolved program is an arithmetic expression or a propositional formula. Koza and his colleagues [30] integrated recursion into GP. One of the major issues is the handling of non-terminating programs. As a generate-and-test approach, GP relies on testing evolved candidate programs against the given examples. If non-termination may appear then a runtime limit is applied. This raises two problems if non-terminating programs are frequently generated: (i) The difficulty of assigning a fitness value to an aborted program and (ii) the runtime uselessly consumed by evaluating non-terminating programs. Wong and Mun [31] deal with this problem by a meta-learning approach to decrease the possibility of evolving non-terminating programs.

Others try to avoid non-termination completely: In her system PolyGP [32], Yu integrates *implicit recursion* through the use of user-provided higher-order functions. Kahrs [33] evolves *primitive recursive* functions over the natural numbers. Binard and Felty [34] evolve programs in System F, a typed lambda calculus where only total recursive functions are expressible. The primitive recursive functions are contained as proper subclass.

Hamel and Shen [35] have developed a method lying in the intersection of ILP, GP and algebraic specification. They evolve (recursive) algebraic specifications, i.e., equational theories over many-sorted signatures, using GP search methods. Instead of providing a fitness function, a target theory is, as in ILP, specified by positive and negative facts—ground equations in this case. Additionally, a background theory may be provided. The fitness function to be maximized is derived from such a specification. Candidate theories satisfying more positive facts, excluding more negative facts, and being of smaller syntactical complexity are preferred.

5.2 ADATE

The ADATE system [36], to our knowledge the most powerful inductive programming system regarding inducible programs, is an evolutionary system in that it maintains a population of programs and performs a greedy search guided by a fitness function. Yet unlike GP, it is especially designed to evolve *recursive* programs and applies sophisticated program transformation operators, search strategy, and program evaluation functions to this end.

Programs are represented in ADATE-ML, a subset of STANDARD ML. Programs are rated according to a user-provided output evaluation function, user provided preference biases, and syntactical and computational complexity.

5.3 Systematic Enumeration of Programs

Two further recent methods, MAGICHASKELLER [37] and the software testing system G∀ST [38] essentially systematically enumerate programs of a certain class.

MAGICHASKELLER uses higher-order functions as background knowledge. Katayama argues that by using higher-order functions, programs can be represented in a compact form and by using strong typing, the problem space is narrowed such that a simple brute-force enumeration of programs could make sense. He furthermore considers MAGICHASKELLER as a base-line which could be used to evaluate the performance of more sophisticated methods. As a first result, Katayama compares MAGICHASKELLER and POLYGP for the problems *Nth*, *Length*, and *Map*, and states that POLYGP, in contrast to MAGICHASKELLER, needs different higher-order functions for each of these problems, needs several runs to find a solution, needs additional parameters to be set, and, nevertheless, consumes more time to induce a solution.

5.4 Discussion

One general advantage of generate-and-test methods is their greater flexibility, in at least to aspects: First regarding the problem space—there are no *principle* difficulties in enumerating even very complex programs. Second regarding the form of the incomplete specification. Whereas the search operators of an analytical technique depend on the specification (e.g., I/O-examples) such that different forms of specification need different search operator techniques, the search is more independent from the specification in generate-and-test methods such that more expressive forms of specification can easily be integrated. In particular, fitness functions in GP or the objective function in ADATE are more expressive than I/O-examples since no fixed outputs need to be provided but general *properties* to be satisfied by computed outputs can be specified.

The disadvantage of generate-and-test methods is that they generally generate far more candidate programs until a solution is found and hence need much more time than data-driven methods to induce programs of equal size. Several analytical and generate-and-test systems have been compared empirically in [39]. A further problem is non-termination. As generated programs need to be tested against the provided examples, non-termination is a serious issue. Higher-order functions or formalisms that a-priori only include total functions are helpful to circumvent this problem.

6 Conclusions and Further Research

In the previous sections, we described several approaches and systems to the inductive synthesis of functional and logic programs and discussed pros and cons and relations between them.

One obvious dimension to classify them is the way of how example data is used: As basis to construct candidate solutions (Section 3) or to test and evaluate independently generated candidates (Section 5). (In ILP, both approaches are found.) The analytical approach tends to faster because many representable programs are a priori excluded from being generated. On the other side, since it strongly depends on the data and the language bias, it is much less robust and flexible regarding the whole problem specification including types of data, preference-, and language biases. Besides further developing both general approaches separately, we think that examining ways to combine them could be useful to achieve a satisfiable combination of robustness, flexibility, expressiveness, and efficiency. Our system IGOR2 and the well-known ILP system PROGOL indicate the potential of such an integration.

One important topic, that certainly has not received sufficient attention in the context of inductive program synthesis, is learning theory, including models of learning and criteria to evaluate candidate programs. PAC-learning, the predominant learning model in machine learning, is well-suited for restricted representation languages and noisy data, hence approximate solutions. Yet in program synthesis, we have rich representation languages, often assume error-free examples, and want have programs that *exactly* compute an intended function or relation. Moreover, efficiency, not only of the induction process, but of the induced program, becomes an important issue. Muggleton's *U-learning* model[6] captures these needs and is probably a good model or initial point to develop learning models for inductive program synthesis.

There has certainly been significant progress since the beginnings in the seventies. Yet inductive program synthesis still is not yet in a status to be applied to real problems. We think that it is now time for a more target-oriented approach. This does not mean to replacing general approaches by problem-dependent ad hoc techniques. We rather think that identifying and promoting specific application fields and domains could help to spark broader interest to the topic as well

[6] The 'U' stands for 'universal'.

as to sensibly identify strengths and weaknesses of existing methods, to extend them and to identify possibilities to integrate them in a useful way.

In the context of software engineering, we think that *test-driven development (TDD)* would be a good starting point to bring IPS to application. The paradigm requires preparing tests "(incompletely) defining" a function *before* coding it. Hence, IPS could smoothly fit in here. Moreover, TDD typically features a strong modularization such that only small entities need to be synthesized.

Within algorithms research, one could try to find (classes) of problems for which "better" than currently known algorithms are expected to exist and to apply IPS methods to them.

References

1. Partridge, D.: The case for inductive programming. Computer 30(1), 36–41 (1997)
2. Flener, P., Partridge, D.: Inductive programming. Automated Software Engineering 8(2), 131–137 (2001)
3. Schmid, U.: Inductive Synthesis of Functional Programs: Universal Planning, Folding of Finite Programs, and Schema Abstraction by Analogical Reasoning. LNCS (LNAI), vol. 2654. Springer, Heidelberg (2003)
4. Summers, P.D.: A methodology for LISP program construction from examples. Journal of the ACM 24(1), 161–175 (1977)
5. Mitchell, T.M.: Machine Learning. McGraw-Hill, New York (1997)
6. McCarthy, J.: Recursive functions of symbolic expressions and their computation by machine, part i. Communications of the ACM 3(4), 184–195 (1960)
7. Smith, D.R.: The synthesis of LISP programs from examples: A survey. In: Biermann, A., Guiho, G., Kodratoff, Y. (eds.) Automatic Program Construction Techniques, pp. 307–324. Macmillan, Basingstoke (1984)
8. Jouannaud, J.P., Kodratoff, Y.: Program synthesis from examples of behavior. In: Biermann, A.W., Guiho, G. (eds.) Computer Program Synthesis Methodologies, pp. 213–250. D. Reidel Publ. Co. (1983)
9. Plotkin, G.D.: A note on inductive generalization. Machine Intelligence 5, 153–163 (1970)
10. Biermann, A.W.: The inference of regular LISP programs from examples. IEEE Transactions on Systems, Man and Cybernetics 8(8), 585–600 (1978)
11. Kitzelmann, E., Schmid, U.: Inductive synthesis of functional programs: An explanation based generalization approach. Journal of Machine Learning Research 7, 429–454 (2006)
12. Kitzelmann, E.: Analytical inductive functional programming. In: Hanus, M. (ed.) Logic-Based Program Synthesis and Transformation. LNCS, vol. 5438, pp. 87–102. Springer, Heidelberg (2009)
13. Muggleton, S.H., De Raedt, L.: Inductive logic programming: Theory and methods. Journal of Logic Programming 19, 20, 629–679 (1994)
14. Nienhuys-Cheng, S.-H., de Wolf, R.: Foundations of Inductive Logic Programming. LNCS (LNAI), vol. 1228. Springer, Heidelberg (1997)
15. Shapiro, E.Y.: Algorithmic Program Debugging. MIT Press, Cambridge (1983)
16. Quinlan, J.R., Cameron-Jones, R.M.: FOIL: A midterm report. In: Brazdil, P.B. (ed.) ECML 1993. LNCS, vol. 667, pp. 3–20. Springer, Heidelberg (1993)

17. Muggleton, S.H., Feng, C.: Efficient induction of logic programs. In: Proceedings of the First Conference on Algorithmic Learning Theory, Ohmsha, pp. 368–381 (1990)
18. Muggleton, S.H.: Inverse entailment and progol. New Generation Computing 13, 245–286 (1995)
19. Flener, P., Yilmaz, S.: Inductive synthesis of recursive logic programs: Achievements and prospects. The Journal of Logic Programming 41(2-3), 141–195 (1999)
20. Aha, D.W., Lapointe, S., Ling, C.X., Matwin, S.: Inverting implication with small training sets. In: Bergadano, F., De Raedt, L. (eds.) ECML 1994. LNCS, vol. 784, pp. 29–48. Springer, Heidelberg (1994)
21. Rios, R., Matwin, S.: Efficient induction of recursive prolog definitions. In: McCalla, G.I. (ed.) Canadian AI 1996. LNCS, vol. 1081, pp. 240–248. Springer, Heidelberg (1996)
22. Idestam-Almquist, P.: Efficient induction of recursive definitions by structural analysis of saturations. In: Advances in Inductive Logic Programming. IOS Press, Amsterdam (1996)
23. Furusawa, M., Inuzuka, N., Seki, H., Itoh, H.: Induction of logic programs with more than one recursive clause by analyzing saturations. In: Džeroski, S., Lavrač, N. (eds.) ILP 1997. LNCS, vol. 1297, pp. 165–172. Springer, Heidelberg (1997)
24. Mofizur, C.R., Numao, M.: Top-down induction of recursive programs from small number of sparse examples. In: Advances in Inductive Logic Programming. IOS Press, Amsterdam (1996)
25. Bergadano, F., Gunetti, D.: Inductive Logic Programming: From Machine Learning to Software Engineering. MIT Press, Cambridge (1995)
26. Flener, P.: Inductive logic program synthesis with DIALOGS. In: ILP 1996. LNCS, vol. 1314, pp. 175–198. Springer, Heidelberg (1997)
27. Jorge, A.M.G.: Iterative Induction of Logic Programs. PhD thesis, Departamento de Ciência de Computadores, Universidade do Porto (1998)
28. Ferri-Ramírez, C., Hernández-Orallo, J., Ramírez-Quintana, M.: Incremental learning of functional logic programs. In: Kuchen, H., Ueda, K. (eds.) FLOPS 2001. LNCS, vol. 2024, pp. 233–247. Springer, Heidelberg (2001)
29. Koza, J.R.: Genetic Programming: On the Programming of Computers by Means of Natural Selection. MIT Press, Cambridge (1992)
30. Koza, J.R., Andre, D., Bennett, F.H., Keane, M.A.: Genetic Programming III: Darwinian Invention & Problem Solving. Morgan Kaufmann, San Francisco (1999)
31. Wong, M., Mun, T.: Evolving recursive programs by using adaptive grammar based genetic programming. Genetic Programming and Evolvable Machines 6(4), 421–455 (2005)
32. Yu, T.: Hierarchical processing for evolving recursive and modular programs using higher-order functions and lambda abstraction. Genetic Programming and Evolvable Machines 2(4), 345–380 (2001)
33. Kahrs, S.: Genetic programming with primitive recursion. In: Proceedings of the 8th annual Conference on Genetic and Evolutionary Computation (GECCO 2006), pp. 941–942. ACM, New York (2006)
34. Binard, F., Felty, A.: Genetic programming with polymorphic types and higher-order functions. In: Proceedings of the 10th annual Conference on Genetic and Evolutionary Computation (GECCO 2008), pp. 1187–1194. ACM Press, New York (2008)
35. Hamel, L., Shen, C.: An inductive programming approach to algebraic specification. In: Proceedings of the 2nd Workshop on Approaches and Applications of Inductive Programming (AAIP 2007), pp. 3–14 (2007)

36. Olsson, J.R.: Inductive functional programming using incremental program transformation. Artificial Intelligence 74(1), 55–83 (1995)
37. Katayama, S.: Systematic search for lambda expressions. In: van Eekelen, M.C.J.D. (ed.) Revised Selected Papers from the Sixth Symposium on Trends in Functional Programming, TFP 2005, vol. 6, pp. 111–126. Intellect (2007)
38. Koopman, P., Alimarine, A., Tretmans, J., Plasmeijer, R.: GAST: Generic automated software testing. In: Peña, R., Arts, T. (eds.) IFL 2002. LNCS, vol. 2670. Springer, Heidelberg (2003)
39. Hofmann, M., Kitzelmann, E., Schmid, U.: A unifying framework for analysis and evaluation of inductive programming systems. In: Proceedings of the Second Conference on Artificial General Intelligence, Atlantis, pp. 55–60 (2009)

Incremental Learning in Inductive Programming

Robert Henderson

Department of Computing, Imperial College London, United Kingdom
rjh09@doc.ic.ac.uk

Abstract. Inductive programming systems characteristically exhibit an exponential explosion in search time as one increases the size of the programs to be generated. As a way of overcoming this, we introduce *incremental learning*, a process in which an inductive programming system automatically modifies its inductive bias towards some domain through solving a sequence of gradually more difficult problems in that domain. We demonstrate a simple form of incremental learning in which a system incorporates solution programs into its background knowledge as it progresses through a sequence of problems. Using a search-based inductive functional programming system modelled on the MagicHaskeller system of Katayama [4], we perform a set of experiments comparing the performance of inductive programming with and without incremental learning. Incremental learning is shown to produce a performance improvement of at least a factor of thirty on each of the four problem sequences tested. We describe how, given some assumptions, inductive programming with incremental learning can be shown to have a polynomial, rather than exponential, time complexity with respect to the size of the program to be generated. We discuss the difficulties involved in constructing suitable problem sequences for our incremental learning system, and consider what improvements can be made to overcome these difficulties.

Keywords: Inductive programming, inductive functional programming, incremental learning.

1 Introduction

Inductive Programming (IP) differs from more conventional machine learning techniques in that it features the use of a general, expressive programming language as a space of hypotheses for describing patterns in data. Herein lies both the attraction and the apparent downfall of IP: having such an expressive hypothesis space allows IP to be used to model complex or recursive patterns that simply cannot be represented with the more conventional methods (feedforward neural networks or decision trees, for example). On the other hand, this expressivity also means that IP methods can become intractable very quickly when applied to larger problems. State of the art IP systems such as ADATE [8], Igor II [6], and MagicHaskeller [4] have shown promise on relatively simple arithmetic and list processing problems, but are not currently capable of synthesising the kinds of complex programs that realistic practical applications would demand. See [3] for a recent evaluation of the capabilities of these systems.

U. Schmid, E. Kitzelmann, and R. Plasmeijer (Eds.): AAIP 2009, LNCS 5812, pp. 74–92, 2010.

How can we solve this dilemma, and get the benefits of a general, expressive hypothesis space as well as a method that is computationally tractable? It has been proposed [12,10] that combining IP with *incremental learning* may provide a solution. An incremental learning system is one that can automatically modify its inductive bias towards a given domain through solving a sequence of successively more difficult problems in that domain. In other words, incremental learning is about gaining the expertise required to solve hard problems through the experience of solving easier ones. If successfully equipped with an incremental learning mechanism, a system should be able to learn to solve complex problems without the need for a human expert to hand-code extensive domain-specific knowledge or algorithms into its workings.

In this paper we present experimental evidence that incremental learning is a viable means for producing orders of magnitude performance improvements in IP. We start with a review of previous work in IP that features incremental learning (Sect. 2). We then describe the particular incremental learning mechanism to be evaluated here (Sect. 3), and give an overview of the IP system that was used in our experiments (Sect. 4). We present the experiments themselves along with their results, and give an explanation for these results in the form of a computational complexity argument (Sect. 5). Finally, we discuss the limitations of our chosen incremental learning mechanism, and consider what improvements are required before it can be of practical use (Sect. 6).

2 Previous Work

Quinlan and Cameron-Jones [9] were probably the first to demonstrate a form of incremental learning in an IP context. They showed how their inductive logic programming system, FOIL, was able to solve more than half of the problems in a sequence of 18 textbook logic programming exercises presented to it in order of gradually increasing difficulty. This was made possible by having the system add each solution program to its background knowledge as it went along. It could therefore potentially re-use solutions to earlier problems as primitive elements in the construction of solutions to later problems.

More recently, Schmidhuber et al. [11] studied an incremental learning mechanism which they termed 'adaptive Levin search'. The idea behind adaptive Levin search is that, in a search-based IP system, the inductive bias can be controlled by weighting the different programming language primitives according to how frequently they should be used. As a system solves a succession of problems, these weights are gradually modified according to how often each primitive actually occurs in solution programs. Thus, the system becomes biased towards re-using primitives that were present in successful programs in the past. Adaptive Levin search was shown to produce some performance improvement on a selection of simple problem sequences.

Schmidhuber later followed up the work on adaptive Levin search with a fully fledged incremental learning IP system called OOPS [10]. OOPS supported both a weight modification mechanism with a similar role to the one in adaptive

Levin search, as well as an ability to invoke chunks of code from past programs in solutions to new problems. However, in the problem sequence that Schmidhuber tested, which involved solving the general 'towers of Hanoi' problem, only the weight modification mechanism was shown to provide a direct performance benefit.

Khan et al. [5] made a brief study into incremental learning in inductive logic programming, under the name of 'repeat learning'. Using the Progol inductive logic programming system, they demonstrated how helper predicates invented in order to solve one problem may be re-used when constructing the solution to another. They chose a problem domain concerning the inference of the general descriptions of moves in chess.

In this paper, we have chosen to focus on the kind of incremental learning mechanism that was employed in FOIL, that in which a system adds solution programs to its background knowledge as it progresses through a problem sequence. As we shall see, this simple method is remarkably powerful. The main drawback of Quinlan's and Cameron-Jones' short study is that they did not provide a direct comparison between scenarios with and without incremental learning. We shall remedy that with the experiments presented here.

3 Incremental Learning Mechanism

We aim to give a convincing demonstration of one simple but effective incremental learning mechanism. The mechanism works as follows: a sequence of successively more difficult, but related, problems is presented to an IP system. The system must solve the problems in the order given, and will incorporate each solution program into its object language as a new primitive function (i.e. into its background knowledge) as it goes along. This addition of these new functions to the system's object language is what constitutes the modification of its inductive bias. For an appropriately designed problem sequence, we would expect the time taken for the system to solve whole the sequence, with the help of incremental learning, to be much less than if it were tasked simply with solving the final problem of the sequence in isolation.

One can see how this mechanism might be expected to work effectively by considering how, particularly in functional programming, it is often natural to express the solution to a complex problem in terms of the solutions to one or more simpler problems already solved. This breaks the program down into smaller, more managable units, and is a technique commonly known as *procedural abstraction* when used by human programmers.

4 Implementation

We implemented, for the purpose of this study, a simple brute-force search based IP system modelled on the MagicHaskeller system of Katayama [4]. We shall refer to our implemented system as 'MagicLisper' (it was written in Common Lisp). In this section, we first review MagicHaskeller and explain our reasons for choosing it, then we describe how our system differs from MagicHaskeller in a few respects. We also talk through an example usage of our system on an IP problem.

4.1 Review of MagicHaskeller

MagicHaskeller is a search-based inductive functional programming system that infers programs from input-output training examples. Its main distiguishing feature is the brute-force algorithm that it uses to synthesise solution programs. More or less, it simply generates and tests all possible programs in its object language in order of length, using a breadth-first search, until it finds one that matches the training examples. This is tractable because of two features of MagicHaskeller's object language. Firstly, the language is strongly typed, with only type-consistent programs being considered by the search algorithm. Secondly, recursion is supported not explicitly, but via the use of certain higher-order primitive operations known as *morphisms* [1]. These morphisms are essentially generalisations of standard functional programming operations such as *map* and *reduce*, and with them, many useful recursive processes can be expressed concisely. Ultimately, these two features combine to produce a search space that contains rather few obviously useless programs, allowing brute-force search to fare well.

For this investigation into incremental learning, we chose to use a system based on MagicHaskeller for two reasons. Firstly, MagicHaskeller's search algorithm is fast; synthesising simple recursive programs takes only a matter of seconds. Secondly, the search algorithm is simple and predictable; it is easy to understand exactly why MagicHaskeller succeeds or fails in finding a solution to a given problem, which helps immensely when one is designing problem specifications. It is for this second reason in particular that we chose MagicHaskeller as our base rather than an alternative such as ADATE or Igor II.

4.2 Differences between MagicLisper and MagicHaskeller

The object language of MagicLisper has the same form as the 'de Bruijn lambda calculus' language used in the version of MagicHaskeller described in [4]. There is one significant structural difference: for the sake of simplicity, MagicLisper's type system does not support parametric polymorphism; instead, every primitive function in its object language has one or more explicit ground types. The default library of primitive functions and constants used by MagicLisper is given in Table 1. Also see Fig. 1 for precise definitions of the morphism primitives.

In this paper we shall use a Lisp-style notation to represent programs. So, for example, the following program (`sum-elems`), which sums the elements of a list, in Haskell notation:

```
(\ a1 -> paralist (\ a2 a3 a4 -> + a4 a2) a1 0)
```

is written in the Lisp notation as:

```
(λ (a1) (paralist (λ (a2 a3 a4) (+ a4 a2)) a1 0))
```

Table 1. The default library of primitive functions and constants used by MagicLisper. The type system consists of: integers (`int`), lists of integers (`list`), and booleans (`bool`). A compound type expression of the form: (λ (a b ...) r) represents a function whose argument types are a, b, etc., and whose return type is r. The role of the weights is to bias the system towards using certain primitives more than others when constructing programs; primitives with lower weights are used more frequently (see Sect. 4.2).

Name	Type	Weight
— The empty list —		
`nil`	`list`	2.1
— List operations —		
`cons`	`(λ (int list) list)`	2.1
`car`	`(λ (list) int)`	3.2
`cdr`	`(λ (list) list)`	3.2
— Integer constants —		
`0`	`int`	3.4
`1`	`int`	3.4
— Integer operations —		
`inc`	`(λ (int) int)`	3.4
`dec`	`(λ (int) int)`	3.4
`+`	`(λ (int int) int)`	3.4
`*`	`(λ (int int) int)`	3.4
— If-then-else —		
`if`	`(λ (bool int int) int)`	2.5
`if`	`(λ (bool list list) list)`	2.5
— Boolean constants —		
`t`	`bool`	3.5
`f`	`bool`	3.5
— Boolean operations —		
`not`	`(λ (bool) bool)`	3.5
`and`	`(λ (bool bool) bool)`	3.5
`or`	`(λ (bool bool) bool)`	3.5
— Integer comparions operations —		
`eql`	`(λ (int int) bool)`	2.0
`<`	`(λ (int int) bool)`	2.0
— Morphisms —		
`paranat`	`(λ ((λ (int int) int) int int) int)`	4.0
`paranat`	`(λ ((λ (int list) list) int list) list)`	4.0
`paranat`	`(λ ((λ (int bool) bool) int bool) bool)`	4.0
`paralist`	`(λ ((λ (int list int) int) list int) int)`	4.0
`paralist`	`(λ ((λ (int list list) list) list list) list)`	4.0
`paralist`	`(λ ((λ (int list bool) bool) list bool) bool)`	4.0
`analist`	`(λ ((λ (list) list) list) list)`	4.5

MagicHaskeller searches through programs in order of length, or more precisely, it searches through programs in order of the total number of functor and lexical variable invocations they contain. In MagicLisper, we generalise on this process by requiring that primitive functors each be assigned a numerical

```
(define (paranat f n x)
  (if (zero? n)
      x
      (f (- n 1) (paranat f (- n 1) x))))

(define (paralist f lst x)
  (if (null? lst)
      x
      (f (car lst) (cdr lst) (paralist f (cdr lst) x))))

(define (analist f lst)
  (let ((pair (f lst)))
    (if (null? pair)
        '()
        (cons (car pair) (analist f (cdr pair))))))
```

Fig. 1. Definitions of MagicLisper's morphism primitives given in the Scheme dialect of Lisp: *natural number paramorphism*, *list paramorphism*, and *list anamorphism*

weight. Programs are synthesised in order of total weight, this being the sum of the weights of their component functor and lexical variable invocations. Lexical variables always receive a weight of 0.4. The weights of the default primitive functors range between 2.0 and 4.5 (see Table 1). As an example of how to calculate the total weight of a program, consider the `sum-elems` program mentioned above, which has a weight of 12:

	paralist	+	a4	a2	a1	0	Total
Weight	4.0	3.4	0.4	0.4	0.4	3.4	12

Note that symbols occuring in lambda parameter lists do not contribute to the calculation.

The weighting feature allows one to manually bias the system towards using certain primitives by assigning them lower weights. This extra flexibility allows our system to potentially handle a larger primitive library than MagicHaskeller, since more rarely used primitives can be given higher weights to minimise their negative impact on the search performance. Note that if one sets all the weights to the same value, our search algorithm reduces to that of MagicHaskeller. In this study, the weights were chosen by hand; however, we note that for a more advanced system it would make sense to have these weights tuned automatically (see Sect. 6.3). To justify our choice of weight values, we have tested MagicLisper's performance on a selection of nine non-incremental problems, both with and without the customised weights (Table 2). The problems all exhibit a significant increase in solution speed due to the custom weights, ranging from a factor of 2.4 to a factor of 165.7.

MagicLisper does not employ the memoisation or fusion rule optimisations of MagicHaskeller. Finally, MagicLisper requires the user to explicitly specify the maximum number of 'steps' for which to test any candidate solution program on a given training example. Each step corresponds to one evaluation by the

Table 2. Some typical problems that MagicLisper can solve without the aid of incremental learning. In each case, between 3 and 5 training examples were given. Solution times were measured in two different scenarios: 'custom weights', in which the lexical variable and primitive weights were set up as described in Sect. 4.2, and 'uniform weights', in which the lexical variable and primitive weights were all set to the value 1. The 'speed-up factor' column gives the proportional increase in speed due to the custom weights: time (uniform weights) divided by time (custom weights). The measurements were made on a 2 GHz Intel Core II Duo desktop PC with 2 GB of RAM running GNU CLISP.

Name	Description	Time / s (custom weights)	Time / s (uniform weights)	Speed-up factor
`append`	Appends two lists together.	< 0.1	14.5	> 145.0
`make-list`	Constructs the list of n instances of a given value.	0.1	13.3	133.0
`length`	Finds the length of a list.	0.2	1.9	9.5
`sum-elems`	Finds the sum of the elements in a list.	0.5	19.9	39.8
`evenp`	Tests if a given integer is even.	0.7	1.7	2.4
`nth`	Finds the nth element of a list.	0.9	26.0	28.9
`last-elem`	Finds the last element of a list.	1.5	248.5	165.7
`member`	Tests if a given value is a member of a list.	6.7	> 251.4	> 37.5
`pow`	Raises one integer to the power of another.	9.6	31.2	3.3

interpreter of a sub-expression within a program, and this 'number of steps' is an approximate specification of the maximum time to spend testing each program.

4.3 Example Usage of MagicLisper

Let us briefly look at MagicLisper in action on a simple problem. Consider the following specification for a function which finds the length of a list:

```
() → 0              [10 steps]
(8) → 1             [20 steps]
(10 4 7 2) → 4      [50 steps]
```

To solve this, MagicLisper first determines the type of the program implied by the specification: in this case, it is a function mapping a list of integers to an integer. It then performs an iterative deepening search through the space of programs matching that type; on the nth iteration, it generates and tests programs whose total weight is less than or equal to n. When testing a program, MagicLisper runs it on each training input in turn, for no more than the specified number of steps in each case. The whole search finishes when MagicLisper finds the program with the smallest weight that satisfies all of the training examples, which is in this case:

```
(λ (a1) (paralist (λ (a2 a3 a4) (inc a4)) a1 0))
```

The above program has a weight of 11.6, so is found on the 12th search iteration.

5 Incremental Learning Experiments

In this section, we describe a set of experiments with MagicLisper that demonstrate the incremental learning mechanism of Sect. 3, that in which solution programs are successively added to the system's object language as new primitives.

5.1 Method and Results

We measured the performance of MagicLisper on four problem sequences, both with and without the aid of incremental learning in each case. Full specifications of these problem sequences along with the experimental results are given in Figs. 2 to 5. Each specification consists of a main problem, and a sequence of sub-problems whose solutions may act as building blocks out of which the solution to the main problem can be constructed. For example, in the `sort` problem sequence (Fig. 4) we tasked our system with inferring an algorithm to sort a list of numbers. Sub-problems included the simpler but related task of taking the smallest element out of a list and bringing it to the front (`extract-least-elem`), and the yet simpler tasks of finding the smallest element in a list (`least-elem`), and of removing a given element from a list (`remove-elem`).

When designing the problem sequences, we used our knowledge of how one might implement the solution programs by hand in order to choose appropriate sub-problems. We used some degree of trial and error in tweaking the problem sequences until incremental learning worked effectively (for example, `remove-first-block` was originally the first stage in our design for the `block-lengths` problem sequence; we added an extra stage, `car-p`, when it became apparent that our system was taking too long to solve `remove-first-block` from the default starting conditions). Also when choosing step counts, we made use of our knowledge of the computational complexities of the desired solutions, as well as a degree of trial and error. For now, let us emphasise the point that readily comprehensible and effective incremental problem specifications often exist. In the next section (Sect. 6) we shall consider in detail the issue of how much human effort is required to produce these specifications, as well as what ways can be developed to reduce or remove the need for this human effort.

deref-list: *dereferences a list of indices into another list.*	
— Training examples —	
`(), (7) → ()`	[20 steps]
`(0), (6) → (6)`	[50 steps]
`(1 0 2), (8 6 4 5) → (6 8 4)`	[200 steps]
— Test examples —	
`(3 2 2 1 3 4 0 5), (77 42 3 -10 8 61) → (-10 3 3 42 -10 8 77 61)`	
`(8 4 7), (9 5 2 5 8 4 1 9 1 7) → (1 8 9)`	

Incremental specification

1.

nth: *returns the nth element of a list.*	
— Training examples —	
`0, (5) → 5`	[15 steps]
`1, (8 6) → 6`	[30 steps]
`3, (4 10 77 34 58) → 34`	[150 steps]
— Test examples —	
`8, (8 4 9 3 7 1 9 2 5 4 7) → 5`	
`4, (11 23 45 15 27 89 102 56) → 27`	

2. **deref-list**

Results

Stage	Time / s	Depth	Solution
`nth`	0.9	12	(λ (a1 a2) (car (paranat (λ (a3 a4) (cdr a4)) a1 a2)))
`deref-list`	3.6	13	(λ (a1 a2) (paralist (λ (a3 a4 a5) (cons (nth a3 a2) a5)) a1 nil))
Total	**4.5**		

Non-incremental: TIMEOUT (950.2 seconds, depth 18)

Fig. 2. The `deref-list` problem sequence: specification and results

For every problem and sub-problem, in order to obtain some guarantee that the program found was indeed the correct general solution, we checked it against a set of test examples. When designing our problem specifications, if any failure occurred at the testing stage, we added new training examples and re-ran the experiment. For the final specifications given in the figures, every solution program has passed all of its test examples.

We recorded the times taken for MagicLisper to solve the stages of each sequence. Total times was determined by adding these values together. Following each sub-problem in a sequence, the inferred solution program was added to the library of primitives and assigned a weight of 2.5, 2.5, 3.5, or 3.0 in the case of problem sequences `deref-list`, `reverse`, `sort`, and `block-lengths` respectively. The library of primitives was reset to its default state between problem

reverse: *reverses a list.*	
— Training examples —	
`() → ()`	[20 steps]
`(8) → (8)`	[40 steps]
`(3 7) → (7 3)`	[150 steps]
`(9 4 7 1) → (1 7 4 9)`	[800 steps]
— Test examples —	
`(2 9 1 7 -3 4 8 9 10 12) → (12 10 9 8 4 -3 7 1 9 2)`	
`(6 4 5 2 1 1 1 8 2) → (2 8 1 1 1 2 5 4 6)`	

Incremental specification

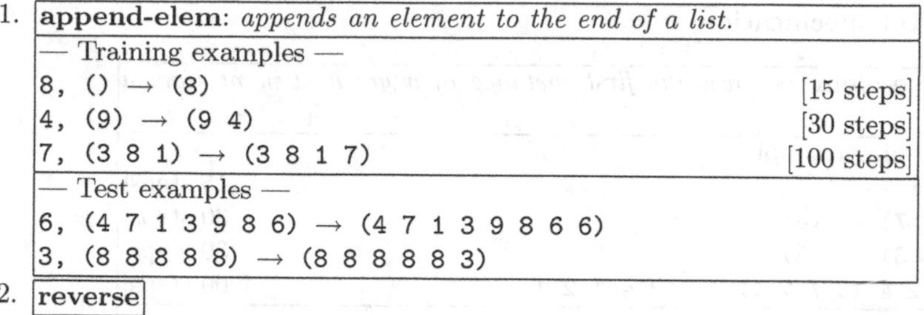

1.

append-elem: *appends an element to the end of a list.*	
— Training examples —	
`8, () → (8)`	[15 steps]
`4, (9) → (9 4)`	[30 steps]
`7, (3 8 1) → (3 8 1 7)`	[100 steps]
— Test examples —	
`6, (4 7 1 3 9 8 6) → (4 7 1 3 9 8 6 6)`	
`3, (8 8 8 8 8) → (8 8 8 8 8 3)`	

2. **reverse**

Results

Stage	Time / s	Depth	Solution
`append-elem`	1.0	12	(λ (a1 a2) (paralist (λ (a3 a4 a5) (cons a3 a5)) a2 (cons a1 nil)))
`reverse`	0.1	10	(λ (a1) (paralist (λ (a2 a3 a4) (append-elem a2 a4)) a1 nil))
Total	**1.1**		

Non-incremental: SOLUTION FOUND (569.6 seconds, depth 19):
(λ (a1) (paralist (λ (a2 a3 a4) (paralist (λ (a5 a6 a7) (cons a5 a7)) a4 (cons a2 nil))) a1 nil))

Fig. 3. The `reverse` problem sequence: specification and results

sequences. We also tested how our system fared when solving each main problem on its own with the default primitive library, i.e. without incremental learning. We allowed at least 500 seconds for every problem; if this time limit was exceeded then the computation was aborted after allowing for the current search iteration to finish, and 'TIMEOUT' was indicated in the results table. Also given in each results table are the search depths, in units of program weight, at which any solution was found or a timeout occurred, as well as the solution programs themselves. The experiments were performed on a 2 GHz Intel Core II Duo desktop PC with 2 GB of RAM running GNU CLISP.

sort: *sorts a list of integers in ascending order.*	
— Training examples —	
`() → ()`	[30 steps]
`(7) → (7)`	[100 steps]
`(4 2) → (2 4)`	[500 steps]
`(9 8 7) → (7 8 9)`	[2000 steps]
`(3 2 3 2 3) → (2 2 3 3 3)`	[10000 steps]
— Test examples —	
`(10 6 -30 7 2 5 -2 3 1 6 4) → (-30 -2 1 2 3 4 5 6 6 7 10)`	
`(1 1 1 8 6 8 6 4 3 3 1 1) → (1 1 1 1 1 3 3 4 6 6 8 8)`	
`(10 2 105 -78 46 45 23) → (-78 2 10 23 45 46 105)`	

Incremental specification

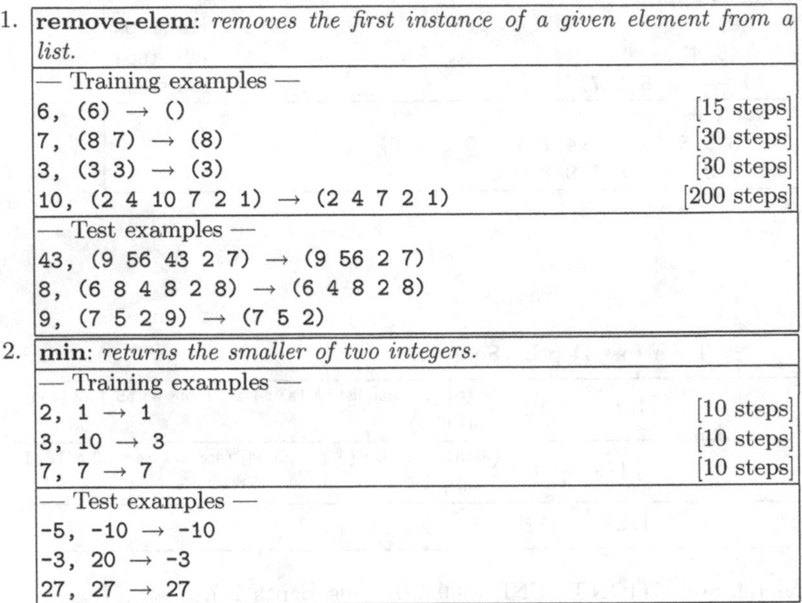

1.

remove-elem: *removes the first instance of a given element from a list.*	
— Training examples —	
`6, (6) → ()`	[15 steps]
`7, (8 7) → (8)`	[30 steps]
`3, (3 3) → (3)`	[30 steps]
`10, (2 4 10 7 2 1) → (2 4 7 2 1)`	[200 steps]
— Test examples —	
`43, (9 56 43 2 7) → (9 56 2 7)`	
`8, (6 8 4 8 2 8) → (6 4 8 2 8)`	
`9, (7 5 2 9) → (7 5 2)`	

2.

min: *returns the smaller of two integers.*	
— Training examples —	
`2, 1 → 1`	[10 steps]
`3, 10 → 3`	[10 steps]
`7, 7 → 7`	[10 steps]
— Test examples —	
`-5, -10 → -10`	
`-3, 20 → -3`	
`27, 27 → 27`	

Fig. 4. The `sort` problem sequence: specification and results

5.2 Analysis

The total times taken for our system to solve the incremental specifications ranged between 1 and 16 seconds. On the other hand, all of the non-incremental scenarios took more than 500 seconds, with a solution only being found at all in the case of `reverse`. This amounts to an increase in speed due to incremental learning of at least a factor of thirty in every case.

On inspection of the solution programs for the incremental sequences, we see that the majority of programs do indeed invoke earlier solutions, as expected. Indeed, for the longer sequences `sort` and `block-lengths` we can visualise a graph of dependencies between the solution programs (Fig. 6).

3. **least-elem**: *returns the smallest element in a list of integers.*

— Training examples —	
(3) → 3	[20 steps]
(8 4 7) → 4	[100 steps]
(9 6 2 9 2) → 2	[200 steps]
— Test examples —	
(10 7 45 5 7 8) → 5	
(77 34 59 34 208) → 34	

4. **extract-least-elem**: *brings the smallest element to front of a list of integers.*

— Training examples —	
(8) → (8)	[50 steps]
(10 4) → (4 10)	[200 steps]
(8 6 2 7 2 5) → (2 8 6 7 2 5)	[2000 steps]
— Test examples —	
(3 2 1 2 3) → (1 3 2 2 3)	
(54 70 14 59 14 20) → (14 54 70 59 14 20)	

5. **sort**

Results

Stage	Time / s	Depth	Solution
remove-elem	7.8	14	(λ (a1 a2) (paralist (λ (a3 a4 a5) (if (eql a3 a1) a4 (cons a3 a5))) a2 a2))
min	0.0	7	(λ (a1 a2) (if (< a2 a1) a2 a1))
least-elem	0.7	13	(λ (a1) (paralist (λ (a2 a3 a4) (min a4 a2)) a1 (car a1)))
extract-least-elem	3.3	14	(λ (a1) (cons (least-elem a1) (remove-elem (least-elem a1) a1)))
sort	4.5	14	(λ (a1) (analist (λ (a2) (paralist (λ (a3 a4 a5) (extract-least-elem a5)) a2 a2)) a1))
Total	**10.3**		

Non-incremental: TIMEOUT (586.6 seconds, depth 19)

Fig. 4. (*continued*)

The timing results indicate that, at worst, incremental learning can greatly improve the performance of IP, while, at best, it is able to make otherwise intractable problems tractable. To see why this should be the case, consider the following computational complexity argument. Assuming that it takes constant time to generate and test each program, then the time taken for MagicLisper's search algorithm to solve a given problem will be proportional to the total number of programs generated. We expect this to be approximately $O[b^d]$, where b

block-lengths: *replaces all blocks of consecutive identical elements in a list with their lengths.*	
— Training examples —	
`() → ()`	[50 steps]
`(8) → (1)`	[200 steps]
`(7 6) → (1 1)`	[700 steps]
`(8 8 3 4) → (2 1 1)`	[5000 steps]
`(6 5 5 4) → (1 2 1)`	[5000 steps]
— Test examples —	
`(7 7 7 7 7 5 5 5 7 7 2 2 4 9 9 9) → (5 3 2 2 1 3)`	
`(5 8 8 4 9 1 2 1 2) → (1 2 1 1 1 1 1 1)`	
`(0 0 0 0 0 7 0 0 0 5 5 5 5 5 5) → (5 1 3 6)`	

Incremental specification

1.

car-p: *tests whether an object is the first element of a list.*	
— Training examples —	
`0, () → f`	[15 steps]
`1, () → f`	[15 steps]
`4, (4) → t`	[15 steps]
`5, (2) → f`	[15 steps]
`8, (8 2) → t`	[15 steps]
`7, (6 2 7) → f`	[15 steps]
— Test examples —	
`7, (8 7 7 6 4 7) → f`	
`3, (3 8 1 4) → t`	

2.

remove-first-block: *removes the first block of consecutive identical elements from a list.*	
— Training examples —	
`(8) → ()`	[30 steps]
`(4 6) → (6)`	[100 steps]
`(1 3 1 3) → (3 1 3)`	[400 steps]
`(9 9 8 6 9 3) → (8 6 9 3)`	[1000 steps]
`(5 5 5 5 4 9) → (4 9)`	[1000 steps]
— Test examples —	
`(7 7 7 7 4 4 3 3 7 8 8 7 2 2) → (4 4 3 3 7 8 8 7 2 2)`	
`(1 6 5 1 2 2 2) → (6 5 1 2 2 2)`	
`(9 9 9 9 9) → ()`	

3.

length: *finds the length of a list.*	
— Training examples —	
`() → 0`	[10 steps]
`(8) → 1`	[20 steps]
`(10 4 7 2) → 4`	[50 steps]
— Test examples —	
`(8 4 7 3 2 9 1 1 2) → 9`	
`(92 -8 7 83 24) → 5`	

Fig. 5. The `block-lengths` problem sequence: specification and results

4. **length-first-block**: *finds the length of the first block of consecutive identical elements in a list.*

— Training examples —

`(8) → 1`	[50 steps]
`(4 6) → 1`	[100 steps]
`(9 9 8 6 9 3) → 2`	[1000 steps]

— Test examples —

`(3 3 3 3 8 7 6 3 4 5) → 4`
`(5 5 5 5 5 5 5 2 2) → 7`

5. **convert-first-block-to-length**: *replaces the first block of consecutive identical elements in a list with its length.*

— Training examples —

`() → ()`	[20 steps]
`(8) → (1)`	[100 steps]
`(7 6) → (1 6)`	[400 steps]
`(8 8 3 4) → (2 3 4)`	[2000 steps]
`(5 5 5 3) → (3 3)`	[2000 steps]

— Test examples —

`(8 8 8 6 6 6 6) → (3 6 6 6 6)`
`(4 1 5 4 2 2) → (1 1 5 4 2 2)`

6. **block-lengths**

Results

Stage	Time / s	Depth	Solution
`car-p`	0.4	11	(λ (a1 a2) (paralist (λ (a3 a4 a5) (eql a3 a1)) a2 f))
`remove-first-block`	0.5	12	(λ (a1) (paralist (λ (a2 a3 a4) (if (car-p a2 a3) a4 a3)) a1 a1))
`length`	0.2	12	(λ (a1) (paralist (λ (a2 a3 a4) (inc a4)) a1 0))
`length-first-block`	6.9	15	(λ (a1) (length (paralist (λ (a2 a3 a4) (cdr a4)) (remove-first-block a1) a1)))
`convert-first-block-to-length`	4.8	14	(λ (a1) (paralist (λ (a2 a3 a4) (cons (length-first-block a1) (remove-first-block a1))) a1 a1))
`block-lengths`	0.1	9	(λ (a1) (analist (λ (a2) (convert-first-block-to-length a2)) a1))
Total	**12.9**		

Non-incremental: TIMEOUT (561.8 seconds, depth 19)

Fig. 5. (*continued*)

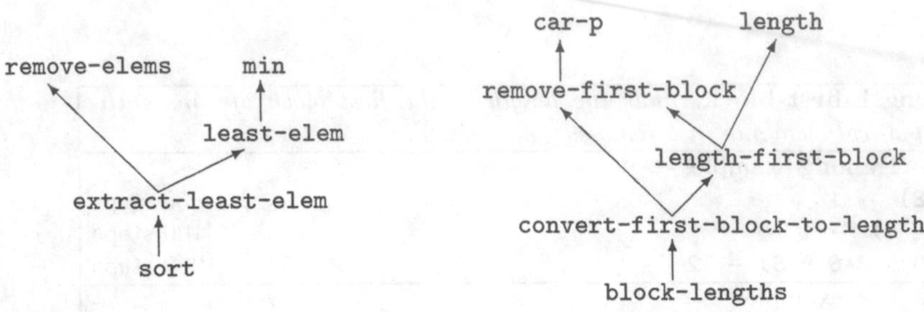

Fig. 6. Dependency graphs for the solutions to the **sort** and **block-lengths** problem sequences. Each arrow $x \longrightarrow y$ means 'program x invokes program y'.

is the search branching factor, roughly proportional to the size of the primitive library, and d is the search depth of the lowest-weight solution program that exists for the problem. Now, if we make an assumption that with incremental learning we can always divide a problem into sub-problems whose solution depths are bounded by a constant d_0, then the time taken to solve the problem in incremental stages is no more than $\mathrm{O}[n(b_0 + n\Delta b)^{d_0}]$, where n is the number of stages, b_0 is the branching factor of the default primitive library and Δb is the increase in the branching factor that occurs each time we add a new primitive. Let us also assume that the number of stages required to satisfactorily break down a problem is roughly proportional to the depth of the lowest-weight solution program that we'd get if the problem were solved non-incrementally, in other words, $n = kd$. This gives us a time taken of $\mathrm{O}[kd(b_0 + kd\Delta b)^{d_0}]$, or simply $\mathrm{O}[d^{d_0+1}]$ with respect to d, if the problem is solved incrementally, compared with $\mathrm{O}[{b_0}^d]$ if it is solved non-incrementally. In this way, IP with incremental learning can allow a system to solve, in polynomial time, problems that take exponential time with non-incremental IP.

6 Limitations and Further Work

The main contribution of this paper has been to demonstrate a simple, working methodology for incremental learning in IP. This methodology involved equipping a brute-force search based IP system with an ability to reuse solution programs by adding them to its primitive library. We showed that this mechanism can be effective by demonstrating its use on four problems, each of which had been broken down into an appropriate sequence of sub-problems. Our IP system was able to solve the problems orders of magnitude more quickly when making using of the incremental sequences than when simply solving the main problems in isolation.

In this section we address the limitations of our simple incremental learning methodology; in particular we talk about the difficulties involved in constructing problem sequences. We consider how to overcome these limitations, and discuss how, by eliminating the need for problem sequences to be designed by a human expert, we aim to enable a much more useful, autonomous form of incremental learning.

6.1 Limitations of the Simple Methodology

The main drawback of the simple incremental learning methodology presented in this paper is the significant amount of human effort and expertise required to design effective problem sequences. Based on our experience designing problem sequences for MagicLisper, we feel that the need for this effort and expertise is largely due to what we shall call 'brittleness' in the system's learning mechanism. In other words, problem specifications must obey certain conditions in order for learning to work, and they 'break easily', i.e. if these conditions are not met perfectly, then the system will fail to find a solution at all.

One source of brittleness in our mechanism is the fact that solutions to sub-problems are only useful if a solution to the main problem can be expressed in terms of them directly. It is not enough for a sub-problem simply to be related to the main problem, for example if their solutions would share some common structure. In consequence, the success or failure of incremental learning is very sensitive to the exact choice and order of sub-problems. Often, the only way to predict if a particular sub-problem will be effective is to use ones knowledge of how one might implement the target program by hand; in other words, using the IP system does not save one much effort over hand-coding the program. Our methodology suffers from brittleness in two other ways too. Firstly, the IP system will not tolerate any error or noise in the training examples. Secondly, if any of the step counts associated with the training examples are too low, the system will again completely fail to find a solution.

6.2 Overcoming the Limitations

The need to specifiy step counts with training examples should be the easiest limitation to overcome. In MagicHaskeller, it is already unnecessary to specify step counts, because the system simply tests all programs until termination, relying on the fact that the primitive library belies the possibility of infinite loops. However, we don't expect this approach to remain feasible as we start to generate more complex programs, because the number of programs that run for a long time before termination will become much larger. Instead, we propose using an algorithm like 'Levin search' [10], in which the iterative deepening nature of our IP search is extended so as to automatically re-test programs for longer and longer step counts as the search progresses.

The need for a solution to a main problem to be expressible directly in terms of solutions to sub-problems could be overcome as follows. Suppose that we modify our incremental learning mechanism such that, instead of adding actual solution programs to the primitive library, it attempts to derive re-usable procedural abstractions from groups of solution programs, and then adds these abstractions as the new primitives. The potential re-usabilility of a procedural abstraction can be measured objectively using a principle of 'minimum description length': if a procedure, when reused in multiple solution programs, serves to reduce the combined size of these programs by more than its own size, then we can deem it a useful abstraction. Though the best way to discover candidate abstractions is an open question, it would seem a reasonable starting point to try a brute-force search. This method of incremental learning would be much more adaptable and generic than our original mechanism, in that it should be able to extract useful inductive bias from almost any kind of shared structure or commonality between solution programs. We know of at least one previous implementation of a similar idea: the 'Duce' system [7] can discover abstractions that encapsulate shared structure among groups of statements in propositional logic.

To overcome the lack of toleration of errors or noise in the training examples, we feel that the most satisfactory solution will ultimately be to reformulate our IP methodology within a probabilistic framework. In such a framework, a program would no longer describe a deterministic mapping from inputs to outputs, rather it would represent a conditional probability distribution over the set of possible outputs given the inputs. Such a reformulation is highly desirable if our aim is to develop a machine learning technique of practical use, since real-world data is usually noisy. Indeed, the development of probabilistic frameworks for IP is an active area of research, particularly within inductive logic programming [2].

In overcoming the above limitations, our eventual goal is to produce an IP methodology capable of performing incremental learning simply from a corpus of data, without the need for that data to be organised into problem sequences by a human expert. To see how this might work, first consider how a system could perform incremental learning if provided with a large bank of related problems of various difficulties, in no particular order. Such a system could repeatedly scan through the problems, briefly attempting to solve each as it goes. Some of the problems might be easy enough to solve immediately, and the system could then use the solutions of these to derive procedural abstractions which it would add to its primitive library. On the next scan through the problem bank, these new primitives should enable the system to solve some problems that were previously out of its reach. Ideally, the process iterates until most of the problems are solved. Consider next how one might extend this idea in order to create a system capable of automonomously learning a model for a complex environment or corpus of data. In a such a situation, it might often be the case that various parts of the environment or corpus can be described by simple models. By analogy with the 'bank of problems' scenario, one may imagine an incremental learning system that initially looks for these simple models, adds abstractions derived from those models to its background knowledge, then searches for more complex models, and so on. We may think of this process as an automation of the scientific method.

6.3 Managing an Expanding Background Knowledge

Let us lastly discuss the issue of how to prevent an incremental learning system from becoming gradually less efficient as the size of its background knowledge increases. Each time a system like MagicLisper adds a new procedure to its primitive library, it increases the branching factor of its search space. As discussed in Sect. 5.2, we expect the time taken for our system to solve a given problem to increase polynomially with the value of this branching factor. Here we suggest two ways to alleviate this potential source of slowdown.

Our first solution would be to enable our IP system to automatically tune the weights of primitives. Not only would this remove the need for a human to choose the weight values, but it would also provide a mechanism for the system to control the size of its background knowledge by 'unlearning' any procedures that turned out to be not so useful in the long term. To perform the tuning, we can adjust weights according to how frequently their associated primitives occur in solution programs, as in 'adaptive Levin search'. If we do this in an online manner, problem by problem, then rarely used primitives will gradually increase in weight until their influence becomes negligible. We can even delete primitives altogether if their weights exceed some threshold.

If an incremental learning IP system is ever to grow a large background knowledge consisting of hundreds or even thousands of primitives, it could do with some means of automatically inventing new data types. Types place constraints on which primitives can be used in combination with which others, and the more of these constraints that we have, the greater the size of the primitive library we can support while still maintaining a low search branching factor. For human programmers, it is natural to define new types (with the `data` keyword in Haskell, for instance) as well as new functions as we build up a software system. Can an IP system do the same in an effective way? We leave this as an open question.

7 Conclusion

In this paper, we have demonstrated a simple but effective incremental learning mechanism for an inductive programming system. It works by having the system incorporate solution programs into its object language as new primitive functions as it progresses through a sequence of problems. The mechanism is capable of producing orders of magnitude improvements in problem solving performance, but at the expense of considerable human effort spent in designing appropriate problem sequences. However, we have sketched a number of possible improvements to the mechanism intended to reduce or remove much of this need for human guidance. Our aim is that this methodology can eventually be developed into a powerful generic machine learning technique by which a system can learn a model of a large, complex dataset in an autonomous fashion.

Acknowledgments. Thank you to my MSc supervisor Michael O'Boyle, for his support and encouragement on this project.

References

1. Augusteijn, L.: Sorting morphisms. In: Swierstra, S.D., Oliveira, J.N. (eds.) AFP 1998. LNCS, vol. 1608, pp. 1–27. Springer, Heidelberg (1999)
2. De Raedt, L., Kersting, K.: Probabilistic inductive logic programming. In: Ben-David, S., Case, J., Maruoka, A. (eds.) ALT 2004. LNCS (LNAI), vol. 3244, pp. 19–36. Springer, Heidelberg (2004)

3. Hofmann, M., Kitzelmann, E., Schmid, U.: A unifying framework for analysis and evaluation of inductive programming systems. In: Proceedings of the Second Conference on Artificial General Intelligence, AGI 2009 (2009)
4. Katayama, S.: Systematic search for lambda expressions. In: Revised Selected Papers from the Sixth Symposium on Trends in Functional Programming, TFP 2005, vol. 6, pp. 111–126. Intellect (2007)
5. Khan, K., Muggleton, S., Parson, R.: Repeat learning using predicate invention. In: Page, D.L. (ed.) ILP 1998. LNCS, vol. 1446, pp. 165–174. Springer, Heidelberg (1998)
6. Kitzelmann, E.: Data-driven induction of recursive functions from input/output-examples. In: Proceedings of the ECML/PKDD 2007 Workshop on Approaches and Applications of Inductive Programming (AAIP 2007), pp. 15–26 (2007)
7. Muggleton, S.: Duce, an oracle based approach to constructive induction. In: IJCAI 1987, pp. 287–292 (1987)
8. Olsson, J.R.: Inductive functional programming using incremental program transformation. Artificial Intelligence 74(1), 55–83 (1995)
9. Quinlan, J.R., Cameron-Jones, R.M.: FOIL: A midterm report. In: Brazdil, P.B. (ed.) ECML 1993. LNCS, vol. 667, pp. 3–20. Springer, Heidelberg (1993)
10. Schmidhuber, J.: Optimal ordered problem solver. Machine Learning 54(3), 211–254 (2004)
11. Schmidhuber, J., Zhao, J., Wiering, M.: Shifting inductive bias with success-story algorithm, adaptive levin search, and incremental self-improvement. Machine Learning 28(1), 105–130 (1997)
12. Solomonoff, R.J.: Progress in incremental machine learning. Given at: NIPS Workshop on Universal Learning Algorithms and Optimal Search. Whistler, B.C., Canada, December 14 (2002), `http://world.std.com/~rjs/pubs.html`

Enumerating Well-Typed Terms Generically

Alexey Rodriguez Yakushev[1] and Johan Jeuring[2,3]

[1] Vector Fabrics B.V., Paradijslaan 28, 5611 KN Eindhoven, The Netherlands
[2] Department of Information and Computing Sciences, Utrecht University, P.O. Box 80.089, 3508 TB Utrecht, The Netherlands
[3] School of Computer Science, Open University of the Netherlands, P.O. Box 2960, 6401 DL Heerlen, The Netherlands

Abstract. We use generic programming techniques to generate well-typed lambda terms. We encode well-typed terms by means of generalized algebraic datatypes (GADTs) and existential types. The Spine approach to generic programming supports GADTs, but it does not support the definition of generic producers for existentials. We describe how to extend the Spine approach to support existentials and we use the improved Spine to define a generic enumeration function. We show that the enumeration function can be used to generate the terms of simply typed lambda calculus.

1 Introduction

This paper discusses the problem of given a type, generate lambda terms of that type. There exist several algorithms and/or tools for producing lambda terms given a type (1; 8; 10). The approach discussed in this paper uses generic programming techniques on Generalized Algebraic Datatypes (GADTs) and existentials to enumerate well-typed lambda terms. The enumeration function is much simpler than previous work; the main problem lies in making generic programming techniques available for GADTs and existentials in functions that produce values of a particular datatype, such as an enumeration function.

Since their introduction in Haskell, Generalized Algebraic Datatypes (GADTs) (3; 13; 16) are often used to improve the reliability of programs. GADTs encode datatype invariants by type constraints in constructor signatures. With this information, the compiler rejects values for which such invariants do not hold during type-checking. In particular, GADTs can be used to model sets of well-typed terms such that values representing ill-typed terms cannot be constructed. Other applications of GADTs include well-typed program transformations, implementation of dynamic typing, staged computation, ad-hoc polymorphism and tag-less interpreters.

Given the growing relevance of GADTs, it is important to provide generic programming support for them. The generation of datatype values using generic programming is of particular interest. Generic value generation has been used before to produce test data, which can be used to check the validity of program properties (9). In generic value generation, the datatype definition acts as a specification for test data. However, this specification is often imprecise, since it gives rise to either values that do not occur in practice, or, worse, ill-formed values (for example, a program fragment with unbound variables). For this reason, QuickCheck (4) allows the definition of custom generators.

U. Schmid, E. Kitzelmann, and R. Plasmeijer (Eds.): AAIP 2009, LNCS 5812, pp. 93–116, 2010.

GADT definitions may specify types more precisely than normal datatypes. In the case of well-typed terms, the constraints in the datatype definition describe the formation rules of a well-typed value. It follows that a generic producer function on a GADT might produce values that are better suited for testing program properties. For example, it should be possible to use a generic value generation function with a GADT encoding lambda calculus, in order to produce a well-typed lambda term with which a tag-less interpreter can be tested.

The *spine* view (6; 7), which is based on "Scrap Your Boilerplate" (11), is the only approach to generic programming in Haskell that supports GADTs. The main idea behind the spine view is to make the application of a data constructor to its arguments explicit. The spine view represents a datatype value by means of two cases: the representation of a datatype constructor, and the representation of the application to constructor arguments. A generic function can then be defined by case analysis on the spine view. Hinze et al. (6) describe how to use the spine view to represent GADT values and define generic functions to consume and produce such values.

Besides GADT definitions, our definition of well-typed terms uses existentially quantified type variables. In particular, the type of expression application is that of the function return type. The argument type is hidden from the application type and is therefore existentially quantified. Under certain conditions, the spine view supports the definition of generic functions that *consume* existentially typed values. Unfortunately, it cannot be used to define a generic function that *produces* them. It follows that the spine view cannot in general be used to define generic enumerators for well-typed terms.

This paper extends the spine view to allow the use of producer functions on existential types. We make the following contributions:

- We show how to support existential types systematically within the spine view. We extend the spine view to encode existentially quantified type variables explicitly. This enables the definition of generic functions that perform case analysis on such types. As a consequence, the extended spine view supports the definition of generic producers that work on existential types. We demonstrate the increased generality by defining generic serialization and deserialization for existential types and GADTs.
- We define a generic enumeration function that can be used with GADTs and existential types. This function can be used to enumerate the well-typed terms represented by a GADT. Consider a GADT that represents terms in the simply typed lambda calculus. The enumeration of terms with type $\mathsf{Expr}\ ((\mathsf{b} \to \mathsf{c}) \to (\mathsf{a} \to \mathsf{b}) \to \mathsf{a} \to \mathsf{c})$ yields the term that corresponds to function composition. The enumeration function requires explicit support for existential types in producers. For that reason it cannot be defined in approaches such as that of Hinze et al. (6).

This paper is organized as follows. Section 2 introduces the spine view and gives several examples illustrating why this view is not suitable to define producers for existential types. Section 3 describes our extensions to the spine view, which enable producer support for existential types. Section 4 uses the extended spine view to define a generic enumeration function. The enumeration function is then used to produce well-typed lambda calculus terms. Section 5 discusses related work, and section 6 concludes.

2 The Spine View

The spine view was introduced by Hinze et al. (7). This view supports the definition of generic functions that consume (such as *show* or *eq*) or transform (such as *map*) datatype values. We introduce the spine view using the generic show function as an example. This function prints the textual representation of a value based on the type structure encoded by the view. To implement this function, we need case analysis on types to implement type-dependent behavior.

2.1 Case Analysis on Types

The spine view uses GADTs to implement case analysis on types. We define a type representation datatype where each constructor represents a specific type:

```
data Type :: * → * where
  Int    :: Type Int
  Maybe  :: Type a → Type (Maybe a)
  Either :: Type a → Type b → Type (Either a b)
  List   :: Type a → Type [a]
  (:→)   :: Type a → Type b → Type (a → b)
```

An overloaded function can be implemented by performing case analysis on types. To perform case analysis on types we pattern match on the type representation values. The GADT pattern matching semantics (13) ensures that the type variable a is refined to the target type of the matched constructor:

```
show :: Type a → a → String
show Int          n         = showInt n
show (Maybe a)    (Just x)  = paren ("Just"  • show a x)
show (Maybe a)    Nothing   = "Nothing"
show (Either a b) (Left x)  = paren ("Left"  • show a x)
show (Either a b) (Right y) = paren ("Right" • show b y)
show (List a)     ((:) x xs) = paren ("(:)" • show a x • show (List a) xs)
show (List a)     []        = "[]"
```

This function prints a textual representation of a datatype value. Note that we choose to print lists in prefix syntax rather than the usual Haskell notation. The operator (•) separates two strings with a white space, and *paren* prints parentheses around a string argument.

2.2 The Spine Representation of Values

Type representations can be used to implement overloaded functions, but such functions are not generic. The user needs to define new *show* cases for every datatype added to the program. To define generic functions, we make use of the spine view.

The spine view represents all datatype values by means of two cases: a constructor and the application of a (partially applied) constructor to an argument. This is embodied in the Spine datatype:

```
data Spine :: * → * where
  Con :: ConInfo a → Spine a
  (:◇:) :: Spine (a → b) → Typed a → Spine b
infixl 0 :◇:
```

The *Con* case of the spine view stores a value constructor of type a together with additional information including the constructor name, the fixity, and the constructor tag. This additional information is stored in the datatype ConInfo. The application case (:◇:) consists of a functional value Spine that consumes a-values, and the argument a paired with its type representation in the datatype Typed. We show Typed, and a simplified ConInfo containing only the constructor name below:

```
data ConInfo a = ConInfo{ conName :: String, conVal :: a }
data Typed a   = (:▷:)   { val :: a, rep :: Type a }
```

To write a generic function, we first convert a value to its Spine representation. We show how to perform this conversion using the type-indexed function *toSpine*:

```
toSpine :: Type a → a → Spine a
toSpine Int          x        = Con (conint x x)
toSpine (Maybe a)    (Just x) = Con (conjust Just) :◇: x :▷: a
toSpine (Maybe a)    Nothing  = Con (connothing Nothing)
toSpine (Either a b) (Left x) = Con (conleft Left) :◇: x :▷: a
toSpine (Either a b) (Right y) = Con (conright Right) :◇: y :▷: b
toSpine (List a)     ((:) x xs) = Con (concons (:))
                                  :◇: x :▷: a :◇: xs :▷: List a
toSpine (List a)     []       = Con (connil [])
```

Because we reuse the constructor information in later sections of the paper, we define ConInfo values separately. We give some examples below:

```
conint :: Int → a → ConInfo a
conint i     = ConInfo (showInt i)

connothing, conjust :: a → ConInfo a
connothing = ConInfo "Nothing"
conjust    = ConInfo "Just"
```

In summary, to enable generic programming using the spine view, we define a GADT for type representations, the Spine datatype, and conversions from datatype values to their spine representations. The conversions for datatypes are written only once, and then the same conversion can be reused for different generic functions. The conversion to the spine representation is regular enough that it can be automatically generated from the syntax trees of datatype declarations[1].

[1] At the time of writing, Template Haskell cannot handle GADT declarations. Our prototype generates the spine representation for a GADT using a manually constructed declaration syntax tree instead of parsing the GADT declaration and processing it via Template Haskell.

Equipped with the spine representation, we can write a number of generic functions. For example, this is the definition of generic *show*:

```
show :: Type a → a → String
show rep x = paren (gshow (toSpine rep x))

gshow :: Spine a → String
gshow (Con con)     = conName con
gshow (con :◇: arg) = gshow con • show (rep arg) (val arg)
```

This function is a simplified variant of the *show* function defined in the Haskell prelude. All datatype values are printed uniformly: constructors are separated from the arguments by means of the • operator, and parentheses are printed around fully applied constructors.

2.3 A View for Producers

We now discuss the definition of generic producers using parsing as an example. In the first part of the paper we use parsing to motivate and illustrate our improvements to the spine approach. With the improvements in place, Section 4 shows the main function of interest in this paper: generic enumeration.

It is impossible to define *read*, the inverse to *show* using the current Spine datatype. We could for example use the following type for *read*:

```
read :: Type a → String → [(a, String)]
```

This function produces all possible parses of type a (paired with unused input) from a representation for the type a and an input string. To write such a generic function, we would need a spine representation to guide the parsing process. Unfortunately, a representation Spine a cannot be used for this purpose. A value of Spine a represents a particular value of type a (for example, a singleton list) rather than the full datatype structure (a description of the cons and nil constructors and their arguments). To enable a generic definition of generic read and other producer generic functions, Hinze et al. (6) introduce the type spine view. This view describes all values of a rather than a particular one.

```
type TypeSpine a = [Signature a]
data Signature :: * → * where
  Sig   :: ConInfo a → Signature a
  (:⊕:) :: Signature (a → b) → Type a → Signature b
infixl 0 :⊕:
```

Here we again have two cases, one for encoding a constructor and another for the application of a (partially) applied constructor to an argument. The application case contains only a type representation and no argument value anymore. A value of TypeSpine a is a list of constructor signatures representing all constructors of the represented datatype. The type-indexed function *typeSpine* produces the type spine representations of all datatypes on which generic programming is to be used.

```
typeSpine :: Type a → TypeSpine a
typeSpine Int          = [Sig (conint i i) | i ← [minBound..maxBound]]
typeSpine (Maybe a)    = [Sig (connothing Nothing), Sig (conjust Just) :⊕: a]
typeSpine (Either a b) = [Sig (conleft Left) :⊕: a, Sig (conright Right) :⊕: b]
typeSpine (List a)     = [Sig (connil []), Sig (concons (:)) :⊕: a :⊕: List a]
```

The generic parsing function *read* builds a parser that deserializes a value of type a:

```
read :: Type a → Parser a
```

For the purposes of this paper, we assume that Parser is an abstract parser type with a monadic interface, with some standard derived functions:

```
return       :: a → Parser a
(>>=)        :: Parser a → (a → Parser b) → Parser b
ap           :: Parser (a → b) → Parser a → Parser b
(>>)         :: Parser a → Parser b → Parser b
noparse      :: Parser a
alternatives :: [Parser a] → Parser a
readInt      :: Parser Int
lex          :: Parser String
token        :: String → Parser ()
readParen    :: Parser a → Parser a
```

The definition of generic read uses *readInt* to read an integer value. For other datatypes, we make parsers for each of the constructor representations and merge all the alternatives in a single parser.

```
read :: Type a → Parser a
read Int = readInt
read rep = alternatives [readParen (gread conrep) | conrep ← typeSpine rep]
```

The generic parser of a constructor is built by induction on its signature representation. The base case (*Sig*) tries to recognize the constructor name and returns the constructor value. The application case parses the function and argument parts recursively and the results are combined using monadic application:

```
gread :: Signature a → Parser a
gread (Sig c)         = token (conName c) >> return (conVal c)
gread (con :⊕: arg)   = gread con `ap` read arg
```

2.4 Generalized Algebraic Datatypes

Recall that generalized algebraic datatypes are datatypes to which type-level constraints are added. Such constraints can be used to encode invariants that datatype values must satisfy. For example, we can define a well-typed abstract syntax tree by having the syntactic categories of constructs in the target type of constructors:

```
data Expr :: * → * where
  EZero   :: Expr Int
  EFalse  :: Expr Bool
  ESuc    :: Expr Int  → Expr Int
  ENot    :: Expr Bool → Expr Bool
  EIsZero :: Expr Int  → Expr Bool
```

We have constants for integer and boolean values, and operators that act on them.

GADTs can easily be represented in the spine view. For instance, the definition of *toSpine* for this datatype is as follows:

```
toSpine (Expr Int)  EZero       = Con (conezero   EZero)
toSpine (Expr Bool) EFalse      = Con (conefalse  EFalse)
toSpine (Expr Int)  (ESuc e)    = Con (conesuc    ESuc)    :◇: e :▷: Expr Int
toSpine (Expr Bool) (ENot e)    = Con (conenot    ENot)    :◇: e :▷: Expr Bool
toSpine (Expr Bool) (EIsZero e) = Con (coneiszero EIsZero) :◇: e :▷: Expr Int
```

where *conezero* etc. represent constructor information. This definition requires the extension of Type with the representation constructors *Expr* and *Bool*. Generic functions defined on the spine view, such as generic show, can now be used on Expr.

What about generic producer functions? These can be used on Expr too, because it is also possible to construct datatype representations for GADTs in the type spine view:

```
typeSpine (Expr Int)  = [Sig (conezero   EZero)
                        ,Sig (conesuc    ESuc) :⊕: Expr Int]
typeSpine (Expr Bool) = [Sig (conefalse  EFalse)
                        ,Sig (conenot    ENot) :⊕: Expr Bool
                        ,Sig (coneiszero EIsZero) :⊕: Expr Int]
```

To parse boolean expressions, we invoke the generic read function as follows:

```
readBoolExpr :: Parser (Expr Bool)
readBoolExpr = read (Expr Bool)
```

The parser for integer expressions would use a different argument for *Expr*. In this example, we are assuming that the expression to be parsed is always of a fixed type. A more interesting scenario would be to leave the type of the GADT unspecified and let it be dynamically determined from the parsed value. This would be useful if the programmer wants to parse some well-typed expression regardless of the type that the expression has.

A possible solution to parsing a GADT without specifying its type argument would be to existentially quantify over that argument in the result of the parsing function. Next, we discuss how the spine view deals with existential types.

2.5 Existential Types and Consumer Functions

In Haskell, existential types are introduced in constructor declarations. A type variable is existentially quantified if it is mentioned in the argument type declarations but omitted in the target type. For example, consider dynamically typed values:

```
data Dynamic :: * where
  DynVal :: Type a → a → Dynamic
```

The type variable a in the declaration is existentially quantified. It is hidden when building a Dynamic value.

The type a is kept abstract when pattern matching a Dynamic value, but by case analyzing the type representation it is possible to dynamically recover the type a. Thus, statically, Dynamic values all have the same type, but, dynamically, the type distinction can be recovered and acted upon.

To represent dynamic values in Spine, we add type representations for Type itself and Dynamic. Hence, we add the following two constructors to Type:

```
Type    :: Type a → Type (Type a)
Dynamic :: Type Dynamic
```

Now, Dynamic values may be represented as follows by the spine view:

```
toSpine Dynamic (DynVal rep val) = Con (condynval DynVal)
                                   :◇: rep :▷: Type rep
                                   :◇: val :▷: rep
```

While Dynamic values may be easily represented, this is not the case for all datatypes having existential types. Recall that in a spine representation, every constructor argument is paired with its type representation in the datatype Typed. In general, in constructors having existential types, it may not be possible to build such a pair because the representation of the existential type may be missing. The constructor *DynVal* is a special case, because it carries the representation type of the existential a. For an example where the representation of a constructor with existential types is not possible, consider adding an application constructor to the expression datatype:

```
EApp :: Expr (a → b) → Expr a → Expr b
```

and consider the corresponding *toSpine* alternative:

```
toSpine (Expr b) (EApp fun arg) = Con (coneapp EApp)
                                  :◇: fun :▷: Expr (a :→ b)
                                  :◇: arg :▷: Expr a
```

This code is incorrect due to the unbound variable *a* which stands for the existential representation. The conclusion here is that the spine view can be used on an existential type, as long as the constructor in which it occurs carries a type representation for it.

2.6 Existential Types and Producer Functions

Unfortunately the spine approach does not support the definition of generic producer functions that build existentially typed values. In particular, This makes it hard to define a generic generator for datatypes with existential types such as Expr in our previous example, and a generator for simply typed lambda calculus as defined in Section 4.

The reason behind this problem is that the generating function has no access to the representation of the existential type. For example, consider the representation for dynamically typed values:

$$typeSpine\ Dynamic = [Sig\ (condynval\ DynVal)\ {:}{\oplus}{:}\ Type\ a\ {:}{\oplus}{:}\ a]$$

What should the representation *a* be? There are two options, we either fix it to a single type representation or we range over all possible type representations. Choosing one type representation would be too restrictive, because *read* would only parse dynamic values of that type and fail on any other type. We try the second option:

$$typeSpine\ Dynamic = [Sig\ (condynval\ DynVal)\ {:}{\oplus}{:}\ Type\ a\ {:}{\oplus}{:}\ a \mid a \leftarrow types]$$

This code does not yet have the behavior we desire. For *typeSpine* to be type-correct, *types* must return a list of representations all having the same type. Because Type is a singleton type (each type has only one value), *types* returns a single type representation. We would like *types* to generate a list of all possible type representations, but different type representations have different types. Therefore, *types* should return representations whose represented type is existentially quantified. To this end, we define the type of boxed type representations:

```
data BType = ∀a.Boxed (Type a)
applyBType :: (∀a.Type a → c) → BType → c
applyBType f (Boxed a) = f a
```

Now we can define the type spine of dynamic values, for which we assume a list of boxed representations (*types*):

```
types :: [BType]
typeSpine Dynamic =[Sig (condynval DynVal) :⊕: Type a :⊕: a | Boxed a ← types]
```

The boxed representations are used to construct a list of constructor signatures that represent a dynamic value of the corresponding type. There are infinitely many type instances of polymorphic types, therefore there are infinitely many Dynamic constructor representations. An infinite type spine is not a desirable representation to work with. The *read* function would try to parse the input using every Dynamic constructor representation. If there is a correct parse, parsing eventually succeeds with one of the representations. However, if there is no correct parse, parsing does not terminate. Moreover, this representation precludes implementing more efficient variants of parsing.

Infinite type spine representations for datatypes with existentials make the use of generic producers on such datatypes unpractical. Before describing a modified type spine view that solves this problem, we explore a couple of non-generic examples to motivate our design decisions.

We start with the parser definition for Dynamic values. In the code above, we can parse any possible dynamic value because there are *DynVal* constructor signatures for all possible types. For each signature, we build a parser that parses the corresponding type representation and a value having that type. Now, rather than parsing the two arguments of the constructor *DynVal* independently, we introduce a dependency on representations. First, we parse the type representation for the existential. Then, we use it to build a parser of the corresponding type and parse the second argument. In this way, we no longer need to have an infinite representation of types because we obtain the representation of the existential during the parsing process:

```
read Dynamic = do
  Boxed a ← readType
  value   ← read a
  return (DynVal a value)
```

To this end, we use a function that parses type representations. Because the result may be of an arbitrary type, *readType* produces a representation that is boxed:

```
readType :: Parser BType
```

We defer the presentation of *readType* to Section 3.3.

The same technique can be used to parse any constructor having an existential type. For example, the definition for parsing expression applications is as follows:

```
read (Expr b) = do
  Boxed a ← readType
  fun     ← read (Expr (a :→ b))
  arg     ← read (Expr a)
  return (EApp fun arg)
```

In this example, the type representation that is parsed is used to build the type representations for the two remaining arguments.

These two examples show that constructors with existential types must be handled differently from other constructors. In such constructors, the constructor argument representations depend on the type representation of the existential type. In our examples, this dependency is witnessed by the dynamic construction of parsers based on the type representation that was previously parsed.

3 An Improved Spine View: Support for Existential Types

We start this section by showing how to extend the spine view for producers to represent existential types explicitly. Then, we show why this extension is also necessary for the consumer spine view.

3.1 The Existential Case for Producer Functions

We have learned two things from the *read* examples for constructors with existential types. First, we need a way to represent existential variables explicitly, so that generic functions can handle existential type variables specifically. And second, there is a dependency from constructor arguments on the existential variable. For example, we can only parse the function and argument parts of an expression application, if we have already parsed the existential type representation. We modify the type spine view to accommodate these two aspects. We extend the constructor signatures in this view with a constructor to represent existential quantification: *AllEx*. The dependency of type b on an existential type a is made explicit by means of a function from type representations of type a to representations of b.

```
data Signature :: * → * where
  Sig   :: a → Signature a
  (:⊕:) :: Signature (a → b) → Type a → Signature b
  AllEx :: (∀a.Type a → Signature b) → Signature b
```

Interestingly, the type variable a is universally rather than existentially quantified. Why is this the case? The type spine view represents all possible values of a datatype, therefore the existential variable must range over all possible types. This also explains the name of the constructor *AllEx*, which stands for all existential type representations.

There is another modification to the type spine view. The *Sig* constructor no longer carries constructor information. Instead, this information is stored at the top-level of the representation:

```
type TypeSpine a = [ConInfo (Signature a)]
```

This change is not strictly necessary but it is convenient. Suppose that the constructor information is still stored in *Sig*. Now, applications that need to perform a pre-processing pass using constructor information (for example, for more efficient parsing) would be forced to apply the function in *AllEx* only to obtain the constructor information. Having this information at the top-level, rather than at the *Sig* constructor, avoids the trouble of dealing with *AllEx* unnecessarily.

The function *typeSpine* has to be modified to deal with the new representation:

```
typeSpine :: Type a → TypeSpine a
typeSpine Int          = [conint i (Sig i) | i ← [minBound..maxBound]]
typeSpine (Maybe a)    = [connothing (Sig Nothing), conjust (Sig Just :⊕: a)]
typeSpine (Either a b) = [conleft (Sig Left :⊕: a), conright (Sig Right :⊕: b)]
typeSpine (List a)     = [connil (Sig []), concons (Sig (:) :⊕: a :⊕: List a)]
typeSpine Dynamic      = [condynval (AllEx (λa → Sig (DynVal a) :⊕: a))]
```

Now let us rewrite the *read* function using the new type spine view. First of all, the constructor is parsed in *read*, because the constructor information is now at the top-level:

```
read :: Type a → Parser a
read Int = readInt
read rep = alternatives [readParen (conParser conrep) | conrep ← typeSpine rep]
  where conParser conrep = token (conName conrep) ≫ gread (conVal conrep)
```

The generic parsing function is not very different for the first two Signature constructors:

```
gread :: Signature a → Parser a
gread (Sig c)         = return c
gread (con :⊕: arg) = gread con ‘ap‘ read arg
```

The existential case is the most interesting one. We first parse the type representation, and then continue with parsing the remaining part of the constructor.

```
gread (AllEx f) = readType >>= applyBType (gread ∘ f)
```

This example effectively captures the *read* examples for dynamically typed values and for expression applications. The type representation is used to build the parser for the remaining constructor arguments. This dependency is expressed using the bind operation on parsers (>>=).

There is one function that we use to read type representations:

```
readType :: Parser BType
```

Because type representations are somewhat special, we deal with them separately in Section 3.3.

3.2 The Existential Case for Consumer Functions

Producer functions need a modified type spine view (TypeSpine) to handle existential types. Do we need to modify the spine view (Spine) for consumers too? After all, we were able to define *toSpine* for Dynamic using the existing view. There is a good reason why we still need to modify the spine view to handle existentials in an appropriate way. Consider the *read* and *show* functions for example. There is a clear dependency on the representation of existential types during parsing. It is not possible (or at least very impractical) to parse a dynamic value without first having the type representation for it. Therefore, existential type representations should appear earlier than the constructor arguments that depend on it in the text input used for parsing. This means that *show* must pretty print the type representation for the existential before the dependent constructor arguments. However, the current spine view makes this difficult because the representation for the existential may appear in any position.

We solve the problem above making the dependence between existential types and constructor arguments explicit. Like the type spine view, the new constructor encodes the dependency on existentials using a function. The type variable is existentially quantified because in this case we are representing a specific constructor value:

```
data Spine :: * → * where
  Con   :: a → Spine a
  (:◇:) :: Spine (a → b) → Typed a → Spine b
  Ex    :: Type a → (Type a → Spine b) → Spine b
```

The pretty printing function is modified to handle the existential case as follows (we omit the remaining *show* code):

```
gshow (Ex a f) = showType a • gshow (f a)
```

The function for printing type representations is explained next:

```
showType :: Type a → String
```

3.3 Handling Type Representations

In the example above, we have used the function *readType* to parse a type representation. The function *readType* returns a boxed representation since the represented type is dynamically determined during parsing. Unfortunately, it is not easy to define producers that return boxed representations using generic programming. If special care is not taken, such functions may loop when invoked. In the following we describe the problem in more detail and we propose a solution.

Parsing type representations. The obvious way to parse a type representation is to do it generically by using the *read* function. To this end, we use generic read to parse boxed type representations:

$$\begin{aligned}&\mathit{readType} :: \mathsf{Parser\ BType}\\&\mathit{readType} = \mathit{read\ BType}\end{aligned}$$

Unfortunately, the function given above is non-terminating. First, remember that BType uses existential quantification, and hence its type spine is:

$$\mathit{typeSpine\ BType} = [\mathit{conboxed}\ (\mathit{AllEx}\ (\lambda a \rightarrow \mathit{Sig}\ (\mathit{Boxed}\ a)))]$$

Since the type spine uses an existential case, *gread* would try to parse a BType-value calling *readType* recursively. Therefore, trying to parse a boxed type representation would lead to parsing an existential type, which leads to parsing a boxed type representation and so on.

How can we solve this problem? A desperate solution would be to give up using generic programming in the definition of *readType*. This approach is undesirable because every generic producer would need to have a type representation case. Worse even, every such case would have to handle all type representation constructors. If there are n generic functions and m represented types, the programmer would need to write $n \times m$ cases. Despite this significant problem, it is worth exploring a non-generic variant of *readType* and try to generalize it.

```
readType = alternatives (map readParen
              [token "Int" ≫ boxed Int
              ,token "Maybe" ≫ readType ≫= applyBType (boxed ∘ Maybe)
              ,token "List" ≫ readType ≫= applyBType (boxed ∘ List)
              ,token "Either" ≫ readType ≫=
               applyBType (λl → readType ≫= applyBType (boxed ∘ (Either l)))
              ])
   where boxed rep = return (Boxed rep)
```

This example shows that parsing a type representation is no different than parsing a normal datatype in that the type argument of the GADT plays no role here. This example also illustrates the verbosity of writing such boilerplate without using generic programming.

The code of *readType* suggests that we could forget the "GADT-ness" of type representations during parsing. This is the first step we take towards being able to define generic producers for boxed representations, namely, defining the datatype of type codes, a non-GADT companion to type representations:

```
data TCode :: * where
  CInt     :: TCode
  CMaybe   :: TCode → TCode
  CEither  :: TCode → TCode → TCode
  CList    :: TCode → TCode
  CArrow   :: TCode → TCode → TCode
  CType    :: TCode → TCode
  CDynamic :: TCode
  CTCode   :: TCode
```

Besides naming and the absence of a type argument, this datatype is identical to type representations. To make the relation between type codes and type representations precise, we introduce two conversion functions. The first function converts a type representation to a type code, erasing the type information in the process:

```
eraseType :: Type a → TCode
eraseType Int        = CInt
eraseType (Maybe a)  = CMaybe (eraseType a)
eraseType (a :→ b)   = CArrow (eraseType a) (eraseType b)
...
```

Conversely, we want to be able to convert from a type code to a type representation. Note, however, that the resulting type-index depends on the value of the type code and hence the result is a boxed representation:

```
interpretTCode :: TCode → BType
interpretTCode CInt          = Boxed Int
interpretTCode (CMaybe a)    = appTCode (Boxed ∘ Maybe) a
interpretTCode (CArrow a b)  = appTCode (λr → appTCode (Boxed ∘ (r :→ )) b) a
...

appTCode :: ∀c.(∀a.Type a → c) → TCode → c
appTCode f code = applyBType f (interpretTCode code)
```

Using type codes it is now possible to implement parsing of type representations generically. To implement *readType*, we parse a type code value and then we interpret it to obtain a type representation:

```
readType :: Parser BType
readType = read TCode >>= return ∘ interpretTCode
```

Here *TCode* is the type representation for type codes, we do not show the spine and type spine views for this datatype as they are no different from that of other datatypes.

Showing a type representation was no problem previously, we could have written *showType* as follows:

```
showType :: Type a → String
showType a = show (Type a) a
```

However, to remain compatible with *read* we use type codes as the means to pretty print type representations:

```
showType :: Type a → String
showType = show TCode ∘ eraseType
```

Summarizing, *readType* is a special function. It cannot be defined by instantiating *read* to boxed representations. Such an instantiation leads to non-termination because parsing a boxed representation uses the existential case of generic parsing, which in turn makes the recursive call to *readType*. To solve this problem, we defined type codes, a non-GADT analogue of type representations. Non-termination is no longer an issue with type codes. To parse a type code we no longer need to parse existential types, which prevents the recursive call to *readType*. This machinery enables the definition of *readType* as a generic program. This machinery can be reused for other generic producers, for example, see the definition of *enumerateType* in Section 4.

3.4 Equality of Type Representations

In this section, we have introduced machinery to handle type representations generically, namely type codes and conversion functions between type codes and type representations. In Section 4, we show an advanced GADT example that requires a last piece of machinery: equality on type representations.

The function *teq* compares two type representations, if the two representations are the same, it returns a proof that the arguments represent the same type.

```
teq :: Monad m ⇒ Type a → Type b → m (TEq a b)
```

The resulting proof, a value of type TEq a b, can be used to convince the type checker that two types a and b are the same at compile time. The type TEq is defined as follows:

```
data TEq :: * → * → * where
  Refl :: TEq a a
```

Two type representations need not be the same, so we use a monad and function *fail* to encode failure in the comparison of two types. The definition of *teq* is as follows:

```
teq Int       Int       = return Refl
teq (Maybe a) (Maybe b) = liftM  cong1 (teq a b)
teq (a :→ c)  (b :→ d)  = liftM2 cong2 (teq a b) (teq c d)
...
teq _         _         = fail "Different reprs"
```

Here, we use *liftM* and *liftM2* to turn congruence functions into functions on monads. Congruence functions are used to lift equality proofs of types to arbitrary type constructors.

```
cong1 :: TEq a b → TEq (f a) (f b)
cong1  Refl      = Refl
cong2 :: TEq a b → TEq c d → TEq (f a c) (f b d)
cong2  Refl         Refl        = Refl
```

3.5 Type Codes and Dependently Typed Programming

In the literature of generic programming based on dependent types, sets of types having common structure are modelled by universes (2). Values known as universe codes describe type structure and an interpretation function makes the relationship between codes and types explicit.

The generic programming approach that this chapter describes would greatly benefit from the use of dependent types. Our approach is slightly redundant due to the necessity of both type representations and type codes. If we were to revise our approach to use dependent types, the generic machinery would be based on type codes only. Previously, the type representation datatype described the relationship between types and the values that represent them. Using dependent types, this relationship would be defined by interpretation on codes and therefore type representations would not be necessary. Furthermore, producers like *readType* would no longer need to generate type representations. It follows that it would not be possible to accidentally define a non-terminating variant of such producers.

4 Application: Enumeration Applied to Simply Typed Lambda Calculus

Generalized algebraic datatypes can encode sophisticated invariants using type-level constraints. We can combine such precise datatypes with generic producer functions, to generate values that have interesting properties. The example of this section combines a datatype representing terms of the simply typed lambda calculus with a generic function that enumerates all the values of a datatype. Using this function we can, for example, generate the terms that have the type of function composition.

4.1 Representing the Simply Typed Lambda Calculus

Terms of the simply typed lambda calculus can be represented as follows:

```
data Lam :: * → * → * where
  Vz  :: Lam a (EnvCons a e)
  Vs  :: Lam a e → Lam a (EnvCons b e)
  Abs :: Lam b (EnvCons a e) → Lam (a → b) e
  App :: Type a → Lam (a → b) e → Lam a e → Lam b e
```

The datatype Lam can be read as the typing relation for the simply typed lambda calculus. A value of type Lam a e represents the typing derivation for a term of type a in an environment e. Environments are encoded by list-like type constructors:

```
data EnvCons a e
data EnvNil
```

Each Lam constructor is a rule of the typing relation. The first constructor (*Vz*) represents a variable occurrence of type a, which refers to the first position of the environment (EnvCons a e). We can build a variable occurrence that refers to a deeper environment position by means of the weakening constructor *Vs*. Lambda abstractions are typed by means of the *Abs* constructor. In this case, a b-expression that is typeable in an environment containing a in the first position can be turned into a lambda abstraction of type a → b. The application constructor is almost like application in our previous example, *EApp*, except that *App* includes a representation for the existential type.

The spine representation for this datatype can be defined as follows:

```
toSpine (Lam a e) Vz                   = convz (Con Vz)
toSpine (Lam a (EnvCons b e)) (Vs tm) = convs (Con Vs :◇: tm :▷: Lam a e)
toSpine (Lam (a :→ b) e) (Abs tm)     = conabs (Con Abs :◇: body)
  where body = tm :▷: Lam b (EnvCons a e)
toSpine (Lam b e) (App arg tm1 tm2) = conapp (Ex arg app)
  where app a = Con (App a) :◇: tm1 :▷: Lam (a :→ b) e :◇: tm2 :▷: Lam a e
```

The type representations are pattern matched in the *Vs* and *Abs* constructors to build the representation in the right hand side. The *App* constructor has an existential type, therefore we use *Ex* in the spine representation. Using the type representation, we can now print lambda terms.

For producer functions, we define the type spine view on Lam as follows:

```
typeSpine (Lam a e) = concat
  [[convz  (Sig Vz) | EnvCons a' e' ← [e], Refl ← teq a a']
  ,[convs  (Sig Vs :⊕: Lam a e') | EnvCons b e' ← [e]]
  ,[conabs (Sig Abs :⊕: Lam b (EnvCons a' e)) | a' :→ b ← [a]]
  ,[conapp (AllEx (λb → Sig (App b) :⊕: Lam (b :→ a) e :⊕: Lam b e))]
  ]
```

We test whether a constructor signature has the desired target type by performing pattern matching on type representations. The cases *Vz* and *Vs* are only usable if the environment type argument is not empty. Additionally, the target type of *Vz* requires the equality of the type and the first position in the environment. Therefore, the *Vz* case invokes type equality (*teq*) on the term type (*a*) and the type of the first environment position (*a'*). The abstraction constructor (*Abs*) requires an arrow type, which is checked by pattern matching against an arrow type representation. The application constructor can always be used, because there is no restriction on the target type of *App*.

This type spine representation is more informative and larger than previous examples. The reason is that the GADT type argument is more complex because of the use of type-level environments. Furthermore, the type constraint in *Vz* requires the use of type equality (*teq*). Fortunately, it is possible to generate the type spine representation by induction on the syntax of the datatype declaration. It would be possible to automate this process using external tools such as DrIFT and Template Haskell if these tools supported GADTs.

4.2 Breadth First Search Combinators

The generic enumeration function generates all possible values of a datatype in breadth first search (BFS) order. The order used in the search corresponds to the search cost of terms generated. The type BFS is used for the results of a breadth first search procedure:

$$\textbf{type}\ \mathsf{BFS\ a} = [[\mathsf{a}]]$$

The type BFS represents a list of multisets sorted by cost. The first multiset contains terms of cost zero, the second contains terms of cost one and so on. Using this datatype, a consumer can inspect the terms up to a certain cost bound and hence the search does not continue if further terms are not demanded. This is useful because the enumeration function returns a potentially infinite list of multisets.

Multiple BFS values can be zipped together by concatenating multisets having terms of equal cost:

$$\begin{aligned}
&zip_{bfs} :: [\mathsf{BFS\ a}] \to \mathsf{BFS\ a}\\
&zip_{bfs}\ []\ \ = []\\
&zip_{bfs}\ xss = \textbf{if}\ all\ null\ xss\ \textbf{then}\ []\ \textbf{else}\ concatMap\ head\ xss' : zip_{bfs}\ (map\ tail\ xss')\\
&\quad \textbf{where}\ xss' = filter\ (\neg \circ null)\ xss
\end{aligned}$$

It is more convenient to manipulate BFS results using monadic notation. Therefore, we define return and bind on BFS:

$$\begin{aligned}
&return_{bfs}\ x = [[x]]\\
&(\gg\!\!=_{bfs}) :: \forall \mathsf{a\ b.BFS\ a} \to (\mathsf{a} \to \mathsf{BFS\ b}) \to \mathsf{BFS\ b}\\
&(\gg\!\!=_{bfs})\ xss\ f = foldr\ (\lambda xs\ xss \to zip_{bfs}\ (map\ f\ xs +\!\!+ [[] : xss]))\ []\ xss
\end{aligned}$$

Return creates a search result that contains a value of cost zero. Bind feeds the terms found in a search *xss* to a search procedure *f*. The cost of the term passed to *f* is added to the costs of that search procedure. Consider, for example, the search results *aSearch* consisting of the terms $\lambda x\ y \to y$ and $\lambda x\ y \to x$ with costs three and four respectively; and a search procedure that produces a term of cost one by adding an abstraction to its argument:

$$\begin{aligned}
&aSearch = [[],[],[],[Abs\ (Abs\ Vz)],[Abs\ (Abs\ (Vs\ Vz))]]\\
&f\ tm \quad\ \ = [[],[Abs\ tm]]
\end{aligned}$$

Then, the expression $(aSearch \gg\!\!=_{bfs} f)$ evaluates to the following:

$$[[],[],[],[],[Abs\ (Abs\ (Abs\ Vz))],[Abs\ (Abs\ (Abs\ (Vs\ Vz)))]]$$

The two terms in the initial search result now have an additional abstraction argument and have costs of four and five respectively.

The cost addition property of bind can be stated more formally as follows:

$$\begin{aligned}
&propBind :: \mathsf{BFS\ a} \to (\mathsf{a} \to \mathsf{BFS\ b}) \to \mathsf{Bool}\\
&propBind\ xss\ f = all\ (all\ costBind)\ (costs\ xss\ f)\\
&\quad \textbf{where}\ costBind\ (c,(c_{xss},c_f)) = c \equiv c_{xss} + c_f\\
&costs :: \mathsf{BFS\ a} \to (\mathsf{a} \to \mathsf{BFS\ b}) \to \mathsf{BFS\ (Int,(Int,Int))}\\
&costs\ xss\ f = cost\ (cost\ xss \gg\!\!=_{bfs} \lambda(c_{xss},x) \to cost\ (f\ x) \gg\!\!=_{bfs} \lambda(c_f,y) \to\\
&\qquad\qquad\qquad return_{bfs}\ (c_{xss},c_f))
\end{aligned}$$

where *cost* annotates each BFS result value with its cost:

```
cost :: BFS a → BFS (Int, a)
cost = zipWith (λsz → map ((,) sz)) [0..]
```

Additionally we use a function that increases the cost of the values found in a search procedure:

```
spend :: Int → BFS a → BFS a
spend n = (!!n) ∘ iterate ([]:)
```

When using a very expensive search procedure, it is useful to increase the cost of terms exponentially:

```
raise :: Int → BFS a → BFS a
raise base xss = traverse 0 xss where
  traverse _   []         = []
  traverse 0   (xs : xss) = [] : xs : traverse 1 xss
  traverse exp (xs : xss) = spend (base^exp − base^(exp−1) − 1)
                                  (xs : traverse (exp + 1) xss)
```

For example, *spend* 2 *aSearch* and *raise* 2 *aSearch* evaluate to:

```
[[],[],[],[],[],[Abs (Abs Vz)],[Abs (Abs (Vs Vz))]]
[[],[],[],[],[],[],[],[],[Abs (Abs Vz)],[],[],[],[],[],[],[],[Abs (Abs (Vs Vz))]]
```

4.3 Generic Enumeration

The generic enumeration function returns values of a datatype, classified by cost in increasing order. The cost of a term is the number of datatype constructors used therein (constructors used in type representations are an exception and we discuss them last in the definition of *enumerateType*).

```
enumerate :: Type a → BFS a
enumerate a = zip_bfs [genumerate (conVal s) | s ← typeSpine a]
```

At the top-level, function *genumerate* is invoked on each constructor signature and the resulting search results are zipped together.

The first case of *genumerate* returns the constructor value as the search result assigning it a cost of one. The second case performs search recursively on the function and argument parts and combines the results using BFS monadic application ap_{bfs} :: BFS (a → b) → BFS a → BFS b.

```
genumerate :: Signature a   → BFS a
genumerate    (Sig c)       = spend 1 (return_bfs c)
genumerate    (fun :⊕: arg) = genumerate fun `ap_bfs` enumerate arg
```

The third case deals with existential types and hence in our particular application it deals with expression application. This case first enumerates all possible types, and then constructs a constructor signature using *f*, for each type, and enumeration is called recursively:

```
genumerate (AllEx f) = enumerateType >>=_bfs genumerate ∘ applyBType f
```

As usual with producer functions, *enumerateType* returns a boxed representation. The enumeration of types is performed on type codes, which *interpretTCode* converts to boxed representations.

$$enumerateType :: \mathsf{BFS\ BType}$$
$$enumerateType = raise\ 4\ (enumerate\ TCode) \gg\!\!=_{bfs} return_{bfs} \circ interpretTCode$$

For the examples in this paper, we are not interested in values that have very complex existential types. Therefore, we keep their size small by assigning an exponential cost to existentials. This also has the effect of reducing the search space, which makes the generation of interesting terms within small cost upperbounds more likely.

4.4 Term Enumeration in Action

For convenience, we define a wrapper function to perform enumeration of lambda terms:

$$enumerateLam :: \mathsf{Type\ a} \rightarrow \mathsf{Int} \rightarrow \mathsf{BFS\ (Lam\ a\ EnvNil)}$$
$$enumerateLam\ a\ cost = take\ (cost + 1)\ (enumerate\ (Lam\ a\ EnvNil))$$

Our term datatype can perfectly deal with open terms. But the user interface becomes simpler if only closed terms are provided. Therefore, the wrapper function only generates closed lambda terms.

A direct invocation of the enumeration function will result in an attempt to generate an infinite number of terms. For convenience, our wrapper function takes a cost upperbound that limits the cost of terms that are reported. Because of lazy evaluation, the search procedure stops when all terms within the cost bound are reported. The user may choose to increase the cost upperbound in subsequent invocations if the desired term is not found.

The language that the Lam datatype represents is very simple. There are no datatypes, recursion, and arithmetic operations. For example, we cannot expect the enumeration function to generate the successor or predecessor functions for naturals if functions of the type Int → Int are requested. In principle, it is not difficult to extend the language by adding the appropriate constants to Lam. For example, we could add naturals and arithmetic operations on them. We could also add list constructors and elimination functions and even recursion operators such as catamorphisms and paramorphisms.

However, we can keep our language simple and still generate many interesting terms. We focus our attention to parametrically polymorphic functions. Although we do not model parametric polymorphism explicitly in Lam, such functions are naturally generated when the requested type is an instance of the polymorphic type. For instance, a request with type Int → Int generates the identity function.

To make the intent of generating polymorphic functions more explicit, we assume a few uninhabited types A, B, C, and D and their respective type representations. For example, representation *A* has type Type A. These types play the role of type variables in polymorphic type signatures.

In our first example, we generate the code for the identity function. The type of the identity function is $\forall a.a \rightarrow a$, which in our notation translates to $A :\rightarrow A$. The function we expect to generate is $\lambda x \rightarrow x$, which in Lam is written as *Abs Vz*. This term consists of two constructors, therefore a cost upperbound of two should suffice to generate it. The application *enumerateLam* $(A :\to A)$ 2 results in:

$[[],[],[Abs\ Vz]]$

It is instructive to sketch the search procedure as it looks for the identity function. First, *enumerate* is called on the identity type with a closed environment. This function calls *genumerate* on all constructor signatures that match the desired type. The two variable cases *Vz* and *Vs* are not considered because they cannot be used with an empty environment. Application can always be used but recall that it requires an existential type representation, so the cost is at least 5, which is more expensive than the function that we are looking for. The abstraction case matches the identity type so enumeration is called recursively to generate the abstraction body. Now, a term of type A is requested with a type A in the first position in the environment. The case *Vz* matches perfectly with this request so the term *Abs Vz* is returned with cost two.

There are infinitely many lambda calculus terms of a given type when that type is inhabited. A simple way to way to obtain a new term is by creating a redex that reduces to the term that we currently have. For example, we can obtain a new identity function by adding a redex in the function body: $\lambda x \to (\lambda x \to x)\ x$. Can this term be found by our enumeration function? Yes, provided that we increase the cost upperbound to include that of our new term. The new term is essentially two identity functions plus an application constructor, which makes a cost upperbound of nine. We evaluate *enumerateLam* $(A :\to A)$ 9 which yields:

$[[],[],[Abs\ Vz],[],[],[],[],[],[],[Abs\ (App\ A\ (Abs\ Vz)\ Vz)]]$

This example shows that the search space is somewhat redundant. A way to speed up term search would be to avoid the generation of redundant terms by adding constraints to Lam. For example, we could avoid redeces by preventing the generation of abstractions in the left part of applications.

Another interesting example is the generation of the application term, which has type ∀a b.(a → b) → a → b. In our notation we write $((A :\to B) :\to A :\to B)$. Let us evaluate *enumerateLam* $((A :\to B) :\to A :\to B)$ 10 to generate an application term:

$[[],[],[Abs\ Vz],[],[],[],[],[],[],[],[Abs\ (Abs\ (App\ A\ (Vs\ Vz)\ Vz))]]$

These are the encodings for the functions $\lambda x \to x$ and $\lambda x\ y \to x\ y$. The careful reader may wonder why the other identity term $\lambda x \to (\lambda x \to x)\ x$, which has cost 8 in the previous example, is not generated. The answer is that the cost of the term includes that of the type representation used in the application constructor. Since this example has a different type, the type representation would be $A :\to B$ rather than A. It follows that the term $\lambda x \to (\lambda x \to x)\ x$ is not generated because it has a cost of 14.

Our last example is function composition. The type of this function is ∀a b c.(b → c) → (a → b) → a → c. To generate composition, we evaluate

last (*enumerateLam* $((B :\to C) :\to (A :\to B) :\to (A :\to C))$ 19)

which yields to the encoding of $\lambda x\ y\ z \to x\ (y\ z)$:

$[Abs\ (Abs\ (Abs\ (App\ B\ (Vs\ (Vs\ Vz))\ (App\ A\ (Vs\ Vz)\ Vz))))]$

5 Related Work

To the best of our knowledge, only the spine approach (6; 7) enables generic programming on generalized algebraic datatypes in Haskell. This is the approach on which the work in this chapter is based. Because both the spine and the type spine view can encode GADTs, both consumer and producer functions can be defined on such datatypes. Interestingly, to properly support GADTs for producer functions, the approach should also support existential types. For example, when reading a GADT from disk, we may want the GADT type argument to be dynamically determined from the disk contents. Therefore, we would existentially quantify over that argument. However, the spine approach supports existential types for consumers but not for producers.

Generalized algebraic datatypes are inspired by inductive families in the dependent types community. We are aware of two approaches (2; 12) that support definitions by induction on the structure of inductive families. Both approaches make essential use of evaluation on the type level to express the constraints over inductive families. Examples of type families on which generic programming is applied include trees (indexed by their lower and upper size bounds), finite sets, vectors and telescopes. Neither approach gives examples for the support of existential types so it is not clear whether these are supported.

Weirich (15) proposes a language that provides a construct to perform runtime case analysis on types. In order to support universal and existential quantification, the language includes analyzable type constants for both quantifiers. This approach supports the definition of consumers and producers. Moreover, if the language is extended with polymorphic kinds it supports quantification over arbitrarily kinded types.

Our approach to defining breadth-first search combinators is not novel. Spivey (14) defines a set of breadth-first search combinators such as monadic join and composition, and proves desirable properties for them. There are many similarities between our work and that of Spivey. It would be interesting to see whether our combinators satisfy the same properties as the combinators proposed by Spivey.

Koopman et al. (10) generate lambda calculus terms by performing systematic enumeration based on a grammar. To reduce the size of the search space, the grammar has syntactic restrictions such as that the applications of certain operands are always saturated, and recursive calls are always guarded by a conditional. The candidate terms are then reported to the user based on whether they satisfy an input-output specification, which is established by evaluation.

Djinn (1) generates lambda calculus terms based on a user-supplied type. This tool implements the decision procedure for intuitionistic propositional calculus due to Dyckhof (5). Similarly, the work of Katayama (8) makes use of a type inference monad to generate well-typed terms. Later, the candidate terms are evaluated and checked against an input-output specification. As in our approach, Djinn and the approach of Katayama generate only well-typed terms so there is no need for a type checking phase to discard ill-typed terms.

The main difference between the work of Koopman et al. (10) and ours is that our generator is typed-based. It follows that our generator never returns ill-typed terms because the search space is reduced by means of type-level constraints in the GADT. Generating ill-typed terms has advantages. For example, Koopman's approach can generate the Y-combinator. On the other hand, ill-typed terms are usually not desirable, so these have to be discarded through evaluation (as in Koopman's work) which slows down the generation algorithm. In Koopman's work the generation of ill-typed terms is prevented to some extent by the syntactic constraints imposed on the grammar.

A type-based generator, such as Djinn, Katayama's generator and our approach, is able to synthesize polymorphic functions without the need for input-output specifications. In contrast, Koopman's generator cannot produce polymorphic functions based solely on type information.

Djinn supports user-defined dataypes. Katayama and Koopman's generators are able to generate recursive programs. Our approach currently generates programs for a rather spartan language. However, it should be possible to add introduction and elimination constants for (recursive) datatypes, and recursion operators such as catamorphisms and paramorphisms.

Both Djinn and our approach enumerate terms guided by type information. However, the two approaches are very different. Djinn has a carefully crafted algorithm that handles the application of functional values in such a way that it is not necessary to exhaustively enumerate the infinite search space. As a consequence, Djinn is able to detect that a type is uninhabited in finite time. In contrast, our approach produces function applications by means of exhaustive enumeration. First, all the possible types of an argument are enumerated, and, for each of them, function and argument terms are enumerated to construct an application. The good side of an exhaustive approach like ours is that it can generate all possible terms of a given type. For example, it can generate all Church numerals, whereas Djinn only generates those corresponding to zero and one. On the bad side, if unbounded, our approach does not terminate when trying to generate a term for an uninhabited type.

We have not performed a careful performance comparison but we believe that our generator may be the slowest of the approaches considered here. Probably the main culprit for inefficiency is the implementation of the existential case. Currently this case enumerates all possible types, even if no applications for that argument type can be constructed. Ill-typed terms are never generated, but resources are nevertheless consumed when attempting to enumerate terms having possibly uninhabited types. It is difficult to make the algorithm smarter about generating types because, being generic, it does not make assumptions about the particularities of lambda calculus. On the other hand, it is possible to reduce the search space by adjusting the definition of Lam. For example, we could forbid the formation of redeces to avoid redundancy of terms, or even adopt the syntactic restrictions used in Koopman's work.

While our approach may be less efficient, it has the virtue of simplicity: the core of the generation algorithm consists of roughly a dozen lines of code and there is no need for an evaluation phase when generating polymorphic functions. Furthermore, it has the advantage of an elegant separation between the grammar constraints and the formulation of the enumeration algorithm. This allows us to use the enumeration function to generate other languages, whereas the other generators are specific to lambda calculus.

6 Conclusions

We have presented an extension of the spine approach to generic programming, which supports the definition of generic producers for existential types. This extension allows the definition of, for example, generic read for datatypes that use existential quantification.

Our approach opens the way for a new application of generic programming. By taking the standard enumeration generic function and extending it with a case for existentials, we obtain a function that enumerates well-typed terms. For example, we can instantiate enumeration to the GADT that represents terms of the simply typed lambda calculus and use the resulting function to search for terms that have a given type. Such an application was not previously possible because producers that handle existential types could not be generically defined.

Acknowledgements. We are grateful to Andres Löh for the productive discussions that inspired this paper. The ST reading club at Utrecht University gave detailed feedback on an earlier version of this paper. We thank the anonymous reviewers for the useful suggestions and comments. We also thank Lambert Meertens, the careful reader who motivated us to improve the explanations in Section 4.4.

References

[1] Augustsson, L.: Announcing Djinn, version 2004-12-11, a coding wizard (2005), `http://permalink.gmane.org/gmane.comp.lang.haskell.general/12747`

[2] Benke, M., Dybjer, P., Jansson, P.: Universes for generic programs and proofs in dependent type theory. Nordic Journal of Computing 10(4), 265–289 (2003)

[3] Cheney, J., Hinze, R.: First-class phantom types. Technical report, Cornell University (2003)

[4] Claessen, K., Hughes, J.: QuickCheck: A Lightweight Tool for Random Testing of Haskell Programs. In: ICFP 2000, pp. 286–279 (2000)

[5] Dyckhoff, R.: Contraction-free sequent calculi for intuitionistic logic. The Journal of Symbolic Logic 57(3), 795–807 (1992)

[6] Hinze, R., Löh, A.: "Scrap Your Boilerplate" revolutions. In: Uustalu, T. (ed.) MPC 2006. LNCS, vol. 4014, pp. 180–208. Springer, Heidelberg (2006)

[7] Hinze, R., Löh, A., Oliveira, B.C.d.S.: "Scrap your boilerplate" reloaded. In: Hagiya, M., Wadler, P. (eds.) FLOPS 2006. LNCS, vol. 3945, pp. 13–29. Springer, Heidelberg (2006)

[8] Katayama, S.: Systematic search for lambda expressions. In: TFP 2005 (2005)

[9] Koopman, P., Alimarine, A., Tretmans, J., Plasmeijer, R.: Gast: Generic automated software testing. In: Peña, R., Arts, T. (eds.) IFL 2002. LNCS, vol. 2670. Springer, Heidelberg (2003)

[10] Koopman, P., Plasmeijer, R.: Systematic synthesis of λ-terms. In: Essays dedicated to Henk Barendregt on the Occasion of his 60th Birthday (2007)

[11] Lämmel, R., Jones, S.P.: Scrap your boilerplate: A practical design pattern for generic programming. In: TLDI 2003, pp. 26–37 (2003)

[12] Morris, P.: Constructing Universes for Generic Programming. PhD thesis, The University of Nottingham (2007)

[13] Peyton Jones, S., Vytiniotis, D., Weirich, S., Washburn, G.: Simple unification-based type inference for GADTs. In: ICFP 2006, pp. 50–61 (2006)

[14] Spivey, M.: Combinators for breadth-first search. Journal of Functional Programming 10(4), 397–408 (2000)

[15] Weirich, S.: Higher-order intensional type analysis. In: Le Métayer, D. (ed.) ESOP 2002. LNCS, vol. 2305, pp. 98–114. Springer, Heidelberg (2002)

[16] Xi, H., Chen, C., Chen, G.: Guarded recursive datatype constructors. In: POPL 2003, pp. 224–235 (2003)

Generalisation Operators for Lists Embedded in a Metric Space

V. Estruch, C. Ferri, J. Hernández-Orallo, and M.J. Ramírez-Quintana

DSIC, Univ. Politècnica de València
Camí de Vera s/n, 46020 València, Spain
{vestruch,cferri,jorallo,mramirez}@dsic.upv.es

Abstract. In some application areas, similarities and distances are used to calculate how similar two objects are in order to use these measurements to find related objects, to cluster a set of objects, to make classifications or to perform an approximate search guided by the distance. In many other application areas, we require patterns to describe similarities in the data. These patterns are usually constructed through generalisation (or specialisation) operators. For every data structure, we can define distances. In fact, we may find different distances for sets, lists, atoms, numbers, ontologies, web pages, etc. We can also define pattern languages and use generalisation operators over them. However, for many data structures, distances and generalisation operators are not consistent. For instance, for lists (or sequences), edit distances are not consistent with regular languages, since, for a regular pattern such as $*a$, the covered set of lists might be far away in terms of the edit distance (e.g. *bbbbbba* and *aa*). In this paper we investigate the way in which, given a pattern language, we can define a pair of generalisation operator and distance which are consistent. We define the notion of (minimal) distance-based generalisation operators for lists. We illustrate positive results with two different pattern languages.

Keywords: Distance-based methods, inductive operators, induction with distances, list-based representations.

1 Introduction

Distance-based (or more generally, instance-based) methods are a powerful tool in the field of machine learning. Several reasons back its popularity, among them, we must stand out its capability to cope with different data representations: these methods are designed on the basis of a similarity principle (similar examples should share similar properties) which makes them easily adaptable to different datatypes via redefining the similarity (distance) function. In this sense, multiple distances and similarity functions can be found in the literature.

However, in the area of Inductive Programming, the use of distances is still at a very incipient state. Inductive Programming is concerned with the automated construction of declarative programs from data. We can distinguish several approaches to this problem according to the knowledge representation adopted. For

U. Schmid, E. Kitzelmann, and R. Plasmeijer (Eds.): AAIP 2009, LNCS 5812, pp. 117–139, 2010.

instance, the field known as *Inductive Logic Programming* (ILP) [13] aims to induce consistent first order theories from data represented as first order objects (atoms or clauses). A natural extension of this comes when we move to higher-order logics [1,12]. The synthesis of functional programs arises when training data consist in a sample of inputs and outputs of a evaluation function [14,16]. A more generic framework corresponds to the induction of functional-logic theories. This paradigm centres on performing induction within a formal context that combines the strengths of logic and functional programming [7,10,9].

In this area, the use of similarity functions and distances has been restricted to ILP, and very specially for machine learning applications of ILP and not for program synthesis. The reason for this limited success of the use of distances in inductive programming is twofold. First, distances and similarities return numerical values which are difficult to integrate with declarative models. A model such as "the sequence *aabb* has been classified as positive since it is similar to the sequence *aaba* which is also positive" cannot reduce the part "similar to" to a traditional declarative notation, since it usually involves an external function $similarity(s_1, s_2)$ and a numerical threshold. In other words, no declarative pattern has been defined to capture the notion of similarity or, at least, to be consistent with the notion. Second, although declarative languages constitute an elegant and powerful framework for program synthesis, they show some limitations when the semantics of the data representation does not match the implicit semantics managed by these declarative languages. An example of this is found when working with lists or sequences. From a declarative point of view, lists are recursively defined in terms of a special item (head) and a tail, which is another (sub)list. This perspective makes it difficult for the search of patterns in data that does not suit this definition. For instance, if we are given the lists *abaca* and *bc*, it is not immediate to learn a pattern of the form $*b*c*$ because of the simple fact that the heads of the lists do not match. Unfortunately, list-based representations appear in many real-world domains, which might put some limits on the applicability of declarative tools. For instance, in bioinformatics, compounds such as amino-acids have a direct representation as sequences of symbols. Furthermore, other much more complex molecules can also be described in terms of sequences by using the so-called 1-D or SMILE representation [17]. Another example is found in text or web mining where documents are usually transformed into sequences of words. Very common software utilities such as command line completion or orthographic correctors work on lists as well.

In general, we could wonder if some of the tools employed in inductive programming (generalisation operators) could be upgraded to deal with list-based representations in a more satisfactory way and overcome this limitation. In [4,6], we consider the possibility by analysing the relationship between distance and generalisation. In [5] we analysed this framework employing distances and generalisations for graphs.

Note that most of the applications that handle sequences usually employ distances in order to find the most similar sequences in data. Distances (and consequently, metric spaces) play an important role in many inductive techniques that have been developed to date. Similarity offers a well-founded inference principle for learning and reasoning since it is commonly assumed that *similar objects have similar properties*. Given the importance of lists as a datatype for knowledge representation, several distances can be found in the literature, being the edit distance [11] the best-known. The drawback is that these methods do not infer a model (or patterns) from data as declarative inductive (or more general, symbolic) learners do.

Therefore, if we were able to find out a connection between distance and generalisation we could, on the one hand, define more suitable generalisation operators to work with structured data in general and with lists in particular; and on the other hand, we could come up with induction techniques capable of transforming distance-based method outputs into symbolic models, and consequently, more comprehensible explanations for the user.

There might be many different ways to establish a connection between distance and generalisation. Ensuring the consistency between them is a compelling one. Note that if the generalisation process is not driven by the distance, this might result in patterns that do not capture the semantics of the distance, so giving wrong explanations about why objects are similar. Let us see an example of this. If we consider the edit distance over the lists *bbab*, *bab* and *aaba*, we see that the list *ab* is close to the previous lists (distances are 2, 1, and 2 respectively). However, a typical pattern that can be obtained by some model-based methods, **ba**, does not cover the list *ab*. The pattern does cover the list *dededfafbakgagggeewdsc*, which is at distance 20 from the three original lists. The pattern and the distance are up to some point inconsistent since those elements that are most similar to the initial examples which are excluded.

Although there are other important works on hybridisation, they tend to ignore the problem of consistency between the semantic of the model learnt and the semantic of the underlying distance. Basically, what we do is to define some simple conditions that a generalisation operator should have in order to behave in a consistent way wrt. a distance. These operators are called distance-based generalisation operators.

In this paper, we address the problem of inducing patterns from lists of symbols embedded in a metric space. In other words, the work we present here can be seen as an instantiation for lists of the general framework aforementioned. It is noteworthy that, even though first-order logic constitutes an elegant and powerful framework for symbolic knowledge representation, lists have a complex and a little intuitive representation by means of first-order formulas which implies that patterns over lists have also a complex representation. This fact makes rather complicated that the ILP techniques can find patterns over lists by applying a generalisation operator like the *lgg*. In fact, one of the consequences derived of this term-based representation is that we need auxiliary predicates to extract requested information which is packed in a term (like *member, head, tail, previous*, , ...). Hence, useful patterns might not be learnt if we have not previously defined the correct auxiliary predicates [3].

This paper is organised as follows. Section 2 contains an overview of our proposal. In Section 3, we analyse how our framework could be used to learn symbolic patterns from lists. To this end, we introduce two different pattern languages: $\mathcal{L}_0$ and another more expressive $\mathcal{L}_1$, and study how to define (minimal) distance-based operators in all of them. Finally, conclusions and future work are given in Section 4.

2 Framework

In this section we summarise the main concepts of our setting which integrates distances and generalisation. For a more detailed presentation of it we refer the reader to [3].

The underlying idea in our proposal is that, in order to have a *true* connection between distance and generalisation, the generalisation process have to take the underlying distance into consideration (or at least the two must be consistent). This special relation is formalised through three notions: *reachability*, *intrinsicality* and *minimality*.

Reachability implies that the generalisation of two elements ought to include those paths (a sequence of elements in the metric space) that allow us to reach both elements from each other by making small "steps". The concept of short step must be understood in the sense of the distance.

The second property arises from the observation that the distance between two elements is always given by the length of the shortest paths. Thus, if we want our generalisation to be compatible with the distance, we need the elements belonging to the shortest paths to be covered by the generalisation. This condition is called *intrinsicality*.

The two above properties have been defined for two elements since they are established in terms of the distance which is a binary function. But generalisation operators are not binary, thus for more than two elements, the connection between distance and generalisation turns a bit unclear. It seems that the properties of reachability and intrinsicality must be extended for this generic case. Distance-based algorithms suggest that it would make sense to impose the notion of intrinsicality for *some* pairs of elements. The pairs of elements that will have to comply with the intrinsicality property will be set by a path or connected graph which we will call *nerve*. Furthermore, we obtain with this a more generic notion of reachability since all the elements in the set are reachable from any of them by moving from one element to another through combinations of (intrinsical) paths.

In Figure 1, generalisations $G1$ and $G2$ do not connect the three elements to be generalised. Only the generalisations $G3$ and $G4$ connect the three elements through combinations of straight segments.

Finally, the last property concerns with the notion of *minimality*, which is understood not only in terms of fitting the set (i.e., semantic minimality) but also as the simplicity of the pattern (i.e., syntactic minimality). In Figure 1, $G3$ is an example of a very specific and rather complicated generalisation of A, B and C.

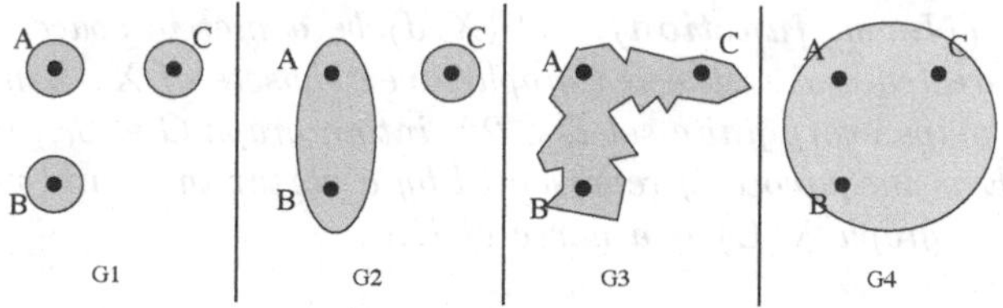

Fig. 1. Generalising the elements $E = \{A, B, C\}$. Elements in E are not reachable through a path of segments in generalisations $G1$ and $G2$. For any two elements in E, generalisations $G3$ and $G4$ include a path of segments connecting them.

2.1 Distance-Based Inductive Operators

Next, we formally show how the three previous notions are employed in order to define the so-called distance-based generalisation operators.

A generalisation of a finite set of elements $E \subset X$ could be seen as any superset of E in X. Therefore, a generalisation operator (denoted by Δ) simply maps sets of elements E into supersets. As known, this superset can be extensionally or intensionally defined, being the latter one more useful from a predictive/explanatory point of view. Symbolic patterns constitute a widely-spread manner of representing intensional generalisations. For instance, the pattern $a*$ denotes all the lists headed by the symbol a. We denote by $\mathcal{L}$ the pattern language and by $Set(p)$ the set of all the elements in X that the pattern $p \in \mathcal{L}$ represents. For instance, $Set(a*) = \{a, aa, ab, \ldots\}$. If necessary, $\mathcal{L}$ expressiveness can always be increased by combining patterns via logical operators (e.g. pattern disjunction). In this work, disjunction is denoted by the symbol $+$ and the expression $p_1 + p_2$ represents the set $Set(p_1) \cup Set(p_2)$. For simplicity, the pattern $p = p_1 + \ldots + p_n$ will be expressed as $p = \sum_{i=1}^{n} p_i$.
Now, we can already introduce the definition of binary distance-based pattern and binary distance-based generalisation operator.

Definition 1 ***(Binary distance-based pattern and binary distance-based generalisation operator).*** *Let (X, d) be a metric space, $\mathcal{L}$ a pattern language, and a set of elements $E = \{e_1, e_2\} \subset X$. We say that a pattern $p \in \mathcal{L}$ is a binary distance-based (db) pattern of E if p covers all the elements between e_1 and e_2*[1]*. Additionally, we say that Δ is a binary distance-based generalisation (dbg) operator if $\Delta(e_1, e_2)$ always computes a binary distance-based pattern.*

As previously said, for the case of more than two elements to be generalised, the concept of "nerve" of a set of elements E is needed to define non-binary *dbg* operators. Informally, a nerve of E is simply a connected[2] graph whose vertices are the elements belonging to E. Observe that if $E = \{e_1, e_2\}$, the only possible nerve is a one-edged graph. Formally,

[1] Given a metric space (X, d) and two elements $e_1, e_2 \in X$, we say that an element $e_3 \in X$ is between e_1 and e_2, or is an intermediate element wrt. d, if $d(e_1, e_2) = d(e_1, e_3) + d(e_3, e_2)$.

[2] Here, the term connected refers to the well-known property for graphs.

Definition 2 ***(Nerve function).*** *Let (X, d) be a metric space and let S_G be the set of undirected and connected graphs over subsets of X. A nerve function $N : 2^X \rightarrow S_G$ maps every finite set $E \subset 2^X$ into a graph $G \in S_G$, such that each element e in E is inequivocally represented by a vertex in G and vice versa. We say the obtained graph $N(E)$ is a nerve of E.*

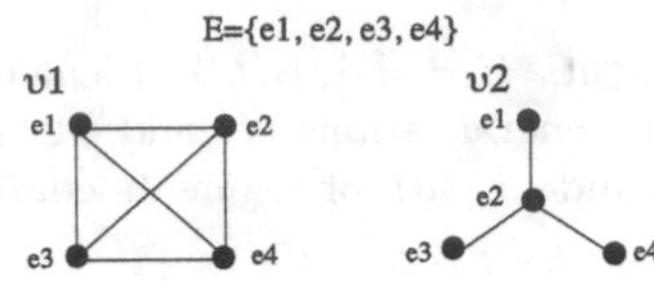

Fig. 2. Two nerves for the set E. **(Left)** ν_1 is a complete graph. **(Right)** ν_2 is a 3-star graph.

Some typical nerve functions are the complete graph, and a radial/star graph around a vertex (see Figure 2).

Recall that the nerve corresponds to the notion of reachability and indicates which intermediate elements must be covered by the generalisations. In a more precise way,

Definition 3 ***(Skeleton).*** *Let (X, d) be a metric space, $\mathcal{L}$ a pattern language, a set $E \subseteq X$, and ν a nerve of E. Then, the skeleton of E wrt. ν, denoted by skeleton(ν), is defined as a set which only includes all the elements $z \in X$ between x and y, for every $(x, y) \in \nu$.*

Consequently, we look for generalisations that include the skeleton. From here, we can define the notion of distance-based pattern wrt. a nerve.

Definition 4 ***(Distance-based pattern and distance-based pattern wrt. a nerve ν).*** *Let (X, d) be a metric space, $\mathcal{L}$ a pattern language, E a finite set of examples. A pattern p is a db pattern of E if there exists a nerve ν of E such that skeleton(ν) $\subset$ Set(p). If the nerve ν is known, then we will say that p is a db pattern of E wrt. ν.*

And, from here, we have:

Definition 5 ***(Distance-based generalisation operator).*** *Let (X, d) be a metric space and $\mathcal{L}$ be a pattern language. Given a generalisation operator Δ, we will say that Δ is a dbg operator if for every $E \subseteq X$, $\Delta(E)$ is a db pattern of E.*

The above definition can be characterised for one nerve function in particular.

Definition 6 ***(Distance-based generalisation operator wrt. a nerve function).*** *Let (X, d) be a metric space and $\mathcal{L}$ a pattern language. A generalisation operator Δ is a dbg operator wrt. a nerve function N if for every $E \subseteq X$ then $\Delta(E)$ is a db pattern of E wrt. $N(E)$.*

In general it is quite hard to prove that a generalisation operator is *db* wrt. any nerve function. Fortunately, for most of the applications it is enough to exist a particular nerve function wrt. Δ is distance-based. If the nerve is known beforehand, we speak of *distance-based generalisation operators wrt. a nerve function N*.

Proposition 1. *Let $\mathcal{L}$ be a pattern language endowed with the operation + and let Δ^b be a binary dbg operator in $\mathcal{L}$. Given a finite set of elements E and a nerve function N, the generalisation operator Δ_N defined as follows is a dbg operator wrt. N.*

$$\Delta_N(E) = \sum_{\forall (e_1, e_j) \in N(E)} \Delta^b(e_i, e_j)$$

Proof. It follows from the definition of *dbg* operator.

2.2 Minimality

Given the definition of *dbg* operator in the previous section, we can now guarantee that a pattern obtained by a *dbg* operator from a set of elements ensures that all the original elements are reachable inside the pattern through intrinsic (direct) paths. However, the generalisation can contain many other, even distant, elements.

An abstract, well-founded and widely-used principle that connects the notions of fitness and simplicity is the well-known MDL/MML principle [15,19]. According to this principle, in our framework, the optimality of a generalisation will be defined in terms of a cost function, denoted by $k(E,p)$, which considers both the complexity of the pattern p and how well the pattern p fits E in terms of the underlying distance.

From a formal viewpoint, a cost function $k : 2^X \times \mathcal{L} \to \mathbf{R}^+ \cup \{0\}$ is a mapping where we assume that E is always finite, p is any pattern covering E and $k(E,p)$ can only be infinite when $Set(p) = X$.

As usual in MDL/MML approaches, most of the $k(E,p)$ functions will be expressed as the sum of a complexity (syntactic) function $c(p)$ (which measures how complicated the pattern is) and a fitness function $c(E|p)$ (which measures how the pattern fits the data E). As said, the most novel point here is that $c(E|p)$ will be expressed in terms of the distance employed.

As $c(p)$ measures how complex a pattern is, this function will strongly depend on the sort of data and the pattern space $\mathcal{L}$ we are dealing with. For instance, if the generalisation of two real numbers is a closed interval containing them, then a simple choice for $c(p)$ would be the length of the interval.

As $c(E|p)$ must be based on the underlying distance, a lot of definitions are based on or inspired by the well-known concept of border of a set[3]. But as the concept of border of a set is something intrinsic to metric spaces, several general definitions of $c(E|p)$ can be given independently from the datatype as shown in Table 1.

[3] Intuitively, if a pattern p_1 fits E better than a pattern p_2, then the border of p_1 (∂p_1) will somehow be nearer to E than the border of p_2 (∂p_2).

Table 1. Some definitions of the function $c(E|p)$: 1-Infimum of uncovered elements, 2-Supremum of covered elements, 3-Minimum to the border, 4-Minimum and maximum to the border

	$\mathcal{L}$	$c(E\|p)$
1	Any	$\sum_{\forall e \in E} r_e$ $r_e = inf_{r \in \mathbf{R}} B(e, r_e) \not\subset Set(p)$
2	Any	$\sum_{\forall e \in E} r_e$ $r_e = sup_{r \in \mathbf{R}} B(e, r_e) \subset Set(p)$
3	Any	$\sum_{\forall e \in E} min_{e' \in \partial Set(p)} d(e, e')$
4	$Set(p)$ is a bound set	$\sum_{\forall e \in E} min_{e' \in \partial Set(p)} d(e, e')$ $+max_{e'' \in \partial Set(p)} d(e, e'')$

Now, we can introduce the definition of minimal distance-based generalisation operator and minimal distance-based generalisation operator relative to one nerve function.

Definition 7 (Minimal distance-based generalisation operator and minimal distance-based generalisation operator relative to one nerve function N). *Let (X, d) and N be a metric space and a nerve function, and let Δ be a dbg operator wrt. N defined in X using a pattern language $\mathcal{L}$. Given a finite set of elements $E \subset X$ and a cost function k, we will say that Δ is a minimal distance-based generalisation (mdbg) operator for k in $\mathcal{L}$ relative to N, if for every dbg operator Δ' wrt. N,*

$$k(E, \Delta(E)) \leq k(E, \Delta'(E)), \text{for every finite set } E \subset X. \quad (1)$$

In similar terms, we say that a dbg operator Δ wrt. a nerve function N is a mdbg operator relative to N if the expression (1) holds for every dbg operator Δ' wrt. N.

The previous definition says nothing about how to compute the *mdbg* operator, and as we will see later, this might be difficult. A way to proceed is to first try to simplify the optimisation problem as much as possible, as the next definition shows:

Definition 8 (Skeleton generalisation operator wrt. a nerve function N). *Let (X, d) be a metric space and N a nerve function. The skeleton generalisation operator $\bar{\Delta}_N$ is defined for every set $E \subset X$ as follows:*

$$\bar{\Delta}_N(E) = argmin_{\forall p \in \mathcal{L}: skeleton(N(E)) = Set(p)} \, k(E, p)$$

which means the simplest pattern that covers the skeleton of the evidence (given a nerve) and nothing more. Clearly, it is a *dbg* operator because it includes the skeleton, but it might not exist because it cannot be expressed.

The following section is devoted to defining *db* and *mdbg* operators for the list data type.

3 Inductive Operators for Lists

Lists or sequences is a widely-used datatype for data representation in different fields of automatic induction such as structured learning, bioinformatics or text mining. In this section, we apply our framework to finite lists of symbols by introducing two cost functions and two pattern languages for this sort of data and studying different *dbg* and *mdbg* operators for each particular combination of language and cost function. Due to space limitations as well as comprehensibility's sake, we sketch those proofs that are excessively long and would make the reading unnecessarily difficult. If needed, a complete detail of them can be found in [3].

3.1 Metric Space, Pattern Languages and Cost Functions

Several distance functions for lists have been proposed in the literature. For instance, the Hamming distance defined for equally-length lists in [8], or the distance in [2], defined for infinite-length lists but which can easily be adapted for finite lists.

However, the most widely used distance function for lists is the edit distance (or Levenshtein distance [11]), which is the one we are working with. Specifically, we set the edit distance in such a way that only insertions and deletions are allowed (a substitution can be viewed as a deletion followed by an insertion or vice-versa).

Two different pattern languages $\mathcal{L}_0$ (single-list pattern language) and $\mathcal{L}_1$ (multiple-list pattern language) will be introduced in this section. The patterns in $\mathcal{L}_0$ are lists that are built from the extended alphabet $\Sigma' = \{\lambda\} \cup \Sigma \cup V$ where λ denotes the empty list, $\Sigma = \{a, b, c, \ldots\}$ is the alphabet (also called ground symbols) from which the lists to be generalised are defined, and $V = \{V_1, V_2, \ldots\}$ is a set of variables. The same variable cannot appear twice in a pattern. Each variable in a pattern represents a symbol from $\{\lambda\} \cup \Sigma$. Finally, the pattern language $\mathcal{L}_1$ is defined from $\mathcal{L}_0$ by means of the operation + (see Subsection 2.1) and aims to improve the expressiveness of $\mathcal{L}_0$. For instance, if we let $\Sigma = \{a, b\}$, then, the patterns $p_1 = aV_1V_2$ and $p_2 = bV_1V_2b$ belong to $\mathcal{L}_0$ where $Set(p_1) = \{aaa, aab, aba, abb, aa, ab, a\}$ and $Set(p_2) = \{baab, babb, bbab, bbbb, bab, bbb, bb\}$. In other words, the pattern p_1 denotes all those lists headed by the symbol a whose length ranges between 1 and 3. In a similar way, p_2 contains all the lists headed and ended by b whose length ranges between 2 and 4. Likewise, the pattern $p_3 = p_1 + p_2$ belongs to $\mathcal{L}_1$ and $Set(p_3) = Set(p_1) \cup Set(p_2) = \{aaa, aab, aba, abb, aa, ab, a, baab, babb, bbab, bbbb, bab, bbb, bb\}$.

With regard to the cost function, it is convenient to discuss some issues about the computation of the semantic cost function $c(\cdot|\cdot)$ for this particular setting. We will do this by means of an example. Suppose we are given the pattern $p = V_1V_2V_3V_4aV_5V_6V_7V_8$ and the element $e = ccaba$ which is covered by p. The computation of $c(e|p)$ is equivalent to find one of the nearest elements to e, namely e', which is not covered by p. Note that e' is not covered by p when the symbol a does not occur in e' (e.g. $e' = ccb$) or the number of symbols before or after each occurrence of a in e' is greater than 4 (e.g. $e' = ccbbbaba$). From this two possibilities, it is clear in this case that $e' = ccb$ is the nearest element to e not covered by p. This simple example allows us to affirm that the calculus $c(e|p)$ can be as complicated as determining the number of times a sequence s_1 occurs in a sequence s_2. Generally speaking, if s_p is the sequence of ground symbols in a pattern p and e' is the nearest element to e not covered by p, then e' will be a supersequence or a subsequence of e which will be obtained by modifying all the occurrences of s_p in e. Of course, as for the general form $c(E|p)$, this operation must be repeated for all the elements in E.

Therefore, if the learning problem requires the use of a cost function (e.g. because we are interested in minimal generalisations), it might be more convenient to approximate $c(E|p)$, instead of handling the original definition. For instance, we propose a naive but intuitive approximation of c inspired on the one we introduced in [3] for sets:

$$c'(E|p = \sum_{i=1}^{n} p_i) = \begin{cases} |E - E_1| + c(E_1|p_k), \exists p_k = V_1 \ldots V_j \\ \quad \text{and } E_1 = \{e \in E : \text{length of } e \leq j\} \\ |E|, \text{ otherwise.} \end{cases}$$

The justification is as follows. If there exists a pattern $p_k = V_1 \ldots V_j$ in p, then it is immediate that for every element e such that its length l is equal to or less than j, its nearest element not covered by p is, at least, at a distance $j - l + 1$, which is the value computed by $c(e|V_1 \ldots V_j)$. Otherwise, we assume that the nearest element of e is, at least, at a distance of 1. Implicitly, we are assuming that the nearest element to e can be obtained by removing (or adding) one specific ground symbol from (to) e.

The simplicity of $c'(\cdot|\cdot)$ will help us to study and compare the computation of the *mdbg* in $\mathcal{L}_0$ and $\mathcal{L}_1$. As for $\mathcal{L}_0$, the cost function is directly defined as $k_0(E,p) = c'(E|p)$ (that is, the complexity of the pattern is disregarded). As for $\mathcal{L}_1$, we use $k_1(E,p) = c_1(p) + c'(E|p)$ where $c_1(p)$ measures the complexity of a pattern $p \in \mathcal{L}_1$ by counting both the ground and variable symbols in p.

3.2 Notation and Previous Definitions

The function $Seq(\cdot)$ defined over a pattern $p \in \mathcal{L}_0$ returns the sequence of ground symbols in p. For example, setting $p = V_1 aa V_2 b$, then $Seq(p) = aab$. The bar notation $|\cdot|$ denotes the length of a sequence (here a sequence can be an element, a pattern, etc.). For instance, in the previous case, $|p| = 5$. The i-th symbol in a sequence p is denoted by $p(i)$. Following with the example, $p(1) = V_1$, $p(2) = a$, $\ldots, p(5) = b$. Any sequence is indexed starting from 1. The set of all the indices of p is denoted by $I(p)$. Thus, $I(p) = \{1, 2, 3, 4, 5\}$. We sometimes use superscript as a shorthand notation to write sequences and patterns. For instance, $V^5 a^3 V^2$ is equivalent to $V_1 \ldots V_5 aaa V_6 V_7$, and $V^2(ab)^3c$ is the same as $V_1 V_2 abababc$. Finally, we will often introduce mappings that are defined from one sequence to another. By $Dom(\cdot)$ and $Im(\cdot)$ we denote the domain and the image, respectively, of a mapping.

The first concept that is required is:

Definition 9 (Maximum common subsequence). *Given a set of sequences $E = \{e_1, \ldots, e_n\}$, and according to [18], the maximum common subsequence (mcs, to abbreviate) is the longest (not necessarily continuous) subsequence of all the sequences in E.*

This concept is already widely used in pattern recognition. Note that the *mcs* of a group of sequences is not necessarily unique. The following definitions will let us work with the concept of common subsequence in a more algebraic fashion.

Definition 10 (Alignment). *Given two elements e_1 and e_2, we say that the mapping $M_{e_2}^{e_1} : I(e_1) \rightarrow I(e_2)$ is an alignment of e_1 with e_2 if:*

i) $\forall i \in Dom(M_{e_2}^{e_1})$, $e_1(i) = e_2(M_{e_2}^{e_1}(i))$
ii) $M_{e_2}^{e_1}$ *is a strictly increasing function in* $Dom(M_{e_2}^{e_1})$.

(Remark 1). If $Dom(M_{e_2}^{e_1}) = \emptyset$, we say that $M_{e_2}^{e_1}$ is the empty alignment of e_1 with e_2. Thus, for every pair of elements we can affirm that there is always at least one alignment between them.
(Remark 2). Note that the alignment definition does not exclude the case $e_1 = e_2$.
(Remark 3). We call $e_1(i) = e_2(M_{e_2}^{e_1}(i))$ a (symbol) matching. Thus, $|Dom(M_{e_2}^{e_1})|$ (or equivalently, $|Im(M_{e_2}^{e_1})|$) is the number of matchings between e_1 and e_2 captured by $M_{e_2}^{e_1}$, and the subsequence obtained by considering the i-th symbols of e_1 where $i \in Dom(M_{e_2}^{e_1})$ is the sequence of matchings. For the sake of simplicity, we denote this sequence by $Seq(M_{e_2}^{e_1})$.

Definition 11 (Optimal alignment). *Given two elements e_1 and e_2, if $Seq(M_{e_2}^{e_1})$ is a mcs of e_1 and e_2, then we say that $M_{e_2}^{e_1}$ is an optimal alignment.*

Since $I(e_1)$ and $I(e_2)$ are finite sets, an alignment $M_{e_2}^{e_1}$ can be written as a $2 \times n$ matrix where n (which we denote as $Rang(M_{e_2}^{e_1})$) is the number of matchings. Hence,

$$M_{e_2}^{e_1} = \begin{pmatrix} a_{11} \ldots a_{1n} \\ a_{21} \ldots a_{2n} \end{pmatrix}$$

where $e_1(a_{1i}) = e_2(a_{2i})$ for all $1 \leq i \leq n$ (condition *i*) from Definition 10) and $a_{1i} < a_{1(i+1)}$ and $a_{2i} < a_{2(i+1)}$ for all $1 \leq i \leq (n-1)$ (condition *ii*) from Definition 10). An element of $M_{e_2}^{e_1}$ placed at row i and column j is denoted by $(M_{e_2}^{e_1})_{ij}$.

Let us illustrate all these ideas by means of an example.

Example 1. Given the elements $e_1 = caabbc$ and $e_2 = aacd$ where $I(e_1) = \{1, 2, 3, 4, 5, 6\}$ and $I(e_2) = \{1, 2, 3, 4\}$. An alignment $M_{e_2}^{e_1}$ (M in short) is

$$M = \begin{pmatrix} 2\,3\,6 \\ 1\,2\,3 \end{pmatrix} \equiv \begin{matrix} c\;a\;a\;b\;b\;c \\ a\;a\;c\;d \end{matrix}$$

Note that M satisfies both conditions from Definition 10. Following with M, we have that $Dom(M) = \{2, 3, 6\}$, $Im(M) = \{1, 2, 3\}$, $Rang(M) = 3$ and $Seq(M) = aac$. Finally, M is an optimal alignment.

Given that different optimal alignments can be defined over two elements e_1 and e_2, we might be interested in obtaining a concrete optimal alignment. To do this, we define a total order over all of them which lets us formally specify which optimal alignment we want.

Definition 12 ***(Total order for optimal alignments).*** *Given two elements e_1 and e_2 and given the optimal alignments $M_{e_2}^{e_1}$ (M in short) and $N_{e_2}^{e_1}$ (N in short) defined as*

$$M = \begin{pmatrix} a_{11} \ldots a_{1n} \\ a_{21} \ldots a_{2n} \end{pmatrix} N = \begin{pmatrix} b_{11} \ldots b_{1n} \\ b_{21} \ldots b_{2n} \end{pmatrix}$$

we say that $M < N$ iff $(a_{11}, \ldots, a_{1n}, a_{21}, \ldots, a_{2n}) <_{LO} (b_{11}, \ldots, b_{1n}, b_{21}, \ldots, b_{2n})$ where $<_{LO}$ is the Lexicographical Order for numerical tuples.

Example 2 Given $e_1 = aab$ and $e_2 = ab$, we define the optimal alignments

$$M_{e_2}^{e_1} = \begin{pmatrix} 1\,3 \\ 1\,2 \end{pmatrix} N_{e_2}^{e_1} = \begin{pmatrix} 2\,3 \\ 1\,2 \end{pmatrix}$$

Then $M_{e_2}^{e_1} < N_{e_2}^{e_1}$.

Every alignment between two elements e_1 and e_2 induces a special pattern p which covers both e_1 and e_2. This pattern is unique and we call it the pattern associated to an alignment.

Definition 13 (Pattern associated to an alignment and optimal alignment pattern). *Let e_1 and e_2 be two elements in Σ^* and let $M_{e_2}^{e_1}$ (M in short) be an alignment of e_1 with e_2. We say that a pattern $p \in \mathcal{L}_0$ is a pattern associated to the alignment M (denoted by p_M), if*
i) $Seq(M) = Seq(p)$
ii) the variable symbols in p are distributed as follows (letting $n = Rang(M)$, $l_1 = |e_1|$, $l_2 = |e_2|$):

- *The number of variables in the pattern p before the first ground symbol is equal to*

$$((M)_{11} - 1) + ((M)_{21} - 1)$$

- *The number of variables between whatever two ground symbols $p(i)$ and $p(j)$ $(i < j)$ in $Seq(p)$ such that there does not exists $i < k < j$ where $p(k)$ is a ground symbol, is equal to*

$$((M)_{1(i+1)} - (M)_{1i} - 1) + ((M)_{2(i+1)} - (M)_{2i} - 1)$$

- *The number of variables after the last ground symbol in p is equal to*

$$(l_1 - (M)_{1n}) + (l_2 - (M)_{2n})$$

If $M_{e_2}^{e_1}$ is an optimal alignment of e_1 with e_2, we say that $p_{M_{e_2}^{e_1}}$ is an optimal alignment pattern.

For instance, the pattern associated to the alignment M in Example 1 is $p_M = V_1aaV_2V_3cV_4$, which is an optimal alignment pattern because M is an optimal alignment. Note that if M is the empty alignment then $p_M = V^{l_1+l_2}$ and $Seq(M) = \lambda$.

The alignment and optimal alignment concepts (Definitions 10 and 11) can be easily extended to cope with patterns. Given two patterns p_1 and p_2, $M_{p_2}^{p_1}$ is an alignment of p_1 with p_2 where only matchings between ground symbols are taken into account, that is, $\forall i \in Dom(M_{p_2}^{p_1}), p_1(i) = p_2(M_{p_2}^{p_1}(i))$, $p(i) \in \Sigma$ and $p_2(M_{p_2}^{p_1}(i)) \in \Sigma$. Analogously, $M_{p_2}^{p_1}$ is an optimal alignment if $Seq(M_{p_2}^{p_1})$ is a *msc* of p_1 and p_2.

To conclude, we introduce a binary bottom-up generalisation operator (called $\uparrow$-transformation) defined over $\mathcal{L}_0$, which allows us to move through the pattern language.

Definition 14. *Given two patterns p_1 and p_2 in $\mathcal{L}_0$ we define the binary mapping*

$$\begin{aligned} \uparrow(\cdot,\cdot) : \mathcal{L}_0 \times \mathcal{L}_0 &\to \mathcal{L}_0 \\ (p_1, p_2) &\to \uparrow(p_1, p_2) = p, \qquad \textit{such that} \end{aligned}$$

1. *Let $M_{p_2}^{p_1}$ (M in short) be the minimum optimal alignment of p_1 with p_2, then $Seq(p) = Seq(M)$.*
2. *If $Seq(M) = \lambda$ then $p = V^{max\{|p_1|,|p_2|\}}$. Otherwise, the distribution of the variables in p is:*
   - *Before the first ground symbol in p, the number of variable is equal to:*
   $$max\{(M)_{11} - 1, (M)_{21} - 1\}$$
   - *Between two consecutive ground symbols in p, the number of variables is equal to:*
   $$max\{(M)_{1(i+1)} - (M)_{1i} - 1, (M)_{2(i+1)} - (M)_{2i} - 1\}$$
   - *After the last ground symbol in p, the number of variables is equal to (letting $n = Rang(M)$, $l_1 = |p_1|$ and $l_2 = |p_2|$):*
   $$max\{l_1 - (M)_{1n}, l_2 - (M)_{2n}\}$$

Example 3. Given the patterns $p_1 = abcV_1$, $p_2 = V_1abcccV_2$ and $p_3 = dV_1$, then $\uparrow(p_1, p_2) = VabcV^3$ and $\uparrow(p_1, p_3) = V^4$.

Proposition 2. *For every pair of patterns p_1 and p_2 in $\mathcal{L}_0$, if $p = \uparrow(p_1, p_2)$ then $Set(p_1) \subset (p)$ and $Set(p_2) \subset (p)$.*

Proof. It directly comes from the definition of the $\uparrow$-transformation.

Next, we explain how to define *dbg* operators for the different pattern languages, and we study the possibility of finding *mdbg* operators for $(\mathcal{L}_0, k_0)$ and $(\mathcal{L}_1, k_1)$.

3.3 Single List Pattern Language ($\mathcal{L}_0$)

One would expect that if $\Delta(E)$ computes a pattern p such that $Seq(p)$ is a *mcs* of the lists in E, then $\Delta(\cdot)$ is a *dbg* operator. However, we find that this operator is not, in general, distance-based. The following example illustrates this:

Example 4. Let $E = \{e_1, e_2, e_3\}$ where $e_1 = c^5a^3b^3$, $e_2 = c^5a^2d^4$ and $e_3 = a^3b^3d^4c^5$ are the elements to be generalised. Initially, we are going to fix a nerve for these elements, namely, the complete nerve (see Figure 3).

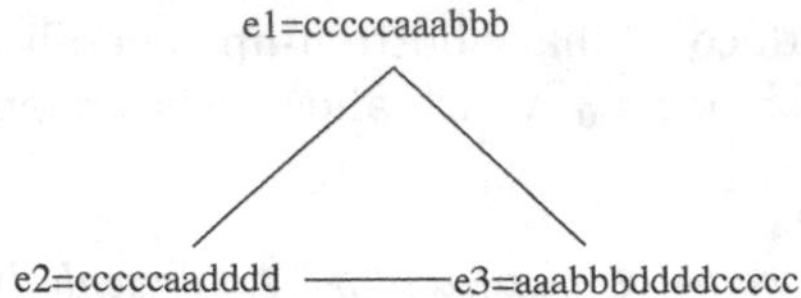

Fig. 3. A complete nerve ν for the evidence $E = \{e_1, e_2, e_3\}$

The pattern $p = V^{10}c^5V^6$ generalises E, and $Seq(p)$ is a *mcs* of the lists in E. However, this pattern is not a *db* pattern of E since, for example, the element a^3b^3 (which is between e_1 and e_3) and the element a^2d^4 (which is between e_2 and e_3) are not covered by p. As a matter of fact, no pattern containing the ground symbol c will be *db* and this result is independent of the nerve chosen.

The explanation for this apparently counterintuitive result is based on how the distance between the different pairs of elements e_i and e_j is calculated. In fact, although all the lists in E have subsequence c^5 in common, this subsequence is never taken into account to compute the distance $d(e_i, e_j)$, for any pair (e_i, e_j) in ν. Therefore, the operator definition we propose next not only uses the concept of *mcs* but also uses others such as the $\uparrow$-transformation and the concept of nerve which ensures the condition of being *db*. First, we deal with the binary generalisation operator, and then we extend it for the n-ary case.

In the first stage, for any two elements e_1 and e_2 to be generalised, we need to somehow find out which patterns in $\mathcal{L}_0$ can cover those elements between e_1 and e_2.

Proposition 3. *Given the elements e_1, e_2 and e, if e is between e_1 and e_2, then there exists an optimal alignment pattern p associated to an optimal alignment of e_1 and e_2 such that $e \in Set(p)$.*

Proof. **(Sketch)** Let $M_e^{e_1}$ and $M_{e_2}^e$ be the optimal alignments of e_1 with e and e with e_2, respectively. We define the mapping M between e_1 and e_2 as the composition of $M_e^{e_1}$ and $M_{e_2}^e$. The goal is to prove first that M is an optimal alignment of e_1 with e_2 and then, see that the associated pattern p_M covers e. For this last step we distinguish two cases: *i)* M is the empty alignment and consequently $p_M = V^{|e_1|+|e_2|}$. According to Proposition 21 in [3], if e is between

e_1 and e_2, then $|e| \leq |e_1| + |e_2|$, hence $e \in Set(p_M)$. *ii)* M is not empty and we aim to prove that the variable symbols in M are distributed in such a way that we can ensure that $e \in Set(p_M)$.

We will use the proposition above along with the $\uparrow$-transformation to define binary *db* operators.

Corollary 1. *Given the elements* e_1 *and* e_2, *if* $\{p_i\}_{i=1}^n$ *is the set of all the optimal alignment patterns of* e_1 *and* e_2, *then the generalisation operator defined as follows is db.*

$$\Delta^b(e_1, e_2) = \uparrow (p_1, \uparrow (p_2, \ldots \uparrow (p_{n-1}, p_n)) \ldots)$$

Proof. For every optimal alignment pattern, we know from Proposition 2, that

$$Set(p_i) \subset Set(\Delta^b(e_1, e_2)) \tag{2}$$

Then, from Proposition 3, we can write that

$$\forall \text{ element } e \text{ between } e_1 \text{ and } e_2 \Rightarrow \exists p_i : e \in Set(p_i) \tag{3}$$

Now, combining (2) and (3), we can affirm that

$$\forall \text{ element } e \text{ between } e_1 \text{ and } e_2 \Rightarrow e \in Set(\Delta^b(e_1, e_2)) \tag{4}$$

Hence, the generalisation operator is distance-based.

Next, we extend Corollary 1 for an arbitrary number of elements.

Corollary 2. *Given a finite set of elements* $E \subset X$ *and a function nerve* N, *the generalisation operator* Δ *defined in Algorithm 1 (where* Δ^b *is defined in Corollary 1) is db wrt.* N.

Proof. For every $(e_i, e_j) \in N(E)$, $Set(\Delta^b(e_i, e_j)) \subset Set(\Delta(E))$ by the definition of the $\uparrow$-transformation. Therefore, for every finite set E, $\Delta(E)$ is distance-based w.r.t. $N(E)$.

Algorithm 1 returns a pattern p such that $Set(\Delta^b(e_i, e_j)) \subset Set(p)$, for every pair of elements in $N(E)$, by iteratively applying the $\uparrow$-transformation over all the patterns $\Delta^b(e_i, e_j)$. The *else*-block is important since it ensures that $Seq(p) \neq \lambda$, if all the sequences $Seq(\Delta^b(e_1, e_j))$ have a subsequence in common. Let us see an example of this.

Example 5. Given $E = \{e_1, e_2, e_3, e_4\}$ where $e_1 = abc$, $e_2 = cabcd$, $e_3 = c$, $e_4 = cab$ and the nerve $N(E) = \{(e_1, e_2), (e_2, e_3), (e_2, e_4)\}$. The binary distance-based generalisations (lines 5-7 in the algorithm) are:

$$\begin{aligned} L[0] &= \Delta^b(e_1, e_2) = VabcV \\ L[1] &= \Delta^b(e_2, e_3) = VcabV \\ L[2] &= \Delta^b(e_2, e_4) = V^3cV^4 \end{aligned}$$

Data: $E = \{e_1, \ldots, e_n\}$, Δ^b (binary *dbg* operator) and ν (a nerve of E)
Result: Distance-based pattern of E wrt. ν

```
1  begin
2      k ← 0;
3      L ← []/ * empty list * /;
4      for (e_i, e_j) ∈ N(E) do
5          L[k] ← Δ^b(e_i, e_j);
6          k ← k + 1;
7      end
8      S ← {a_i ∈ Σ : ∀0 ≤ j ≤ k : a_i ∈ Seq(L[j]);
9      if S = ∅ then return V^{max{|L[j]|:∀0≤j≤k}} ;
10     else
11         p ← First(L);
12         Remove(L, p);
13         while L ≠ ∅ do
14             Find p_i ∈ L: ∃a_j ∈ S, a_j ∈ Seq(↑ (p, p_i));
15             p ←↑ (p, p_i);
16             Remove(L, p_j);
17         end
18         return p;
19     end
20 end
```

Algorithm 1. An algorithm to compute a *db* pattern of a set of lists E wrt. a nerve ν

If we applied the $\uparrow$-transformation in any arbitrary order over the set of binary patterns, we could obtain for example:

$$\begin{aligned} p &\leftarrow VabcV \\ p &\leftarrow \uparrow (p, VcabV) = V^2abV^2 \\ p &\leftarrow \uparrow (p, V^3cV^4) = V^9 \end{aligned}$$

However, if the $\uparrow$-transformation is applied as the algorithm indicates (lines 8-17), then $S = \{c\}$ and the patterns would be merged in the following order:

$$\begin{aligned} p &\leftarrow \uparrow VabcV \\ p &\leftarrow \uparrow (p, V^3cV^4) = V^3cV^4 \\ p &\leftarrow \uparrow (p, VcabV) = V^3cV^4 \end{aligned}$$

With regard to the computation of *mdbg* operators in $(\mathcal{L}_0, k_0)$, the algorithm above always return the *mdbg*. On the one hand, if all the binary patterns have a subsequence in common, the algorithm computes a distance-based pattern p such that $Seq(p) \neq \lambda$ and the function $c'(E|p) = |E|$ which attains a minimum value. On the other hand, the algorithm returns a pattern with variable symbols only, and whose length is the minimum length required to be distance-based. Therefore, p is minimal as well.

3.4 Multiple List Pattern Language ($\mathcal{L}_1$)

We will define *dbg* operators in $\mathcal{L}_1$ via Δ_N (Proposition 1). The binary operator Δ^b required by Δ_N is the one introduced in Corollary 1. An example of how this operator works is shown below:

Example 6. Given a finite set of elements $E = \{e_1, e_2, e_3, e_4\}$ where $e_1 = a^2b^2d$, $e_2 = da^2c^2$, $e_3 = c^2db^2$ and $e_4 = ad$ and the nerve $N(E) = \{(e_1, e_2), (e_1, e_3), (e_1, e_4)\}$.

$$\Delta^b(e_1, e_2) = p_1 = Va^2V^5$$
$$\Delta^b(e_1, e_3) = p_2 = V^5b^2$$
$$\Delta^b(e_1, e_4) = p_3 = VaV^3d$$

Finally,

$$\Delta_N(E) = Va^2V^5 + V^5b^2 + VaV^3d$$

Observe that the solution for this example in $\mathcal{L}_0$ is just a pattern consisting of variable symbols only, which shows the utility of $\mathcal{L}_1$. Next, let us see how to obtain *mdbg* operators in $\mathcal{L}_1$.

Since the only way we know to define a distance-based operator in $\mathcal{L}_1$ consists in fixing a nerve beforehand, it is reasonable to study how to define *mdbg* operators relative to a nerve function. However, the calculus of the *mdbg* operator is not easy at all. Basically, the question is whether the *mdbg* operators relative to a nerve function N can be defined in terms of Δ_N and the $\uparrow$-transformation. However, this result seems hard to be established. On the one hand, we ignore how to explicitly define most of the Δ^b operators (since Corollary 1 only establishes a sufficient condition) and on the other hand, we must take into consideration some inherent limitations of the $\uparrow$-transformation:

1. The *mdb* pattern might not be found by applying the $\uparrow$-transformation over Δ_N if this one uses the binary operator Δ^b defined in Corollary 1: we will illustrate this by means of an example.

   Example 7. Given the set $E = \{e_1, e_2, e_3\}$, where $e_1 = a_1a_2a_3$, $e_2 = a_1a_6a_7$ and $e_3 = a_2a_4a_5$, and $N(E) = \{(e_1, e_2), (e_1, e_3)\}$. The optimal alignment patterns which are associated to (e_1, e_2) and (e_1, e_3), respectively, are a_1V^4 and Va_2V^3. Then a_1V^4 is a *db* pattern of (e_1, e_2) (since it is the only optimal alignment pattern) and Va_2V^3 is a *db* pattern of (e_2, e_3) (since it is the only optimal alignment pattern). Hence, the pattern $p = a_1V^4 + Va_2V^3$ is *db* w.r.t. $N(E)$. However, the pattern $p' = a_1V^4 + a_2V^3$ is distance-based (the only element between e_1 and e_2, which is not covered by a_2V^3, is $a_1a_2a_4a_5$ but this is covered by a_1V^4) but $Set(p') \not\subset Set(p)$. The *mdb* pattern for E will have $|p'|$ or even fewer symbols and this will never be achieved by the $\uparrow$-transformation over the optimal alignment patterns.

   Therefore, given that Δ^b is defined from the concept of optimal alignment patterns and Δ_N is defined from Δ^b, it is not possible that the *mdbg* operator can be expressed in terms of the $\uparrow$-transformation and Δ_N.

2. The *mdbg* pattern might not be found by applying the ↑-transformation over *skeleton*($N(E)$): from the previous point, we could think that the *mdb* pattern cannot be found because the optimal alignment patterns are excessively general. However, if it was so, it would mean that starting the search from something extremely specific, namely the skeleton, the *mdb* pattern should be found. However, this is not true as the next example reveals:

Example 8. Given $E = \{e_1, e_2, e_3, e_4, e_5\}$ where $e_1 = ac^3b^2$, $e_2 = ab^2$, $e_3 = ab^2ce$, $e_4 = d$ and $e_5 = fgh$ and the nerve depicted below:
If we group the elements according to its similarity and then apply the ↑-transformation over the different groups, the pattern obtained would attain a lower value for $k_1(E, \cdot)$. Taking this strategy into account, we can distinguish several meaningful grouping criteria. For instance, those elements which contain the subsequence *abb* (G_1) and those which do not (G_2). That is,

$$G_1 = \{ac^3b^2, acb^2, ac^2b^2, ab^2, \ldots, ab^2d\}$$
$$G_2 = \{dfgh, fdgh, fgdh, fghd\}$$

In this particular case, it does not matter how the elements in the groups are ranked in order to apply the ↑-transformation since the final result remains invariable. Thus, we can write

$$p_1 = \uparrow(G_1) + \uparrow(G_2) = VaV^3bVbV^2 + VfVgVhV$$

For any other binary splitting, we would have elements having no subsequence in common in the same group (e.g. *abb* and *dfgh*). The shortest patterns would be

$$p_2 = aV^3b^2V^2 + V^4$$
$$p_3 = V^6$$

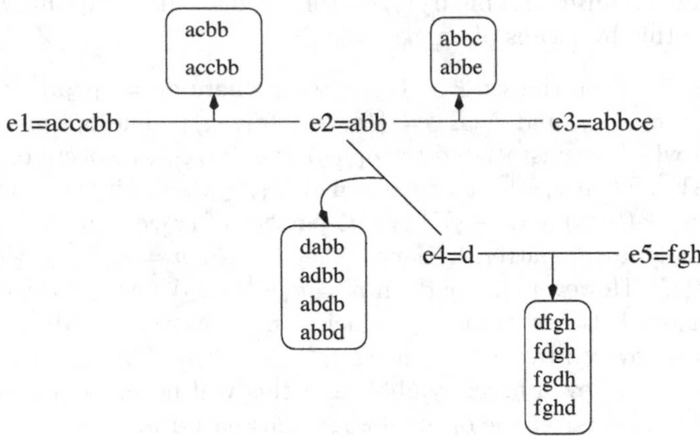

Fig. 4. A naive generalisation of the set E w.r.t. the nerve N(E). Circled elements are the intermediate elements.

Using three groups, another interesting possibility can be explored. For instance, $G_1 = \{fgh\}$, those elements containing the subsequence d (G_2) and the remaining ones (G_3). Depending on the order of the elements in G_2 we could obtain by applying the *uparrow*-transformation.

$$p_4 = V^5 + aV^3b^2V^2$$
$$p_5 = V^3dV^3 + aV^3b^2V^2 + fgh$$

Finally, it is not worth using more than three groups because of the excessive length of the pattern obtained. Evaluating the different patterns, we have that:

$$k_1(E,p_1) = c(p_1) + c'(E|p_1) = 17 + 5 = 22$$
$$k_1(E,p_2) = c(p_2) + c'(E|p_2) = 12 + 10 = 22$$
$$k_1(E,p_3) = c(p_3) + c'(E|p_3) = 6 + 17 = 23$$
$$k_1(E,p_4) = c(p_4) + c'(E|p_4) = 13 + 13 = 26$$
$$k_1(E,p_5) = c(p_5) + c'(E|p_5) = 18 + 5 = 23$$

But the following patterns are also distance-based for E:

$$p_6 = V^3cV^2 + V^4$$
$$p_7 = aV^5 + V^4$$

where

$$k_1(E,p_6) = c(p_6) + c'(E|p_6) = 10 + 10 = 20$$
$$k_1(E,p_7) = c(p_7) + c'(E|p_7) = 10 + 10 = 20$$

However, neither p_6 nor p_7 can be derived from a $\uparrow$-transformation since this tends to extract the longest common subsequence. Observe that all the elements which have the subsequence c or a also contain the subsequence abb in common.

From this previous analysis, we can conclude that the $\uparrow$-transformation is not enough in itself to explore the search space. We need a generalisation tool which is not based on the concept of the longest common subsequence. For this purpose, we introduce the so-called inverse substitution.

Definition 15 ***(Inverse subtitution).*** *Given a pattern p in $\mathcal{L}_0$ or in $\mathcal{L}_1$ an inverse substitution σ^{-1} is a set of indices where each index denotes a ground symbol in p to be changed by a variable. Thus, $p\sigma^{-1}$ represents the new pattern which is obtained by applying σ^{-1} over p.*

Basically, an inverse substitution just changes ground symbols by variables. For example, given $p = VaabV$ and $\sigma^{-1} = \{2,4\}$ then $p\sigma^{-1} = V^2aV^2$. Now, we are in conditions to introduce the next proposition:

Proposition 4. *Given a finite set of elements $E = \{e_1, \ldots, e_n\}$ and a nerve function N. If we set $S = skeleton(N(E))$ then there exists a partition P of the set S and a collection of inverse substitutions $\{\sigma_1^{-1}, \ldots, \sigma_n^{-1}\}$ such that the pattern*

$$p = \sum_{\forall P_i = \{e_{k_i}\}_{k_i=1}^{m_i} \in P} \uparrow (\{e_{k_i}\sigma_{k_i}^{-1}\}_{k_i=1}^{m_i})$$

is a mdb pattern of E relative to $N(E)$.

Proof. **(Sketch).** We can assume that there exists a pattern $p = \sum_{i=1}^{n} p_i$ such that $k(E, p)$ attains a minimum value. The pattern p induces a partition of $E = \cup E_i$ in such a way that $e_i \in E_i$ iff $e_i \in Set(p_i)$. Next, we remove repeated elements in the different E_i in order to make sure that the subsets E_i are pairwise disjoints. Finally, the proposition can be proved using the concepts of inverse substitution and $\uparrow$-transformation over the partition we have set.

This latter proposition leads to an exhaustive search algorithm in order to compute the *mbdg* operator. This algorithm turns out to be useless in general due to the size of the search space (the number of different possibilities for the partition of $skeleton(N(E))$ and substitutions). In fact, for a particular version of $\mathcal{L}_1$, we have proved that this optimisation problem is NP-Hard (see [3]).

Hence, the other option is to approximate the calculus of the *mdb* patterns. To do this, we use a greedy search schema driven by the cost function. That is, for each iteration, the $\uparrow$-transformation is applied over the pair of patterns that reduces th cost function most. This idea is formalised in the Algorithm 2 and illustrated in Example 9.

Input: $E = \{e_1, \ldots, e_n\}$, Δ^b (binary *dbg* operator) and N (nerve function)
Output: A pattern which approximates a *mdb* pattern of E w.r.t. $N(E)$

$\tilde{\Delta}_N(E)$
begin
  $k \leftarrow 1$;
  for $(e_i, e_j) \in N(E)$ **do**
    $p_k \leftarrow \Delta^b(e_i, e_j)$;
    $k \leftarrow k + 1$;
  end
  $p = \sum_{k=1}^{n} p_k$;
  do
    $k_p \leftarrow k_1(E, p)$;
    $p' \leftarrow argmin\{k_1(E, p_{ij}) : \forall 1 \leq i, j, \leq n, p_{ij} = \uparrow(\{p_i, p_j\}) + (p - p_i - p_j)\}$;
    $k'_p \leftarrow k_1(E, p')$;
    if $k_{p'} < k_p$ **then** $p \leftarrow p'$;
  while $k_{p'} < k_p$
  return p;
end
//The notation $p - p_i - p_j$ employed in the algorithm means all the patterns in p except p_i and p_j.;

Algorithm 2. A greedy algorithm which approximates the *mdbg* operator

Example 9. Let E and $N(E)$ be the set of examples and the nerve employed in Example 6. Remember that,

$$p_1 = \Delta^b(e_1, e_2) = Va^2V^5$$
$$p_2 = \Delta^b(e_1, e_3) = V^5b^2$$
$$p_3 = \Delta^b(e_1, e_4) = VaV^3d$$

and

$$p = Va^2V^5 + V^5b^2 + VaV^3d$$

see lines 4-8 in the algorithm. Next, we have to apply the $\uparrow$-transformation over each pair of binary generalisations and we choose the one which attains a lower value of $k_1(E, \cdot)$ (see lines 9-14). In our case, we must consider two possibilities:

$$\begin{aligned} p_1 &= \uparrow (Va^2V^5, V^5b^2) + VaV^3d = V^8 + VaV^3d \\ &= V^8 \\ p_2 &= \uparrow (Va^2V^5, VaV^3d) + V^5b^2 = VaV^6 + V^5b^2 \end{aligned}$$

Since $k_1(E, p_2) = 19$ is less than $k_1(E, p_1) = 27$, we choose the pattern p_2. The process stops when the pattern cannot be further improved. Note that the next iteration leads to

$$\uparrow (VaV^6, V^5b^2) = V^8$$

which performs worse than p_2. Therefore, the algorithm returns p_2.

4 Conclusions and Future Work

We have followed the connection between two major concepts in inductive programming, the concept of distance and generalisation, when applied to lists. This work is based in a correct integration of distance-based methods with symbolic inductive learners we introduced in [4][6]. This proposal relies on the novel concept of (minimal) distance-based generalisation operator, which aims to induce consistent (minimal) patterns from data embedded in a metric space.

The main contribution of this paper consists in studying how to apply our framework in order to infer consistent symbolic patterns from a particular structured data type (lists) and a distance function (edit distance). More concretely, we have seen how to define (minimal) distance-based generalisation operators for this domain. To do this, we have introduced two different pattern languages $\mathcal{L}_0$ and $\mathcal{L}_1$. The first language is made up of patterns which consist of finite sequences of ground and variable symbols. The language $\mathcal{L}_1$ extends $\mathcal{L}_0$ in that the disjunction of patterns is permitted. Additionally, we have defined a cost function for each language in order to study the minimality of the patterns we can obtain.

We have proved that for more than two sequences, the widely-used concept of *maximum common subsequence* does not necessarily lead to distance-based generalisation operators. In order to obtain this sort of operators, we need to introduce a new concept: namely, the concept of sequence associated to an optimal alignment. This kind of sequences leads to certain patterns that when combined, allows us to define distance-based operators. As for the minimality of these operators, we have shown this is a computational hard problem in $\mathcal{L}_1$. For this reason, we have introduced a greedy search algorithm which allows us to approximate minimal generalisations.

There are some work ahead to ease the integration of these generalisation operators into inductive programming tools. For instance, the computational complexity of the greedy search algorithm which approximates minimal patterns is a concern. This has a quadratic complexity with the number of subpatterns in the pattern obtained by Proposition 1. Unfortunately, this operation still has a high cost, if we want to run our algorithm over large data sets. Thus, it would be convenient to try other heuristics with a lower complexity that ensure a good approximation. Another one is devoted to the pattern languages that have been investigated. Note that both $\mathcal{L}_0$ and $\mathcal{L}_1$ are subfamilies of regular languages. A very interesting line of work would consist in extending all the results presented in this paper in order to include pattern representations based on other more expressive subfamilies of regular languages. By doing this, we could obtain not only new grammar inference algorithms but also new grammar learners that would ensure the consistency of the inferred model wrt. the underlying distance, something which does not happen when traditional grammar learners are applied.

Acknowledgments

This work was partially supported by the EU (FEDER) and the Spanish Government MEC/MICINN, under grant TIN 2007-68093-C02, the Spanish project "Agreement Technologies"(CONSOLIDER-INGENIO CSD2007-00022) and the Valencian project PROMETEO/2008/051.

References

1. Bowers, A.F., Giraud-Carrier, C.G., Lloyd, J.W.: Classification of individuals with complex structure. In: Proc. of the 17th International Conference on Machine Learning (ICML 2000), pp. 81–88. Morgan Kaufmann, San Francisco (2000)
2. Edgar, G.A.: Measure, Topology and Fractal Geometry. Springer, Heidelberg (1990)
3. Estruch, V.: Bridging the gap between distance and generalisation: Symbolic learning in metric spaces. PhD Thesis, DSIC-UPV (2008), `http://www.dsic.upv.es/~vestruch/thesis.pdf`
4. Estruch, V., Ferri, C., Hernández-Orallo, J., Ramírez-Quintana, M.J.: Distance based generalisation. In: Kramer, S., Pfahringer, B. (eds.) ILP 2005. LNCS (LNAI), vol. 3625, pp. 87–102. Springer, Heidelberg (2005)
5. Estruch, V., Ferri, C., Hernández-Orallo, J., Ramírez-Quintana, M.J.: Distance based generalisation for graphs. In: Proc. Work. of Machine and Learning with Graphs, pp. 133–140 (2006)
6. Estruch, V., Ferri, C., Hernández-Orallo, J., Ramírez-Quintana, M.J.: Minimal distance-based generalisation operators for first-order objects. In: Muggleton, S.H., Otero, R., Tamaddoni-Nezhad, A. (eds.) ILP 2006. LNCS (LNAI), vol. 4455, pp. 169–183. Springer, Heidelberg (2007)
7. Ferri, C., Hernández-Orallo, J., Ramírez-Quintana, M.J.: Incremental learning of functional logic programs. In: Kuchen, H., Ueda, K. (eds.) FLOPS 2001. LNCS, vol. 2024, pp. 233–247. Springer, Heidelberg (2001)
8. Hamming, R.W.: Error detecting and error correcting codes. Bell System Technical Journal 26(2), 147–160 (1950)

9. Hernández-Orallo, J., Ramírez-Quintana, M.J.: Inverse narrowing for the induction of functional logic programs. In: 1998 Joint Conference on Declarative Programming, APPIA-GULP-PRODE 1998, A Coruña, Spain, July 20-23, pp. 379–392 (1998)
10. Hernández-Orallo, J., Ramírez-Quintana, M.J.: A strong complete schema for inductive functional logic programming. In: Džeroski, S., Flach, P.A. (eds.) ILP 1999. LNCS (LNAI), vol. 1634, pp. 116–127. Springer, Heidelberg (1999)
11. Levenshtein, V.I.: Binary codes capable of correcting deletions, insertions, and reversals. Soviet Physics Doklady 10, 707–710 (1966)
12. Lloyd, J.W.: Learning comprehensible theories from structured data. In: Mendelson, S., Smola, A.J. (eds.) Advanced Lectures on Machine Learning. LNCS (LNAI), vol. 2600, pp. 203–225. Springer, Heidelberg (2003)
13. Muggleton, S.H.: Inductive logic programming: Issues, results, and the challenge of learning language in logic. Artificial Intelligence 114(1-2), 283–296 (1999)
14. Olsson, R.: Inductive functional programming using incremental program transformation. Artifificial Intelligence 74(1), 55–81 (1995)
15. Rissanen, J.: Hypothesis selection and testing by the MDL principle. The Computer Journal 42(4), 260–269 (1999)
16. Schmid, U.: Inductive synthesis of Functional Programs-Universal Planning, Folding of Finite Programs, and Schema Abstraction by Analogical Reasoning. Springer, Heidelberg (2003)
17. Swamidass, S.H., Chen, J., Bruand, J., Phung, P., Ralaivola, L., Baldi, P.: Kernels for small molecules and the prediction of mutagenecity, toxicity and anti-cancer activity. Bioinformatics 21, 359–368 (2005)
18. Rivest, R., Cormen, T.H., Leiserson, C., Stein, C. (eds.): Introduction to Algorithms. MIT Press, Cambridge (2000)
19. Wallace, C.S., Dowe, D.L.: Minimum Message Length and Kolmogorov Complexity. Computer Journal 42(4), 270–283 (1999)

Porting IGORII from MAUDE to HASKELL

Martin Hofmann, Emanuel Kitzelmann, and Ute Schmid

Cognitive Systems Group, University of Bamberg
{martin.hofmann,emanuel.kitzelmann,ute.schmid}@uni-bamberg.de

Abstract. This paper describes our efforts and solutions in porting our IP system IGOR 2 from the termrewriting language MAUDE to HASKELL. We describe how, for our purpose necessary features of the homoiconic language MAUDE especially the treatment of code as data and vice versa, can be simulated in HASKELL using a stateful monad transformer which makes type and class information available. With our new implementation we are now able to use higher-order context during our synthesis and extract information from type classes useable as background knowledge. Keeping our new implementation as close as possible to our old, we could keep all features of our system.

1 Introduction

Inductive programming (IP) dares to tackle a problem as old as programming itself: Help the human programmers with their task of creating programs, solely using evidence of an exemplary behaviour of the desired program. Contrary to deductive program synthesis, where programs are generated from an abstract, but complete specification, inductive program synthesis is concerned with the synthesis of programs or algorithms from incomplete specifications, such as input/output (I/O) examples. Focus is on the synthesis of *declarative*, i.e., logic, functional, or functional logic programs. The aims of IP are manifold. On the one hand, research in IP provides better insights in the cognitive skills of human programmers. On the other hand, powerful and efficient IP systems can enhance software systems in a variety of domains—such as automated theorem proving and planning—and offer novel approaches to knowledge based software engineering such as model driven software development or test driven development, as well as end user programming support in the XSL domain (1).

Beginnings of IP research addressed inductive synthesis of functional programs from small sets of positive I/O examples only (2). One of the most influential classical systems was THESYS (3) which synthesised linear recursive LISP programs by rewriting I/O pairs into traces and folding of traces based on recurrence detection. Currently, induction of functional programs is covered by the analytical approaches IGOR 1 (4), and IGOR 2 (5) and by the evolutionary/generate-and-test based approaches ADATE (6) and MAGICHASKELLER (7).

Analytical approaches work example-driven, so the structure of the given I/O pairs is used to guide the construction of generalised programs. They are typically very fast and can guarantee certain characteristics for the generated programs

U. Schmid, E. Kitzelmann, and R. Plasmeijer (Eds.): AAIP 2009, LNCS 5812, pp. 140–158, 2010.

such as minimality of the generalisation w.r.t. to the given examples and termination. However they are restricted to programs describable by a small set of I/O pairs.

Generate-and-test based approaches first construct one or more hypothetical programs, evaluate them against the I/O examples and then work on with the most promising hypotheses. They are very powerful and usually do not have any restrictions concerning the synthesis able class of programs, but are extremely time consuming.

Two decades ago, some inductive logic programming (ILP) systems were presented with focus on learning recursive logic *programs* in contrast to learning classifiers: FFOIL (8), GOLEM (9), PROGOL (10), and the interactive system DIALOGS (11). Synthesis of functional logic programs is covered by the system FLIP (12).

IP can be viewed as a special branch of machine learning because programs are constructed by inductive generalisation from examples. Therefore, as for classification learning, each approach can be characterised by its restriction and preference bias (13). However, IP approaches cannot be evaluated with respect to some covering measure or generalisation error since (recursive) programs must treat *all* I/O examples correctly to be an acceptable hypothesis.

The task of writing programs writing programs—pardon the pun—is *per se* reflexive, so it is virtually self-suggesting to use reflexive, also called homoiconic languages. Unfortunately only a few homoiconic languages are declarative and adequate for IP, e.g. LISP and MAUDE. Nevertheless, they lack interesting features like polymorphic types with type classes or higher-order functions. State-of-the-art functional languages with a large community and good library support as e.g. HASKELL do not provide reflexive features, though.

Nevertheless, we value the pros of a state-of-the-art functional language more and so grasp the nettle and build our own homoiconic support. This paper describes our efforts and solutions in porting our IP system IGOR 2 from the term rewriting language MAUDE to HASKELL facing problems in simulating reflexive properties. This is done mainly to overcome MAUDE's restricted higher-order context, but also to use information about type classes as background knowledge. IGOR 2's key features are kept unchanged. They are

- termination by construction,
- handling arbitrary user-defined data types,
- utilisation of arbitrary background knowledge,
- automatic invention of auxiliary functions as sub programs,
- learning complex calling relationships (tree- and nested recursion),
- allowing for variables in the example equations,
- simultaneous induction of mutually recursive target functions.

Furthermore it provides insights in less theoretical but more pragmatic implementation details of the systems. The next Section 2 gives an overview of the theory behind IGOR 2 and its strong linkage to MAUDE, and in Section 3 we describe the library specification of our new implementation in HASKELL. We conclude with an outlook on future work in Section 5.

2 Igor 2 and Maude

IGOR 2's (14) main objective is to overcome the strong limitations—only a small fixed set of primitives and no background knowledge, strongly restricted program schemas, linearly ordered I/O examples—of the classical analytical approach but not for the price of a generate-and-test search. This is realized by integrating analytical techniques into a systematic search in the program space. A prototype is implemented in MAUDE. Please note that in the following chapter we adopt the MAUDE syntax, where, contrary to HASKELL variables are in upper case and constructor symbal are in lower case.

2.1 The Igor 2-Algorithm

We only sketch the algorithm here. For a more detailed description see (14).

IGOR 2 represents I/O examples, background knowledge, and induced programs as *constructor (term rewriting) systems (CSs)* over many-sorted (typed) first-order signatures. Signatures for CSs are the union of two disjoint subsignatures called *defined function symbols* and *constructor symbols*, respectively. Terms containing only constructor symbols (and variables) are called *constructor terms.* A CS is a set of directed equations or rules of the form $F(p_1, \ldots, p_n) \rightarrow t$ where F is a defined function symbol, the p_i are constructor terms and t is a term. This corresponds to *pattern matching* over user-defined data types in functional programming. A CS is evaluated by term rewriting. Terms that are not rewritable—these include, in particular, all constructor terms—are called *normal forms.* For CSs representing I/O examples or background knowledge hold the additional restriction that right-hand sides (rhss) are constructor terms. This particularly means that also background knowledge must be provided in an extensional form, i.e. as non-recursive I/O examples.

In order to construct *confluent* CSs, i.e., CSs with *unique* normal forms, IGOR 2 assures that patterns of rules belonging to one defined function are *disjoint*, i.e., do not unify. IGOR 2's inductive bias is—roughly speaking—to prefer CSs with fewer disjoint patters, i.e., CSs that partition the domain into fewer subsets. With respect to this preference bias, IGOR 2 starts with one *initial rule* per target function. An initial rule is the *least general generalisation*—with respect to the subsumption order $t \geq t'$ (t *subsumes* or *is more general than* t'), if there exists a substitution σ with $t\sigma = t'$—of the provided I/O examples. Initial rules entail the I/O examples with respect to equational reasoning and are *correct with respect to the I/O examples* in this sense. However, an initial rule may contain variables in its right-hand side (rhs) not occurring in its left-hand side (lhs), i.e. pattern. We call such variables *unbound* and rules and their rhs containing them, *open.* Unbound variables may be instantiated arbitrarily within rewriting such that CSs containing open rules do not represent *functions.* Hence, CSs are transformed during the search by taking an open rule r out of a CS and replacing it by a set of new rules R such that (i) either the unbound variables are eliminated in the rhs of r in R or r is completely discarded from R, and (ii) the resulting CS is still correct with respect to the I/O examples and equational reasoning. Different sets R may be possible as replacements for an open rule, i.e., a refinement operator takes an open rule r and yields a set of sets R of rules. In one search step, an open and best rated CS with respect to the preference bias and one open rule from it is chosen. Then all refinement operators are applied to r yielding a set of sets of rules each. The union of these sets is the set of possible replacements R of r. Now r is replaced in each CS containing it by each possible R. A goal state is reached if all best rated CSs are closed. This set constitutes the solution returned by IGOR 2.

There are three transformation operators: (i) The I/O examples belonging to the open initial rule are partitioned into subsets and for each subset, a new initial rule (with a more specific pattern than the original rule) is computed. (ii) The open rhs is replaced by a (recursive) call to a defined function. The arguments of the call may again contain calls to defined functions. Hence, computing the arguments is considered as a new subproblem. (iii) If the open rhs has a constructor as root, i.e., does not consist of a single unbound variable, then all subterms containing unbound variables are treated as subproblems. A new auxiliary function is introduced for each such subterm. We will explain all of them in the following paragraphs.

Splitting an open rule. The first operator partitions the I/O examples belonging to a rule into subsets such that the patterns of the resulting initial rules are disjoint more specific than the pattern of the original rule. Finding such a partition is done as follows: A position in the pattern p with a variable resulting from generalising the corresponding subterms in the subsumed example inputs is identified. This implies that at least two of the subsumed inputs have different constructor symbols at this position. Now all subsumed inputs are partitioned such that all of them with the same constructor at this position belong to the same subset. Together with the corresponding example outputs this yields a partition of the example equations whose inputs are subsumed by p. Since more than one position may be selected, different partitions leading to different sets of new initial rules may result.

For example, let

$$\begin{aligned} reverse([]) &= [] \\ reverse([X]) &= [X] \\ reverse([X,Y]) &= [Y,X] \end{aligned}$$

be some examples for the *reverse*-function. The pattern of the initial rule is simply a variable Q, since the example input terms have no common root symbol. Hence, the unique position at which the pattern contains a variable and the example inputs different constructors is the root position. The first example input consists of only the constant [] at the root position. All remaining example inputs have the list constructor *cons* as root. Put differently, two subsets are induced by the root position, one containing the first example, the other containing the two remaining examples. The least general generalisations of the example inputs of these two subsets are [] and $[Q|Qs]$ resp. which are the (more specific) patterns of the two successor rules.

Introducing (Recursive) Function Calls and Auxiliary Functions. In cases (ii) and (iii) help functions are invented. This includes the generation of I/O-examples from which they are induced. For case (ii) this is done as follows: Function calls are introduced by matching the currently considered outputs, i.e., those outputs whose inputs match the pattern of the currently considered rule, with the outputs of any defined function. A defined function is either the target function, a function from the background knowledge, or an auxiliary function invented on the fly. If all current outputs match, then the rhs of the current unfinished rule can be set to a call of the matched defined function. The argument of the call must map the currently considered inputs to the inputs of the matched defined function. For case (iii), the example inputs of the new defined function also equal the currently considered inputs. The outputs are the corresponding subterms of the currently considered outputs.

For an example of case (iii) consider the last two *reverse* examples as they have been put into one subset in the previous section. The initial rule for these two examples is:

$$reverse([Q|Qs]) = [Q2|Qs2] \tag{1}$$

This rule is unfinished due two the two unbound variables in the rhs. Now the two unfinished subterms (consisting of exactly the two variables) are taken as new subproblems. This leads to two new examples sets for two new help functions *sub*1 and *sub*2:

$$\begin{aligned} sub1([X]) &= X \\ sub1([X,Y]) &= Y \\ sub2([X]) &= [] \\ sub2([X,Y]) &= [X] \end{aligned}$$

The successor rule-set for the unfinished rule contains three rules determined as follows: The original unfinished rule (1) is replaced by the finished rule:

$$reverse([Q|Qs]) = [sub1([Q|Qs]) \mid sub2[Q|Qs]]$$

And from both new example sets an initial rule is derived.

Finally, as an example for case (ii), consider the example equations for the help function *sub*2 and the generated unfinished initial rule:

$$sub2([Q|Qs]) = Qs2 \tag{2}$$

The example outputs, $[]$, $[X]$ of *sub*2 match the first two example outputs of the *reverse*-function. That is, the unfinished rhs $Qs2$ can be replaced by a (recursive) call to the *reverse*-function. The argument of the call must map the inputs $[X]$, $[X, Y]$ of *sub*2 to the corresponding inputs $[]$, $[X]$ of *reverse*, i.e., a new help function, *sub*3 is needed. This leads to the new example set:

$$\begin{aligned} sub3([X]) &= [] \\ sub3([X,Y]) &= [X] \end{aligned}$$

The successor rule-set for the unfinished rule contains two rules determined as follows: The original unfinished rule (2) is replaced by the finished rule:

$$sub2([Q|Qs] = reverse(sub3([Q|Qs]))$$

Additionally it contains the initial rule for *sub*3.

2.2 Igor 2's Use of Maude's Term Rewriting and Homoiconic Capabilities

In the functional subpart of MAUDE, a module essentially defines an order-sorted signature[1] Σ, a set of variables X, and a term rewriting system over Σ and X. Hence, IGOR 2's I/O examples, background knowledge, and induced programs are valid and evaluateable MAUDE modules. Since I/O examples, background knowledge, and induced CSs are input and output respectively, i.e., *data* for IGOR 2, we need some *homoiconic* capabilities: A MAUDE program (IGOR 2) needs to handle MAUDE programs as data. This is facilitated by MAUDE's meta-level. For all constructs of MAUDE modules—signatures, terms, equations, and complete modules—sorts and constructors to represent them are implemented in the META-LEVEL module and its submodules in MAUDE's standard library. Furthermore, functions to transform terms etc. to their meta-representation—`upTerm`, `upEqs`, and `upModule`—are predefined there. Meta-represented terms, equations, modules and so on are *terms* of types `Term`, `Equation`, `Module` etc. and may be rewritten by a MAUDE program like any other term.

Let us examine in some more detail, how terms and equations are meta-represented in MAUDE: Constants and variables are meta-represented by quoted identifiers containing name and type of the represented constant or variable. E.g., `upTerm(nil)` where `nil` is a constant of sort `List` yields the constant `'nil.List` of sort `Constant` which is a subsort of `Term` and `upTerm(X)` where `X` is a variable of sort `List` yields the constant `'X:List` of sort `Variable` which is also a subsort of `Term`. Other terms are represented by a quoted identifier as root and a list of meta-terms in brackets as arguments. E.g., `upTerm(Reverse(nil))` yields the term `'Reverse['nil.List]` of sort `Term`.

The constructor in mixfix notation for representing an equation is `eq_=_[_]`. where the first two placeholders (_) may take a term in meta-representation each (the rhs and lhs of the equation) and the third _ an attribute set (belonging to an equation). The resulting term is of sort `Equation`.

Now consider a MAUDE module `M` containing the two equations

```
eq reverse(nil) = nil .
eq reverse(cons(X,nil)) = cons(X,nil) .
```

where X is a variable of sort `Item`. Applying `upEqs('M, false)` then yields:

```
eq 'Reverse['nil.List] = 'nil.List [none] .
eq 'Reverse['cons['X:Item,'nil.List]] =
       'cons['X:Item,'nil.List] [none] .
```

This is a term of the sort `EquationSet`.

Also concepts of rewriting, e.g., matching and substitutions, are implemented for the meta-level. For example,

[1] Order-sorted signatures are a non-trivial extension of many-sorted signatures. In an order-sorted signature, the sorts partially ordered into sub- and supersorts.

```
metaMatch(upModule('M,false), 'X:List,
        'cons['Y:Item,'nil.List], nil, 0)
```

yields the term

```
'X:List <- 'cons['Y:Item,'nil.List]
```

of sort `Assignment` which is a subsort of `Substitution`.

3 Igor 2 in Haskell

As LISP, MAUDE is a dynamically typed, homoiconic language. This means that (i) the majority of its type checking is done at run-time so type information is available at this point, and, as seen in the previous section, (ii) it supports treating 'code as data' and vice versa 'data as code' very well. This is quite useful for program synthesis, because the data structure to represent hypotheses about possible programs can directly be treated as code and evaluated, and of course the other way round too. Any piece of code can be lifted into a data structure and be modified. Furthermore, names of functions or data type constructors can be reified, so the interpreter's symbol table is accessible at runtime. This makes it possible get the constructors of an arbitrary data type or the type of a function at run-time without much effort.

From the viewpoint of IP, HASKELL has on this matter its weak spot. As a typical statically typed language, types are only necessary until type checking is done. Once a piece of code has passed the type checker, type information can safely be dropped. Although this improves efficiency for compiled programs, when doing program synthesis, this information is necessary though. Lifting code to a meta-level and back, as done with MAUDE's `upXYZ` functions is only available quite restricted. Also reification cannot be done so easily since again, there is no access to the symbol table after type checking. There are various library extensions for HASKELL especially for GHC, to alleviate these problems, e.g. Template Haskell (TH) (15) for compile-time metaprogramming and `Data.Dynamic` and `Data.Typeable` to allow for dynamic typing. Why they are not useful for us though, we will explain in the following..

Usually, in HASKELL expressions are represented as an algebraic data type:

```
data Exp
  = VarE Name
  | ConE Name
  | LitE Lit
  | AppE Exp Exp
```

Template Haskell's dual quasi-quoting (`[||]`) and splicing (`$`) operators would provide us with the means to transform code into such an algebraic data type and these expressions back into code, similar to MAUDE's `upXYZ` functions. So `[|1|]` would be `LitE (IntegerL 1)` inside the TH's `Q` monad and `$(LitE (IntegerL 1))` would be replaced by the `Integer` value `1` by the compiler. However, this is only done at compile-time and without types of the quoted code itself. This simply comes from TH's use case to be able to write code-generating macros, so the purpose of quoting and splicing is really to coerce expressions into real code at compile-time and evaluate it at run-time instead of having an algebraic representation of that code at run-time.

Similarly, the dynamic typing library extension of HASKELL is not appropriate for us, too. Its main idea is by creating a type class `Typeable` to be able to compare the type of arbitrary and unknown values. For example the function `toDyn :: Typeable a => a -> Dynamic` from `Data.Dynamic`. Without knowing the type of an arbitrary value, but being a member of `Typeable`, a representation of its type can be created and e.g. compared. However, in our case we are not interested in a type representation of an expression, but of the type representation of an expression when interpreted as code.

In the rest of this section we will look at the HASKELLspecific details of the new IGOR 2 implementation.

3.1 Expressions, Types, and Terms

Finally, there is nothing else for us but to write our own expression type and tag it with an also algebraic representation of its underlying type.

```
type Name = String
data TExp
  = TVarE Name Type
  | TConE Name Type
  | TLitE Lit Type
  | TAppE TExp TExp Type
  | TWildE Type
data Lit
  = CharL Char
  | IntL Int
  | StringL String
```

So a typed expression is either a variable, a constant, a literal, or an application of them. For simplicity let a `Name` be just a `String`. Neglecting the types for the moment, the expression `(:) 1 ((:) 2 [])`[2] would be represented as follows:

```
TAppE (TAppE (TConE ":")
             (TLitE (IntL 1)))
      (TAppE (TAppE (TConE ":")
                    (TLitE (IntL 2)))
             (TConE "[]"))
```

The algebraic data type of a type looks similar, where a type is either a type variable, a type constant, an arrow, or an application of them.

```
type Cxt = [Type]
data Type
   = ForallT [Name] Cxt Type
```

[2] aka `1:2:[]`. or `[1,2]`.

```
  -- variables in scope, class context, type
  | VarT Name
  | ConT Name
  | ArrowT
  | AppT Type Type
```

Additionally, there is a forall type, allowing us to restrict a type variable to a certain type class. As a short example, the type `(Show a):: a -> [Int]` is represented as the following algebraic expression:

```
ForallT ["a"] [AppT (ConT "Show")
                (VarT "a")]
    (AppT (AppT ArrowT (VarT "a"))
          (AppT ListT (ConT "Int")))
```

For our convenience, we also create the `class Typed` to easily have access to a type of an expression or the like.

```
class Typed t where
  typeOf :: t -> Type
instance Typed TExp where
  -- omitted
```

For `TExp`, the function `typeOf` is just a projection on the last argument, i.e. the type of an expression constructor.

To work with `TExp` and `Type` in the sense of terms we make them all instances of a `class Term` which provides the basis for fundamental operations on terms. The function `sameSymAtRoot` compares two term only at their root symbol, `subterms` returns all immediate subterms of a term and `root` is the inverse of it such that `root t (subterms t)= t`. The functions `isVar`, `toVar`, and `fromVar` provide a type independent way to check for variables, access their name and create a variable from a name.

```
class (Eq t) => Term t where

  sameSymAtRoot :: t -> t -> Bool
  subterms      :: t -> [t]
  root          :: t -> ([t] -> t)
  isVar         :: t -> Bool
  toVar         :: t -> Name -> t
  fromVar       :: t -> Name

instance Term Type where
  -- omitted
instance Term TExp where
  -- omitted
```

Both, `Types` and `TExp` are instances of the `class Term`.

3.2 Specification Context

Up to now, we have seen how to represent expressions and types, but as mentioned earlier, this is not sufficient, since synthesis of a program takes place in a certain context. A small specification, which is itself a HASKELL module, could e.g. look like the following listing.

```
module FooMod where

data Peano = Z | S Peano
 deriving (Eq, Ord)

count :: [a] -> Peano
count []     = Z
count [a]    = S Z
count [a,b] = S S Z
```

Such a given specification is parsed and the IO examples for `count` are translated into `TExp`-expressions. Furthermore, all data type definition with their constructors and types have to be stored in a record modelling the context of this specification, i.e. all types and functions which are in scope. Since the standard `Prelude` is assumed to be allways in scope, their types and constructors are included statically. We use a named record for managing the context, where each field in this record is a `Map` from `Data.Map` storing the relevant key value pairs.

```
import qualified Data.Map as M

data SynCtx = SCtx
   { sctx_types      :: (M.Map Name Type)
   -- function name maps to its type
   , sctx_ctors      :: (M.Map Name Typo)
   -- constructor name maps to its type
   , sctx_classes    :: (M.Map Name [Name])
   -- class name maps to its superclasses
   , sctx_members  :: (M.Map Name [Name])
   -- class name maps to member functions names
   , sctx_instnces :: (M.Map Type [Name])
   -- type maps to classes
   , sctx_typesyns :: (M.Map Type Type)
 }deriving(Show)
```

It is common practise to hide the relevant plumbing of stateful computation inside a state monad (16), and so do we. While we are at it we can start stacking monads with monad transformers (17) and add error handling. Later we will go on in piling monads, and because this is the bottom one it is self-evident to the add the error monad here. Our context monad now looks as follows with an accessor function `lookIn` for our convenience.

```
type C a = StateT SynCtx (ErrorT String a)
```

```
(lookIn) :: (Ord a) =>
    a -> (SynCtx -> M.Map a b) -> C b
(lookIn) n f = gets f >>= \m ->
    maybe (fail "Not in context!")
          return
          (M.lookup n m)
```

The function `lookIn` can now be used, preferably infix, wherever we need information about names or types. For example, the expressions **"Peano"**`lookIn` `sctx_classes` yields the names of the classes `Peano` is an instance of, here [**"Eq"**,**"Ord"**].

3.3 Using Terms

The cornerstones of our synthesis algorithm are unification and anti-unification. Due to our type-tagged expression, computing the *most general unifier* or the *least general generalisation* of two terms will become stateful, when considering polymorphic types with type classes. Not only the terms have to be unified or generalised, but with respect to their types. For this purpose we create the classes `Unifiable` and `Antiunifiable` and make both `TExp` and `Type` instances of them.

Substitutions which replace variables by terms are essential when unifying or antiunifying terms. Let a `Substitution` be a list of pairs, such that the variable with the name on the left side is replaced by the term on the right side of the pair. Then we define our unification monad `U t` again as a monad transformer as follows.

```
type Substitution t = [(Name,t)]
nullSubst = []

type U t = StateT (Substitution t) C ()
```

Note that the last argument of `StateT` is the unit type. Consequently, a computation inside `U t` has no result, or put differently, the result is the state itself, i.e. the substitution which is modified on the way. Therefore, when computing the *most general unifier* (`mgu`) or the substitution with which two terms match `matchingS`, `unify` and `match` respectively are executed in the `U t` monad with the empty substitution as initial state. As result the final state is returned.

```
class (Term t) => Unifiable t where

 unify      :: t -> t -> U t

 mgu        :: t -> t -> C (Substitution t)
 mgu x y = execStateT (unify x y) nullSubst

 match      :: t -> t -> U t
```

```
matchingS :: t -> t -> C (Substitution t)
matchingS x y =
      execStateT (match x y) nullSubst

equal     :: (Unifiable t) =>
                t -> t -> C Bool
equal y x = matchingS x y >> return . null
      `catchError` \_ -> return False
```

Remember that we stacked the `U t` monad on top of our context monad `C` which supports error handling. So if two terms do not unify or match respectively, then `fail` is invoked inside `C`, otherwise a potentially empty substitution is returned inside `C`. The function `matchingS` returns the substitution that matches the first term on the second term and `equal` returns `True` if the computation inside `U t` succeeds with an empty substitution, `False` otherwise.

The `class Antiunifier` looks similar, but instead of a `Substitution` it uses the data type `VarImg` as state. `VarImg` stores a list of terms, i.e. the so called image, together with the variable subsuming these terms.

```
type VarImg t = [([t],Name)]
nullImg = []

type AU t = StateT (VarImg t) C t
```

However, unlike in the `U t` monad, there is a result of a computation in the `AU t` monad: The *least general generalisation* of the given terms. With the function `antiunify` we throw the state away and return the result of the monadic computation.

```
class (Term t) => Antiunifiable t where

    aunify            :: [t] -> AU t

    antiunify         :: [t] -> C t
    antiunify t       =
      runStateT (aunify t) nullImg
```

The types `TExp` and `Type` are now added as instances to these type classes. We omit the concrete implementations, since they are straight forward following the structure of the algebraic data types. All that is left to say that two `TExps` only unify/match/antiunify if and only if their types unify/match/antiunify.

3.4 Rules, Hypotheses, and Other Data Types

Now let us introduce the basic data types for the synthesis.

First of all we have a `Rule`, with a list of `TExps` on the left-hand side (`lhs`) and one `TExp` on the right-hand side (`rhs`).

```
data Rule = R { lhs :: [TExp]
              , rhs :: TExp }
```

Usually we are talking about a certain rule, a rule covering some I/O examples of a specific function. Therefore we need to store information about this specific function and the covered I/O examples together with the `Rule` in a covering rule `CovrRule`.

```
data CovrRule = CR
    { name  :: Name
    , rule  :: Rule
    , covr  :: [Int] }
```

The accessor functions `name`, `rule`, and `covr` return the name of the function, the rule itself, and the indices of the covered I/O examples. A `CovrRule` makes therefore only sense, when there is something the indices refer to. The data structure `IOData` answers this purpose. It is more or less a map, relating function names to list of rules, i.e. the I/O examples. Let for simplicity be `IOData` just a synonym.

```
type IOData = M.Map Name [Rule]
```

The indices in a `CovrRule` are just the position of rules in the list stored under a name. The indices should not be visible outside `IOData`. For this purpose there are a couple of functions to create and modify `CovrRule` referring to a certain `IOData`. We refrain from the concrete implementations here.

```
getAll :: Name -> IOData
       -> Maybe [CovrRule]
getNth :: Name -> IOData
       -> Int -> Maybe CovrRule
```

As the names suggest, `getAll` is simply a lookup and returns just a list of covering rules, each covering one I/O pair, and `getNth` just picks the nth of all. The following functions are used to breakup and fuse covering rules. So `breakup` returns a list of covering rule, each covering one I/O pair of those covered by the original one, and `fuse` is the inverse of it, fusing many covering rules into one which covers all their I/O pairs.

```
breakup :: CovrRule -> IOData -> [CovrRule]
fuse    :: [CovrRule] -> C CovrRule
```

We have to be inside the `C` monad for fusing, because we need to antiunify the rules to be covered.

Hypotheses are the most fundamental data record storing a list of open covering rules, the closed rules as a list of declarations `Decl`, for each function one, and all calling dependencies between all functions to prevent the system to generate non-terminating programs. Let `CallDep` be the type of a calling dependency, which encapsualtes the information which function calls which.

```
type Decl = (Name,[Rule])
data Hypo  = HH { open     :: [CovrRule]
                , clsd     :: [Decl]
                , callings :: CallDep }
```

The basic idea behind calling dependencies is that if function f calls function g, then f depends on g ($f \rightarrow g$). The argument(s) of a call could either increase, decrease or remain in their syntactic size, thus the dependency could be of either type LT, EQ, or GT ($\xrightarrow{<}, \xrightarrow{=}, \xrightarrow{>}$).

Calling dependencies are transitive, so if $f \rightarrow g$ and $g \rightarrow h$ then also $f \rightarrow h$. The kind of the transitive dependency has the maximal type of all compound dependencies with the obvious ordering LT < EQ < GT.

If already a calling dependency $f \rightarrow g$ exists, the following possibilities for g calling f are allowed:

$$
\begin{aligned}
f \xrightarrow{>} g &\Rightarrow g \text{ is not allowed to call } f \\
f \xrightarrow{=} g &\Rightarrow g \xrightarrow{<} f \\
f \xrightarrow{<} g &\Rightarrow g \xrightarrow{<} f \text{ or } g \xrightarrow{=} f \\
f = g &\Rightarrow f \xrightarrow{<} f
\end{aligned}
$$

If there is no such calling dependency, all possibilities are allowed. To check, whether a call is admissible and to get all allowed possible calls two functions exist.

```
admissible   :: (Name,Ordering,Name) -> CallDep -> Bool
allowedCalls :: Name -> CallDep -> M.Map Name [Ordering]
```

The first one checks if the given (new) calling dependency is admissible, and the second returns for each function in a CallDep which additional calls to it are allowed. If a function is not mentioned in the Map returned by allowedCalls, anything goes.

3.5 Comparing Rules and Hypotheses

To compare rules and hypotheses to decide which to process we establish the class Rateable with the member function rate which returns for each member an Int value inside C.

```
class Rateable r where
   rate :: r -> C Int
```

Hypotheses should be rated with regard to their number of different partitions, i.e. patterns on the left-hand side of all their rules that do not match any other pattern. This is motivated by some kind of Occam's razor, preferring programs with few rules.

```
instance Rateable Hypo where
   rate h        =  numberOfPartitions h


numberOfPartitions  :: Hypo -> RatingData
numberOfPartitions h =  liftM length $
    foldM leastPatterns $ allRules h
  where
```

```
leastPatterns [] p        = return [p]
leastPatterns (p1:ps) p2 = do
p1gtp2 <- match `on` lhs p1 p2
p2gtp1 <- match `on` lhs p2 p1
if p1gtp2 then return (p2:ps)
  else if p2gtp1 then return (p1:ps)
       else liftM (p1:)(leastPatterns ps p2)
```

Covering rules are rated with regard to the longest chain of function calls they are in, so preferring rules causing less nested function calls. To compute the length of this longest path in the call dependencies, always a `CallDep` is required.

```
instance Rateable (CallDep,CovrRule) where
   rate (cd,cr)  =  return.length (longestPath (name cr) cd)
```

3.6 The Synthesis Monad

For searching a space of hypotheses we need to maintain a data structure representing this search space. In each step, the best hypothesis w.r.t to a certain heuristic is selected and from it an appropriate rule, again w.r.t an *a priori* defined heuristic is chosen. Refining one rule results in multiple sets of rules, because multiple refinement operators are used and each operator may result itself in multiple rules.

So let r be a rule and $\rho_1 \ldots \rho_n$ are refinement operators, then are $\rho_i(r)$ the rules resulting in applying ρ_i to r. If R is the set of all rules occurring in any hypothesis h, then is H the set of all hypotheses, with H included in the powerset of R, where each h is treated as a set of rules. Applying the refinement operators to a rule r in R results in $R' = R \setminus \{r\} \cup \{\rho_1(r), \ldots, \rho_n(r)\}$, thus changing H to $H' = H \setminus \{h|r \in h\} \cup \{h_i|h_i = h \setminus \{r\} \cup \rho_i(r)\}$ for $i = 1 \ldots n$.

This makes the implementation of our search approach lack elegance when compared to breadth-first search combinators proposed by Spivey (18; 19), where the space for breadth-first search can be defined as an infinite list. Katayama for example efficiently uses this approach (20; 7), because he is able to define his search space intensionally *a priori*.

Following the current implementation, this is not applicable for us. Hypotheses represent partial or unfinished programs, so our search space changes over time, because refinement operators may but need not finish a hypotheses. Rather it is refined to multiple, also unfinished, successor hypotheses. Thus, refining one rule may affect multiple hypotheses and change the ordering in the search space after each step.

Therefore we need to pull the whole search space explicitly through all our computations. Again, we use a stateful transformer on top of our `C` monad.

```
data Igor = Igor { iodata :: IOData
                 , searchSpace :: HSpace}

type I a = StateT Igor C a
```

```
modifyHS :: (HSpace -> HSpace) -> IM()
modifyHS f = modify (\igor@(Igor _ sp _) ->
                igor{searchSpace = f sp})

modifyIO ::(IOData -> IOData) -> IM()
modifyIO f = modify (\igor@(Igor io _ _) ->
                igor{iodata = f io})
```

The data structure Igor bundles the data structures IOData, known from section 3.4 to manage the various IO examples and HSpace, a priority queue on hypotheses w.r.t. to their heuristical rating. HSpace also supports efficient access to hypotheses by their rules to facilitate updating hypotheses after one refinement step. Igor serves as state for the monad I. The functions modifyHS and modifyIO allow us to modify HSpace and IOData inside I.

The main loop returns a list of equivalent programs inside I, w.r.t. the given heuristic, explaining the IO examples of the target function. Each program consists of a list of declarations Decl where each Decl defines one function by at least one Rule. First it fetches the currently best hypotheses, extracts the call dependencies and the unfinished rules from this hypothesis. If there are no open rules in all candidate hypotheses, the loop is exited and the candidate hypotheses are returned as result. Otherwise one rule is chosen for refinement, refined using the call dependencies and thus modifying the search space. After all, the loop is entered again.

```
type Prog = [Decl]

enterLoop :: I [Prog]
enterLoop =  do
  chs         <- currentBestHypos
  (deps ,crs) <- chooseOneHypo chs
  if (null crs) then stopWith chs
    else chooseOneRule crs >>= refine deps >> enterLoop
```

Finally, refine computes all refinements, introduced in Section 2, of the given unfinished rule with refineRule and propagates the result, a set of all possible refinements, to the whole search space and updates all affected hypotheses with propagate.

```
refine :: CallDep -> CovrRule -> I ()
refine cd cr =
    refineRule cd cr >>= (modifyHS .) . propagate $ cr

refineRule :: CallDep -> CovrRule -> IM [(CovrRules ,[Call])]
refineRule cd cr = do
    parts <- partition cr
    cllfs <- callFunction cd cr
    subfs <- inventSubfunction cr
    return $ parts ++ subfs ++ cllfs
```

4 Empirical Results

To test our new implementation (in the following named as IGOR 2_H) against the old we have chosen some usual example problems on lists. As usually, they incorporate different recursions patterns, simple linear as in *last* or mutual recursive as in *odd/even*. Most of the problems suggest for inventing auxiliary function as e.g. *lasts*, *repeatlst*, *sort*, *reverse*, *oddpos* but only *reverse* explicitly needs to it to be solvable.

Most of the problems have the usual semantics on lists and can be found in a standard library of a functional Language. Table 1 shows a short explanation of each of them nevertheless.

Table 1. Problem descriptions

add	is addition on Peano integers,
append	appends two lists,
drop	drops the first n elements of a list,
evenpos	are all elements in a list which index is even,
init	are all elements but the last of a list,
last	is the last element in a list,
last	maps *last* over a list of lists,
length	is the length of a list as Peano integer,
odd/even	defines *odd* and *even* mutually recursive on Peano integers,
oddpos	are all elements in a list which index is odd,
repeatfst	overwrites all elements in a list with the first,
repeatlst	overwrites all elements in a list with the last,
reverse	reverses a list,
shiftl	shifts all elements in a list one position to the left,
shiftr	shifts all elements in a list one position to the right,
sort	sorts a list of Peano integers using insertion into a sorted list,
swap	changes the position of two consecutive elements in a list,
switch	changes the position of the first and the last element,
take	takes the first n elements from a list, and
weave	merges two lists into one by alternating their elements.

The tests were run on a laptop with a 1.6Ghz Intel Pentium processor with 2GB RAM using Ubuntu 8.10. IGOR2.2 with MAUDE 2.4 and version 0.5.9.4 of the HASKELL implementation have been used. All programs as well as the used specification and a batch file for the HASKELL implementation can be downloaded from our webpage[3].

Keeping in mind that MAUDE is an interpreted language and IGOR 2_H is compiled, it is not surprising that the new implementation is faster. A speedup by the factor of 10 or more in most of the cases is more than expected, though. Table 2 shows all runtimes and the approximte ratio of old to new.

[3] `http://www.cogsys.wiai.uni-bamberg.de/effalip/download.html`

Table 2. Runtimes on different problems in seconds

	IGOR 2	IGOR 2_H	$\frac{\text{IGOR 2}}{\text{IGOR } 2_H}$ *		IGOR 2	IGOR 2_H	$\frac{\text{IGOR 2}}{\text{IGOR } 2_H}$ *
add	0.236	0.076	3	*repeatfst*	0.052	0.004	13
append	46.338	0.080	579	*repeatlst*	0.100	0.004	25
drop	0.084	0.004	21	*reverse*	0.617	0.032	19
evenpos	0.056	0.004	14	*shiftl*	0.084	0.008	11
init	0.024	0.004	6	*shiftr*	0.308	0.020	15
last	0.024	0.001	24	*sort*	0.148	0.012	12
lasts	6.744	0.020	337	*swap*	0.108	0.008	14
length	0.028	0.001	28	*switch*	2.536	0.036	70
odd/even	0.080	0.004	20	*take*	1.380	0.012	115
oddpos	18.617	0.048	388	*weave*	0.348	0.036	13

* rounded to nearest proper fraction

5 Conclusion

We introduced the new program design of our system IGOR 2, which has been ported from MAUDE to HASKELL. We described how, for our purpose necessary, features of the homoiconic language MAUDE can be simulated in HASKELL using a stateful monad transformer. Although we can not model MAUDE's full reflexive capabilities, we can simulate all functionality necessary in our use case. With our new implementation we paved the way to use higher-order context during our synthesis and extract information from types and their classes usable as background knowledge. Keeping our new implementation as close as possible to our old, it was possible to keep all features of our system as e.g. termination by construction of both synthesised programs and IGOR 2-algorithm, minimality of generalisation, using arbitrary user-defined data types and background knowledge, and others.

For the future we plan to utilise universal properties of higher-order functions such as *fold*, *map* and *filter* to introduce certain recursion schemes as programming patterns when applicable. In this context we will make use of type information which is now accessible. Furthermore, it should be promising to reconsider the current algorithm to make use of lazy data structures to better take advantage of the benefits of lazy evaluation. Memoization could also be helpful to avoid propagating the change of a rule over the whole search space.

References

[1] Hofmann, M.: Automatic Construction of XSL Templates – An Inductive Programming Approach. VDM Verlag, Saarbrücken (2007)

[2] Biermann, A.W., Kodratoff, Y., Guiho, G.: Automatic Program Construction Techniques. The Free Press, NY (1984)

[3] Summers, P.D.: A methodology for LISP program construction from examples. Journal ACM 24, 162–175 (1977)

[4] Kitzelmann, E., Schmid, U.: Inductive synthesis of functional programs: An explanation based generalization approach. Journal of Machine Learning Research 7, 429–454 (2006)
[5] Kitzelmann, E.: Data-driven induction of recursive functions from I/O-examples. In: Kitzelmann, E., Schmid, U. (eds.) Proceedings of the ECML/PKDD 2007 Workshop on Approaches and Applications of Inductive Programming (AAIP 2007), pp. 15–26 (2007)
[6] Olsson, R.J.: Inductive functional programming using incremental program transformation. Artificial Intelligence 74(1), 55–83 (1995)
[7] Katayama, S.: Systematic search for lambda expressions. In: van Eekelen, M.C.J.D. (ed.) Revised Selected Papers from the Sixth Symposium on Trends in Functional Programming, TFP 2005, vol. 6, pp. 111–126. Intellect (2007)
[8] Quinlan, J.R.: Learning first-order definitions of functions. Journal of Artificial Intelligence Research 5, 139–161 (1996)
[9] Muggleton, S., Feng, C.: Efficient induction of logic programs. In: Proceedings of the 1st Conference on Algorithmic Learning Theory, Ohmsma, Tokyo, Japan, pp. 368–381 (1990)
[10] Muggleton, S.: Inverse entailment and Progol. New Generation Computing, Special issue on Inductive Logic Programming 13(3-4), 245–286 (1995)
[11] Flener, P.: Inductive Logic Program Synthesis with Dialogs. In: Muggleton, S. (ed.) Proceedings of the 6th International Workshop on Inductive Logic Programming, Stockholm University, Royal Institute of Technology, pp. 28–51 (1996)
[12] Hernández-Orallo, J., Ramírez-Quintana, M.J.: Inverse narrowing for the induction of functional logic programs. In: Freire-Nistal, J.L., Falaschi, M., Ferro, M.V. (eds.) Joint Conference on Declarative Programming, pp. 379–392 (1998)
[13] Mitchell, T.M.: Machine Learning. McGraw-Hill Higher Education, New York (1997)
[14] Kitzelmann, E.: Analytical inductive functional programming. In: Hanus, M. (ed.) LOPSTR 2008. LNCS, vol. 5438, pp. 87–102. Springer, Heidelberg (2009)
[15] Sheard, T., Jones, S.P.: Template metaprogramming for Haskell. In: Chakravarty, M.M.T. (ed.) ACM SIGPLAN Haskell Workshop 2002, pp. 1–16. ACM Press, New York (2002)
[16] Wadler, P.: The essence of functional programming. In: Conference Record of the Nineteenth Annual ACM SIGPLAN-SIGACT Symposium on Principles of Programming Languages, Albequerque, New Mexico, pp. 1–14 (1992)
[17] King, D., Wadler, P.: Combining monads. Mathematical Structures in Computer Science, pp. 61–78 (1992)
[18] Spivey, J.M.: Combinators for breadth-first search. J. Funct. Program. 10(4), 397–408 (2000)
[19] Spivey, M., Seres, S.: The algebra of searching. In: Proceedings of a symposium in celebration of the work of. MacMillan, Basingstoke (2000)
[20] Katayama, S.: Efficient exhaustive generation of functional programs using montecarlo search with iterative deepening. In: Ho, T.-B., Zhou, Z.-H. (eds.) PRICAI 2008. LNCS (LNAI), vol. 5351, pp. 199–210. Springer, Heidelberg (2008)

Automated Method Induction: Functional Goes Object Oriented

Thomas Hieber and Martin Hofmann

University Bamberg - Cognitive Systems Group,
Feldkirchenstr. 21, 96050 Bamberg, Germany
thomas-wolfgang.hieber@stud.uni-bamberg.de,
martin.hofmann@uni-bamberg.de
http://www.uni-bamberg.de/kogsys/

Abstract. The development of software engineering has had a great deal of benefits for the development of software. Along with it came a whole new paradigm of the way software is designed and implemented - object orientation. Today it is a standard to have UML diagrams translated into program code wherever possible. However, as few tools really go beyond this we demonstrate a simple functional representation for objects, methods and object-properties. In addition we show how our inductive programming system IGORII cannot only understand those basic notions like referencing methods within objects or using a simple protocol called *message-passing*, but how it can even learn them by a given specification - which is the major feature of this paper.

1 Introduction

IGORII is a system for synthesizing recursive functional programs, which learns potentially recursive functions solely from input/output (I/O) examples. Since IGORII is naturally based in functional programming, the main focus of this paper lies on finding a way to use IGORII for program inference in an object oriented background, which requires to express the behaviour of objects and method calls by I/O examples. In order to do so, it is necessary to find a way to express object oriented programs in a functional way and as mainstream software for daily use is commonly not created with functional programming languages it is about time to raise the question whether it is possible to adapt object oriented language features to a functional, *Inductive Programming* setting.

In addition, it is necessary to enable an object oriented programmer to provide input to the synthesis system as unobtrusive as possible. For this purpose, an interface for Eclipse will allow a programmer to use annotations in order to provide input for our induction process, thus seamlessly integrating with software engineering tools like *Rational Software Architect (RSA)*. More practical concerns regarding the plug-in itself can be found in [1].

In this paper we will be introducing the concept of *Constructor Term Rewriting Systems (CTRS)* with respect to IGORII and how it can be used in order

U. Schmid, E. Kitzelmann, and R. Plasmeijer (Eds.): AAIP 2009, LNCS 5812, pp. 159–173, 2010.

to construct a simple algebra to represent object orientation in a functional environment. After this we are going to show some examples to demonstrate how this can be done practically with the help of IGORII. The last chapter takes one step further explaining how this approach has been integrated in a prototype plug-in for the *Eclipse IDE.*

2 Status Quo

In the past 30 years, many different inductive programming (IP) systems have been developed, many of them sharing a functional approach. The extraction of programs from input/output examples started in the the seventies and has been greatly influenced by Summers' [2] paper on the induction of *LISP* programs. After the great success of *Inductive Logical Programming (ILP)* on classification learning in the nineties, research on IP shifted more to this area. Prominent ILP systems for IP are for example FOIL [3], GOLEM [4] or PROGOL [5] - systems which make use of *Prolog* and predicate logic.

Later, the functional approach was taken up again by the analytical approaches IGORI [6], and IGORII [7] [8] and by the evolutionary/generate-and-test based approaches ADATE [9] and MAGICHASKELLER [10].

All in all you can subsume the concern of *Inductive Programming* as the search for algorithms which use as little additional information as possible to generate correct computer programs from a given minimal specification consisting of input/output examples. Similar to classifier learning, *IP* systems can be characterised by a *preference* and a *restriction bias* [11].

At the same time functional languages have had to face the development in programming paradigms which led to many approaches to support object orientation. Established functional languages have their own object oriented extensions like OCaml [12] or OOHaskell ([13]). Additionally there are various approaches to include an object system in a functional language without changing the type system or the compiler (see e.g. [13] for a Haskell related overview).

For our purpose we do not need such sophisticated techniques (yet), therefore we content ourselves with taking on a quite naïve and very simplified perspective, though sufficient for our case, and treat objects merely as tuples.

On the other hand there are some very powerful tools for object oriented programmers which support automated code-generation to a certain extent and the community for *Automated Software Engineering* is very productive to take this even further. In this context it is inevitable to have a look at program synthesis since we ideally do not want to stop at automatically generating class files from UML diagrams like IBM's *RSA*, or generate a GUI by 'WYSIWYG' editors such as *NetBeans* or *Visual Studio.*

3 Constructor Term Rewriting

For our purpose it shall be sufficient to define a functional program as a set of equations consisting of pairs of terms over a many-sorted signature Σ . We are going to adapt the common nomenclature as used in [14] when describing the concepts below using *terms* and *term rewriting.* A *signature* is defined as a set of function symbols Σ and a set of variables $\mathcal{X}$ which are used to form terms. In other words, terms over Σ and $\mathcal{X}$ are denoted $\mathcal{T}_\Sigma(\mathcal{X})$ whereas variable free terms (ground-terms) are just labelled $\mathcal{T}_\Sigma$. Since Σ is many-sorted, all our terms are typed.

One important differentiation to be alert of is that function symbols can either be datatype *constructors* or (user-)defined *functions.* In this fashion $\Sigma = \mathcal{C} \cup \mathcal{F}, \mathcal{C} \cap \mathcal{F} = \emptyset$, where $\mathcal{C}$ contains the constructors and $\mathcal{F}$ the defined function symbols. Our inductive programming system IgorII represents result programs as a set of recursive equations (rules) over a signature Σ. These rules consist of a left-hand side (lhs) and a right-hand side (rhs). While a rhs consists of regular Σ terms $\mathcal{T}_\Sigma(\mathcal{X})$, the lhs has the form $F(p_1, ..., p_n)$ and is called the *function head* with $F \in \mathcal{F}$ being the name of the function implemented by the current rewrite rule (plus some others). The $p_i \in \mathcal{T}_\mathcal{C}(\mathcal{X})$ consist of constructors and variables only.

$Var(t)$ are all variables of a Term t. The constructor terms p_i on the lhs of an equation may contain variables and are called *pattern.* All variables on the rhs of an equation are required to occur in the pattern on the lhs. We say that such variables are *bound* (or *unbound* otherwise). A *substitution* is a function $\sigma : \mathcal{X} \to \mathcal{T}_\Sigma(X)$. For our purpose, we write it in postfix and extend it to terms replacing all contained variables simultaneously. So $t\sigma$ is the result of applying the *substitution* σ to term t, i.e., applying σ to each $v \in Var(t)$. If $s = t\sigma$, then t is called a *generalization* of s and we say that t *subsumes* s and s matches t by σ, respectively. Given two terms t_1 and t_2 and a substitution σ such that $t_1\sigma = t_2\sigma$, we say that t_1 and t_2 *unify.* Given a finite set of terms $S = s, s', s'', ...$ then there exists a term t which subsumes all terms in S and which itself is subsumed by any other term also subsuming all terms in S. The term t is called the *least general generalisation* (lgg) [15] of the terms in S. To generalise a lggs to a set of equations, we tacitly treat the equal sign as a constructor symbol with the lhs and the rhs as arguments

The operational semantics of a set of equations in the above mentioned form are best described in terms of a *term rewriting system* (TRS). An equation can be read as a *simplification* (or *rewrite*) *rule* replacing a term matching the lhs by the rhs. TRS which equations have the above described form are called *constructor term rewriting systems* (*CTRS*). From now on, we use the terms equation and rule as well as equation set and *CTRS* interchangeably throughout the paper, depending on the context. Let i be the vector $i_1, ..., i_n$. Evaluating an n-ary function F for an input i consists of repeatedly rewriting the term $F(i)$ w.r.t. the rewrite relation R implied by the *CTRS* until the term is in *normal form,* i.e., cannot be rewritten further. A sequence of (in)finitely many rewrite steps $t_0 \to_R t_1 \to_R ...$ is called *derivation.* If a derivation starts with term t and results in a normal form s this is written $t \xrightarrow{!}_R s$. We say that t normalises to s and call s the normal form of t. In order to define a function on a domain (a set of ground terms) by a CTRS, no two derivations starting with the same ground term may lead to different normal forms, i.e., normal forms must be unique. A sufficient condition for this is that no two lhss of a CTRS unify; this is a sufficient condition for a CTRS to be *confluent*. A CTRS is *terminating* if each possible derivation terminates. A sufficient condition for termination is that the arguments/inputs of recursive calls strictly decrease within each derivation and w.r.t. a well founded order.

Each rewrite rule may be augmented with a condition that must be met to apply the conditional rule. A term rewriting system or constructor system is called conditional constructor term rewriting system (CCTRS) respectively if it contains at least one conditional rule. A condition is an ordered conjunction of equality constraints $v_i = u_i$ with $v_i, u_i \in \mathcal{T}(X)$. Each u_i must be grounded if the lhs of the rule is instantiated and if all equalities $v_j = u_j$ with $j < i$ evaluate to true, then u_i evaluates to some ground normal form. For the v_i must hold (i) either the same as for the u_i or (ii) v_i may contain unbound variables but then it must be a constructor term. In the first case also v_i evaluates to some ground normal form and the equality evaluates to true if both normal forms are equal. In the second case the equality evaluates to true if v_i and the ground normal form of u_i unify. Then the free variables in v_i are bound and may be used in the following conjuncts and the rhs of the rule. We write conditional rules in the form: $l \to r \Leftarrow v_1 = u_1, ..., v_n = u_n$. The ! indicates negation, thus $!(v_i = u_i)$ holds if both normal forms do not unify. Rules without a condition are called unconditional. If we apply a defined function to ground constructor terms $\mathcal{F}(i_1, ..., i_n)$, we call the i_i inputs of $\mathcal{F}$. If such an application normalises to a ground constructor term o we call o output. A CCTRS is terminating if all rewriting processes end up in a normal form. In order to implement functions the outputs are required to be unique for each particular input vector. This is the case if the TRS is confluent.

4 Igor

IGORII is a prototype for constructing recursive functional programs from few non-recursive, possibly non-ground example equations describing a subset of the input/output (I/O) behaviour of a function to be implemented. For all of the example specifications in IGORII the signatures of the following functions shall be established:

$$[\,] : \to List \tag{1}$$

$$cons : Element \times List \to List \tag{2}$$

$$s : Nat \to Nat \tag{3}$$

$$0 : \to Nat \tag{4}$$

$$t : \to Boolean \tag{5}$$

$$f : \to Boolean \tag{6}$$

Here is a simple example of how the list-function *even* would be presented to the system as I/O examples. Please note that constructor symbols and function names are in lower case, variables in upper case.

```
even(0) = t
even(s(0)) = f
even(s(s(0))) = t
even(s(s(s(0)))) = f
even(s(s(s(s(0))))) = t
```

The induction of a correct program in IGORII is organised as a best-first search. During a search, a hypothesis is a set of equations entailing the example equations but potentially with unbound variables in the right-hand side. Starting from an initial hypothesis, successively the best hypothesis, w.r.t. some preference bias, is selected and an unfinished rule is chosen and replaced by its successor rules. This is continued until the current best hypothesis does not contain any unbound variables.

Initial Rule. The initial hypothesis contains one rule per target function. This rule is a *least general generalisation* (lgg) of the example equations. The lgg for the previous *even*-examples is:

```
even (N) = B
```

Without getting into theoretical details, it should be sufficient to know for now that constructor symbols or sub-terms occurring at the same position in all equations are kept, everything else is substituted by variables. We say, that the rule covers all previous examples, because the pattern on the lhs subsumes each lhs of the examples. Of course, this rule is not a functional program, because it contains an unbound variable on the rhs. To remedy this, the initial hypothesis is stepwise re-defined. For this purpose, IGORII employs three transformation operators:

1. The I/O examples belonging to the open initial rule are partitioned into subsets and for each subset, a new initial rule (with a more specific pattern, or left-hand side, than the original rule) is computed.
2. If the open rhs has a constructor as root, i.e., does not consist of a single unbound variable, then all sub-terms containing unbound variables are treated as sub-problems. A new auxiliary function is introduced for each such sub-term.
3. The open right-hand side is replaced by a (recursive) call to a defined function. The arguments of the call may be computed by new auxiliary functions. Hence, computing the arguments is considered as a new sub-problem.

Splitting an open rule. The first operator partitions the I/O examples belonging to a rule into subsets such that the patterns of the resulting initial rules are disjoint and more specific than the pattern of the original rule. Finding such a partition is done as follows:

A position in the pattern p with a variable resulting from generalising the corresponding sub-terms in the subsumed example inputs is identified. This implies that at least two of the subsumed inputs have different constructor symbols at this position. Now all subsumed inputs are partitioned such that all of them with the same constructor at this position belong to the same subset. Together with the corresponding example outputs this yields a partition of the example equations whose inputs are subsumed by p. Since more than one position may be selected, different partitions leading to different sets of new initial rules may result.

Introducing (Recursive) Function Calls and Auxiliary Functions. In cases (2) and (3) auxiliary functions are invented. This includes the generation of I/O-examples from which they are induced. For case (2) this is done as follows: Function calls are introduced by matching the currently considered outputs, i.e., those outputs whose inputs match the pattern of the currently considered rule, with the outputs of any defined function. If all current outputs match, the rhs of the current unfinished rule can be set to a call of the matched defined function. The argument of the call must map the currently considered inputs to the inputs of the matched function. For case (3), the example inputs of the new defined function also equal the currently considered inputs. The outputs are the corresponding sub-terms of the currently considered outputs.

Terms matching the lhs of a rule, where a variable can subsume any sub-term of the accordant type, can be replaced by the rhs of this rule. This procedure is repeated until the term does not match any more lhs.

Example. Using the data type specification and the I/O examples given below, we will sketch the IGORII algorithm by developing a solution for the list-function *even*. Starting from the initial rule

```
even(N) = B
```

The IGORII algorithm successively develops a solution that is correct and complete w.r.t. the I/O examples using the previously described operators.

In the first step, the example set is partitioned w.r.t. root constructor symbol in the first argument.

```
even(0) = t
even(s(N)) = B
```

The second rule now covers all examples but the first one. In a second step, again a partition is introduced. Now the constructor symbol of the first subterm below the root position discriminates the I/O examples.

```
even(0) = t
even(s(0)) = f
even(s(s(N))) = B
```

The first and the second rule are the base cases of the target function, both covering only one I/O example. The third rule, becoming the recursive call, covers the rest. Following the second partition of the rule set, an auxiliary function is introduced since the rhs contains a constructor symbol:

```
even(0) = t
even(s(0)) = f
even(s(s(N))) = sub1(s(s(N)))
sub1(s(s(N)) = even(N)
```

This result computed by IGORII is a correct and complete w.r.t. the I/O examples, recursive solution to the problem.

Up to this point it should be clear how in the context of a CTRS, IGORII develops a correct functional solution from a set of non–recursive I/O examples. What is left to do now is how we can manage to encapsulate the functional flavour in an object oriented protocol since we are trying to bring those two paradigms together.

5 Igor and Object Orientation

In order to model object oriented processes in a functional way we are going to use two *Constructor Term Rewriting Systems (CTRSs).* This is done for quite a simple purpose: *encapsulation.* One *CTRS* will be employed to model object orientation as a simple protocol, the other one will be used to encapsulate the problem domain as described in section 3. This is as much as we need to understand for now as we are going to come back to that later on.

The two *CTRSs* are going to be defined like this:

$$C_{OO} : \Sigma = \mathcal{F} \cup \mathcal{C} \cup \{\mathcal{D}\}, \mathcal{X}, \mathcal{E} \tag{7}$$

$$C_P : \Sigma' = \mathcal{F}' \cup \mathcal{C}', \mathcal{X}', \mathcal{E}' \tag{8}$$

The first equation describes the object oriented protocol which will be introduced in this section. One main difference to the second one has to be remarked, since $\mathcal{D}$ represents a *constant* which will be used as place holder for terms over C_{OO}

The second equation defines the *CTRS* describing terms in the problem domain. They shall be related to each other in a way that C_P is a proper Sub CTRS of C_{OO}.

The concepts *Super Constructor Term Rewriting System* (C_{OO}) and *Sub Constructor Term Rewriting System* (C_P) shall be defined like this:

Definition 1. C_P is a Sub CTRS of C_{OO} ($C_P \subset C_{OO}$), iff

$$\begin{aligned} \Sigma' \subset \Sigma \; s.t. \; \mathcal{F}' \subset \mathcal{F} \; and \; \mathcal{C}' &\subset \mathcal{C} \\ \mathcal{X}' &\subset \mathcal{X} \\ \mathcal{E}' &\subset \mathcal{E} \end{aligned}$$

Definition 2. C_{OO} is a Super CTRS of C_P, iff

$$C_P \subset C_{OO}$$

5.1 The Super CTRS

Since the aim of this paper is to define an algebraic definition of a simple object oriented protocol, the major part of this section is concerned with the *Super CTRS* and how it models object orientation. Before we proceed it is important to point out that it is not in the focus of this work to create a full-scale model of object orientation. Rather have we singled out a couple of interesting mechanics and put them together to a tiny fragment of object orientation, the one which is concerned with identifying methods and properties in an object and interacting with them.

For this we establish the already known concepts of methods and properties (a.k.a. member-variables) along with a protocol we call *message-passing*, which is used by objects in order to interchange data. The relevant parts contained in the protocol will now be described by relating them to Σ of C_{OO}. For this we need the constant $\mathcal{D}$, constructors $\mathcal{C}$ and the functions $\mathcal{F}$ themselves.

$$data :\rightarrow Data \tag{9}$$

Data will be treated as constant throughout the object oriented protocol, since it is used to have it as wild card for terms of the problem domain it should be self evident that it strictly consists of terms in C_P, in other words $T_{\Sigma'}(\mathcal{X}')$. This is also the actual trick which makes the two domains independent of each other, which should become clear in the course of this section.

The definition of an object in our algebra would look like this:

$$object : Identifier \times PropList \times MethodList \rightarrow Object \tag{10}$$

The constructor's arguments are the object's *Identifier*, a *List* of properties (object resident member variables) and a *List* of (object resident) methods. Later on it is going to be of importance whether an object contains a method or not - this is specified with the help of this constructor.

As the object constructor needs a list of properties to be provided it is time to find out how they can be constructed.

$$property : Identifier \times Data \rightarrow Property \tag{11}$$

Just like before, a property must be labelled with an *Identifier*, the value on the other hand seems rather obscure. *Data* is used to abstract the information contained within the property. This is a crucial section in this protocol since it is the 'wrapper' for our *Sub CTRS*. So, whenever *Data* is used it should be clear that it is the 'packaging' for terms of our problem domain and the only way to combine it with the object oriented protocol. Because it is intended to draw a clear distinction between the two *CTRSs* it is important to understand that using *Data* on the level of object oriented communication is more than enough and all to be aware of at this stage.

There are two more constructors left to define, the first is the one for a *Method*:

$$method : Identifier \times Message \rightarrow Method \tag{12}$$

As it is already evident that a method will have to be identified later on, an *Identifier* needs to be declared for it as done for *Object* and *Property.* The second argument is called *Message* and this is the important part in our protocol when it comes to object interaction. As soon as an object needs to call a method or get the value of a property on any other object (or even itself), it will send a *Message* which contains some kind of data.

The nature of the data becomes clear looking at the constructor of the *Message*:

$$message : Data \rightarrow Message \tag{13}$$

As seen in the *Property* constructor the actual nature of the data transported between objects is abstracted. And this should be quite self evident now since it has been the intention to keep the object oriented protocol strictly apart from the actual data processed with it's help. It is not necessary to know what is inside *Data,* since the only concern for now is how to transport it from one object to another.

This brings us to the concept of *message-passing.* The idea behind it is quite literal the exchange of messages, whenever we are trying to access an object's property or call one of it's methods. Before it is possible to call a function or a property's value they have to be looked up in the target objects' property list/method list.

This can be done by the two following functions:

$$Match\_method : Identifier \times MethodList \rightarrow Method \tag{14}$$

$$Match\_prop : Identifier \times PropList \rightarrow Property \tag{15}$$

For convenience, things are sped up now since it is not hard understanding how to access to the two lists containing the target object's methods/properties. And for now it is not a problem as it is our main focus to clarify how to access a method or a property given a random object. Those functions should demonstrate that a positive match of identifiers within an object's method/property list will return the method/property we are trying to address and raise an exception otherwise.

All that is left to do is to request either the value of it, or call it with a list of method arguments.

It has just been mentioned that the part where the method/property list from an object are extracted - so this is the formal approach in our protocol:

$$Call : Object \times Identifier \times Message \rightarrow Message \tag{16}$$

Up to now the development of signatures in C_{OO} has been delivered and it is intriguing to find out how to proceed further, since the protocol is far away from being complete. The major part of the work left to do will be carried out by IGORII, who will take those signatures and induce the according functions with the help of some simple I/O examples.

5.2 The Sub CTRS

As already pointed out, the *Sub CTRS* is entirely separated from the object-oriented message protocol. This means that it can encapsulate virtually *anything* without interfering with the *Super CTRS*. And this is where the beauty of our approach lies in since we have now successfully separated the way to represent a problem domain structurally from the way it is represented semantically. Since IGORII can only understand functional problem specifications it seems quite rational to have them represented using only terms over a functional algebra – in this case it is C_P.

6 Examples

In section 5 the introduction of two *CTRSs* has been used in order to define a simple object-oriented protocol encapsulating a functional problem domain. However, only signatures have been defined by now. And in order to receive the mechanics of the object-oriented methods like *Match_method*, *Match_prop* and *Call* the inductive programming system IGORII is going to be used to infer those methods just from a few I/O examples. When constructing I/O examples for the system, we use the signatures defined in section 5, which we will include again below:

$$Match\_method : Identifier \times MethodList \rightarrow Method \tag{17}$$

$$method : Identifier \times Message \rightarrow Method \tag{18}$$

The first method to infer is *Match_method*, however, in order to express an unsuccessful match, an *exception* shall be defined beforehand in the following manner:

$$exc : \rightarrow Method \tag{19}$$

Mind that the constant *exception* has not been defined earlier, it is just a placeholder for any kind of imaginable procedure to capture a 'no-match'. Apart from that, the *matching* process is passed a variable as identifier as well as a list of methods which of course would have been taken from an existing object. In case the requested identifier is matched by a resident method within the method list, the according method is returned, otherwise an exception is thrown.

The examples for the method itself read as follows:

```
match_method(Id1 []) = exc
match_method(Id2 []) = exc

match_method(Id1 cons(method(Id1 msg) [])) = method(Id1, msg)
match_method(Id1 cons(method(Id2 msg) [])) = exc
match_method(Id2 cons(method(Id1 msg) [])) = exc
match_method(Id2 cons(method(Id2 msg) [])) = method(Id2, msg)

[...]
```

IGORII takes those examples and constructs the following set of equations:

```
1) match_method(Id1 []) = exc

2) sub1(Id1 cons(method(Id2 msg) Restlist)) =
   Id1 <== !(Id1 = Id2)

3) sub2(Id1 cons(method(Id2 msg) Restlist)) =
   Restlist <== !(Id1 = Id2)

4) match_method(Id1 cons(method(Id2 msg) Restlist)) =
   match_method(sub1(Id1 cons(method(Id2 msg)
   sub2(Id1 cons(method(Id2 msg) Restlist) ))))
   <== !(Id1 = Id2)

5) match_method(Id1 cons(method(Id2 msg) Restlist) ) =
   method(Id1 msg) <== (Id1 = Id2)
```

The same result is returned for *Match_method*, which will be left out here since it is almost identical to *Match_method*. Moving one step further we are going to find out whether the *Call* method can be induced as easily - the answer is yes!

Remember the signature of *Call*:

$$Call : Object \times Identifier \times Message \rightarrow Message \tag{20}$$

Now it has been demonstrated that IGORII can not only understand, but also induce the simple object—oriented protocol which is reason enough to try and insert some terms from the problem domain into our specification. For this the example from section 4 is used, so the functional I/O examples for *even* will be encapsulated within an object oriented specification. As the signature requests an actual *Object* to be part of the call, it is going to be inserted as the variable *O* of the type *Object*. This is enough for our purpose here, since it is never used and remains constant within all our examples.

```
Call(O even message(0)) = message(t)
Call(O even message(s(0))) =  message(f)
Call(O even message(s(s(0)))) = message(t)
Call(O even message(s(s(s(0))))) = message(f)
Call(O even message(s(s(s(s(0)))))) = message(t)
```

The result is as straightforward as before, but notice how the *message-passing* is used consistently:

```
1) call(O even message(0)) = message(t)

2) call(O even message(s(0))) = message(f)

3) call(O even message(s(s(X1)))) =
   call(sub19 message(s(s(X1))))

4) sub19(message(s(s(X1))))  = message(X1)
```

Here it is clearly evident that the object-oriented terms do not obstruct IGORII in any way, an explanation as to why will be given shortly. Another more complex example has the system induce an operator which is very famous in object orientation - the *iteration*. For the sake of readability those examples are not wrapped in messages and within calls. That this is no big problem will be clear at the end of this section, so bear with us for now and just look at the example:

```
iterate([]) = []
iterate(cons(A [])) = cons(call(A))
iterate(cons(A cons(B []))) = cons(call(A) cons(call(B) []))
iterate(cons(A cons(B cons(C [])))) =
cons(call(A) cons(call(B) cons(call(C) [])))
```

The very abstract idea is that a rather abstract *Call* (which could be any defined method) is applied to every object within a list. As expected, IGORII comes up with a recursive solution to this problem:

```
1) iterate([]) = []

2) iterate(cons(Object Restlist)) =
   cons(sub1(cons(Object Restlist)) sub2(cons(Object Restlist)))

3) sub1(cons(Object Restlist)) = call(Object)

4) sub2(cons(Object Restlist)) =
   iterate(sub5(cons(Object Restlist)))

5) sub5(cons(Object Restlist)) = Restlist
```

As mentioned before have we reduced the complexity of our *Call* signature in order to increase readability of the examples. One question when dealing with all the object-orientation might have been urging all the time: *Isn't this a lot of overhead?*

Therefore we are going to combine the signatures of *Object*, *Call*, *Message* and *Method*, generating a *Call* of the signature:

$$Call : Object \times Identifier \times Message \rightarrow Message \tag{21}$$

Into the call (lines 1–8), an *Object* (line 3) is inserted, containing an identifier *OId*, an (empty) property list and two methods *even* and *odd* (all in line 3). When we would now call the function *even* (line 5) with a *Message* containing a singleton list as argument (line 7) it would look like this:

```
1: (
2:   # <-- Object: Identifier x PropList x MethodList
3:   (OId [] cons((even bool ([] [])) (odd bool ([] []))))
4:   # <-- Identifier
5:   even
6:   # <-- Message
7:   message(0
8: )
9: # <-- Message
10: = message(t)
```

This looks very bloated and one might wonder if all this is prone to slow down IGORII during the synthesizing? For this let us have a look how it anti-unifies the terms gradually:

```
(
 (OId [] cons((even bool ([] []) ) (odd bool ([] []))))
 even
 message(succ(0))
)
= message(f)

(
 (OId [] cons((even bool ([] [])) (odd bool ([] []))))
 even
 message(succ(succ(0)))
)
= message(t)
```

after anti-unification:

```
(
   (OId [] cons((even bool ([] [])) (odd bool ([] []))))
   even
   message(succ(t))
)
```

Looking at those examples you find the answer to the question if the protocol's overhead is impeding the system and at the same time you get the key aspect of all the examples and the increasing complexity: **it doesn't matter**! From this it will also be plain to understand why the iteration example has been kept quite simple with no *message-passing* involved at all. It would just be additionaly code around the problem specification itself. And that is the one which matters to IGORII, since it does not even use the terms from C_{OO} in any way.

7 AutoJAVA

All the theory so far has clarified the fact that a functional inductive programming system as IGORII can be confronted with problems outside the functional context. You may have noticed that we are still delivering the problems in a functional way, since this is the only format the system can understand. But it should be obvious that after successfully modeling a very small protocol of object oriented flavour we could enlarge this tiny model into a larger one, much more like a real object oriented protocol.

In order to use our findings in a practical way, a prototype plug-in for eclipse was designed which was aimed to enable a programmer to characterise the behaviour of a function in an abstract way (I/O examples) and having IGORII create a program from this specification, which would be wrapped into our C_{OO}[1].

8 Conclusion

Not only have we successfully modelled objects, methods, properties and messages - we also had igor synthesize all of them. So machine learning approaches have been used in order to have a system learn how to describe generic processes within programming languages. We provided a showcase of how functional programming can be combined with object orientation. The prototype plug-in *AutoJAVA* should prove this to be true and opens up many paths for future expansion. As the problem specification can be embedded within the annotations of a program's method an entry point for large-scale applications such as IBMs *RSA* has been created. A developer can annotate his UML diagrams and have those annotations transferred into the auto-generated code, so you could imagine IGOR using the specification during the code generation filling in a method's implementation.

All in all there has to be said that even though the results presented in this paper do not seem very novel or breathtaking. But they nevertheless show that by enabling functional programs to deal with object orientation we can play to the strengths of both paradigms. It feels like that we have created a foundation for some more thorough steps which might gradually improve the methodology and finally result in a larger scale prototype which actually produces Java code instead of functional programs.

[1] See more on `http://www.cogsys.wiai.uni-bamberg.de/effalip/download.html`

References

1. Hieber, T.: Transportation of the JEdit plug-in ProXSLbE to eclipse. Technical report, Otto Friedrich University of Bamberg (2008)
2. Summers, P.D.: A methodology for LISP program construction from examples. Journal of the ACM 24(1), 161–175 (1977)
3. Quinlan, J.R., Cameron-Jones, R.M.: FOIL: A midterm report. In: Brazdil, P.B. (ed.) ECML 1993. LNCS, vol. 667, pp. 3–20. Springer, Heidelberg (1993)
4. Muggleton, S., Feng, C.: Efficient induction of logic programs. In: Proceedings of the 1st Conference on Algorithmic Learning Theory, Ohmsma, Tokyo, Japan, pp. 368–381 (1990)
5. Muggleton, S.: Inverse entailment and Progol. New Generation Computing, Special issue on Inductive Logic Programming 13(3-4), 245–286 (1995)
6. Kitzelmann, E., Schmid, U.: Inductive synthesis of functional programs: An explanation based generalization approach. Journal of Machine Learning Research 7, 429–454 (2006)
7. Kitzelmann, E.: Data-driven induction of recursive functions from I/O-examples. In: Kitzelmann, E., Schmid, U. (eds.) Proceedings of the ECML/PKDD 2007 Workshop on Approaches and Applications of Inductive Programming (AAIP 2007), pp. 15–26 (2007)
8. Hofmann, M., Kitzelmann, E.: I/o guided detection of list catamorphisms – towards problem specific use of program templates in ip. In: Proceedings of the ACM SIGPLAN 2010 Workshop on Partial Evaluation and Program Manipulation (PEPM 2010) (to appear, 2010)
9. Olsson, R.J.: Inductive functional programming using incremental program transformation. Artificial Intelligence 74(1), 55–83 (1995)
10. Katayama, S.: Systematic search for lambda expressions. In: van Eekelen, M.C.J.D. (ed.) Revised Selected Papers from the Sixth Symposium on Trends in Functional Programming, TFP 2005, vol. 6, pp. 111–126. Intellect (2007)
11. Mitchell, T.M.: Machine Learning. McGraw-Hill Higher Education, New York (1997)
12. Rémy, D., Vouillon, J.: Objective ML: An effective object-oriented extension to ML (1998); A preliminary version appeared in the proceedings of the 24th ACM Conference on Principles of Programming Languages (1997)
13. Kiselyov, O., Laemmel, R.: Haskell's overlooked object system. CoRR (2005); informal publication
14. Terese: Term Rewriting Systems. Cambridge Tracts in Theoretical Computer Science, vol. 55. Cambridge University Press, Cambridge (2003)
15. Plotkin, G.: A note on inductive generalisation. In: Meltzer, B., Michie, D. (eds.) Machine Intelligence 5, pp. 153–163. Edinburgh University Press, Edinburgh (1969)

Recent Improvements of MagicHaskeller

Susumu Katayama

University of Miyazaki
1-1 W. Gakuenkibanadai, Miyazaki, Miyazaki 889-2155, Japan
skata@cs.miyazaki-u.ac.jp

Abstract. MagicHaskeller is our inductive functional programming library based on systematic search. In this paper we introduce two recent improvements to MagicHaskeller, i.e. 1) clarification and extension to arbitrary-rank polymorphism of its algorithm, and 2) efficiency improvement in its filtration algorithm that removes redundancy in the search results.

1 Introduction

Inductive functional programming deals with the problem of automatically generalizing ambiguous program specifications such as a set of input/output (I/O) pairs to concrete functional programs. There are three mainstream inductive functional programming systems: Igor 1/2 system developed at University of Bamberg which implements an analytical approach that quickly generates programs by analyzing given I/O pairs [Kitzelmann(2007)], ADATE system by Roland Olsson which applies an evolutionary approach resembling to multistart local search to program synthesis under monomorphic settings [Olsson(1995)], and our MagicHaskeller system [Katayama(2005b)] which first enumerates type-correct expressions systematically and picks up an expression that satisfies the specification.

Research on inductive functional programming has started about forty years ago, but we have to say that no fully-automated usable system has been developed yet. We think one of the reasons is that unbiased search without guidance was not realistic because computers were not powerful enough when the research started, and as a result the steady approach of starting with simple systematic search and adding heuristics one by one has not been considered enough.

Indeed, when searching systematically and exhaustively, the number of programs explodes exponentially in the limit as the program size increases, but other search-based approaches should also suffer from the same explosion, unless the search is adequately biased for each problem. Then, how can you choose an adequate heuristic evaluation function for computer programs? The percentage of inputs for which correct outputs are returned might be a good candidate, but it has not been evaluated in comparison with non-heuristic search. Our concern is that use of heuristics has been taken for granted, and until recently systematic search has not been paid attention to.

U. Schmid, E. Kitzelmann, and R. Plasmeijer (Eds.): AAIP 2009, LNCS 5812, pp. 174–193, 2010.

Based on the above speculation, we decided the following policy for developing MagicHaskeller as an algorithm for exhaustive search for programs under Hindley-Milner type system:

1. we should first implement systematic exhaustive search as efficiently as possible;
2. then we may add heuristics one by one if necessary, carefully confirming their effectiveness, extending the class of programs that can be synthesized with small amount of computational complexity.

If a research field is immature and researchers are working on toy problems, use of heuristics without discretion can easily lead to some kind of search bias around the known answers and make it difficult to evaluate the work objectively. MagicHaskeller can avoid this common pitfall by avoiding heuristics and sticking to systematic search.

MagicHaskeller is still under development, and there is lots of room for improvements. One major issue we consider is that although we insist it searches systematically and exhaustively, we have not done enough theoretical discussion on such a property, and it is questionable if our papers have successfully persuaded their readers to believe they are really exhaustive. As a first step to solve this problem, we gave a proof-theoretic re-interpretation to the algorithm, and as its side effect, extended the type system to support arbitrary-rank polymorphism. Also, we introduce research on efficiency improvement in its filtration algorithm that removes redundancy in the search results.

The organization of the rest of this paper is as follows: first in Section 2, we further introduce MagicHaskeller. Each of the following two sections describe the two new improvements, and Section 5 concludes the whole paper.

2 MagicHaskeller: Inductive Functional Programming System by Systematic Search

2.1 Policy

MagicHaskeller[Katayama(2005b)] is an implementation of systematic exhaustive generation of programs. Another feature of MagicHaskeller is that it is designed with usability in mind, and usually all you have to do for synthesizing expressions is just to write a boolean function which specifies the program to be generated, that is a higher-order function that returns *True* if the correct program is given as an argument. Also, the user can use the general-purposed primitive set the library provides, and usually there is no need to tailor the library for each synthesis. The reason we think usability is important is just because we think using an automatic programming system must be easier than writing the target program directly.

2.2 Library and Use Cases

[Katayama(2006)] introduced the earliest library interface to MagicHaskeller. Also, the paper showed some interesting use cases which were made possible by the introduction of the library interface, such as finding recursive definitions from closed-form solutions, use of user-defined types, interaction with QuickCheck[Claessen and Hughes(2000)]. Because they are quite useful for quickly giving a good picture of the tool, this section is devoted also for introducing some of them, adapted to the current library definition.

The most typical and easy way to use the library is under the environment of Glasgow Haskell Compiler interactive (GHCi). Tables 2–3 show example uses of the library. Most API functions reside in module `MagicHaskeller`, and useful predefined functions are defined in module `MagicHaskeller.LibTH` (Table 1). Unless you are doing something special, you should first run `MagicHaskeller.LibTH.init075`, which sets the generic primitive set that includes all the constructors and paramorphisms of lists, natural numbers, booleans, and *Maybe* monad, and then execute `printAny` (or `printOne` if you want to measure the execution time) with an argument which specifies the program you want, that is a predicate (i.e. a boolean function) that takes a program and returns *True* if the program satisfies your need. For example, Table 2 shows an example of generating a generalized program that takes `"abc"` as input and returns `"abcba"` as output, and shows that it returns `"abcdcba"` for `"abcd"`.

The fact that the specification is not limited to I/O pairs is an advantage of generate-and-test approaches like MagicHaskeller, and it can, for example, find recursive definitions from a closed-form solution. Table 3 shows an example of finding a recursive definition of function f that satisfies

$$f(n) = \frac{\phi^n - (1-\phi)^n}{\sqrt{5}},$$

$$\phi = \frac{1+\sqrt{5}}{2}.$$

Since we have not implement refactoring, it is still difficult to see what are generated as f at a glance, but it is actually the fibonacci function!

If you do not feel bothered, you can specialize the primitive component library to speed up the search. Table 4 shows an example of using only 0, successor function, the paramorphism of natural numbers, and addition.

2.3 Algorithm

The algorithm behind MagicHaskeller is defined in [Katayama(2005a)] and its updated version [Katayama(2007)]. Although those papers define it without ambiguity by referring to pieces of code in Haskell, for some unknown reasons it is often misunderstood. The most common misunderstanding I hear is that the algorithm first generates all the possible expressions, including ill-typed ones, and then filters out those incorrect programs, though actually the algorithm never generate such ill-typed programs, nor even ill-typed subexpressions. For this reason, in this paper I try defining it in a different way in later sections, i.e., in relation to intuitionistic logic via Curry-Howard isomorphism.

For now, I give an intuitive explanation of the algorithm behind MagicHaskeller.

Table 1. Some of the useful predefined functions defined in `MagicHaskeller.LibTH`

```
{-# LANGUAGE TemplateHaskell #-}
module MagicHaskeller.LibTH (module MagicHaskeller.LibTH, module MagicHaskeller) where
import MagicHaskeller
initialize, init075 :: IO ()
initialize = do setPrimitives (list ++ nat ++ mb ++ bool ++
                  $(p [| (hd :: (->) [a] (Maybe a), (+) :: Int -> Int -> Int) |]))
                setDepth 10
init075 = do setPG $ mkMemo075 (list ++ nat ++ mb ++ bool ++
               $(p [| ((+) :: Int -> Int -> Int) |]))
             setDepth 10
  -- Specialized memoization tables. Choose one for quicker results.
mall, mlist, mlist', mnat, mlistnat :: ProgramGenerator pg => pg
mall = mkPG (list ++ nat ++ mb ++ bool ++ $(p [| (hd :: (->) [a] (Maybe a), (+) :: Int -> Int -> Int) |]))
mlist = mkPG list
mlist' = mkPG list'
mnat = mkPG (nat ++ $(p [| (+) :: Int -> Int -> Int |]))
mlistnat = mkPG (list ++ nat ++ $(p [| (+) :: Int -> Int -> Int |]))
hd :: [a] -> Maybe a
hd []      = Nothing
hd (x : _) = Just x
mb, nat, list', list, bool, boolean, eq, lists :: [Primitive]
mb = $(p [| (Nothing :: Maybe a, Just :: a -> Maybe a, maybe :: a -> (b -> a) -> (->) (Maybe b) a) |])
nat = $(p [| (0 :: Int, succ :: Int -> Int, nat_para :: (->) Int (a -> (Int -> a -> a) -> a)) |])
  -- Nat paramorphism
nat_para :: Integral i => i -> a -> (i -> a -> a) -> a
nat_para i x f = np (abs i)
  where np 0 = x
        np i = let i' = i - 1
               in f i' (np i')
list' = $(p [| ([] :: [a], (:) :: a -> [a] -> [a], foldr :: (b -> a -> a) -> a -> (->) [b] a) |])
list  = $(p [| ([] :: [a], (:) :: a -> [a] -> [a], list_para :: (->) [b] (a -> (b -> [b] -> a -> a) -> a)) |])
  -- List paramorphism
list_para :: [b] -> a -> (b -> [b] -> a -> a) -> a
list_para []       x f = x
list_para (y : ys) x f = f y ys (list_para ys x f)
bool = $(p [| (True, False, iF :: (->) Bool (a -> a -> a)) |])
iF :: Bool -> a -> a -> a
iF True t f = t
iF False t f = f
boolean = $(p [| ((&&) :: Bool -> Bool -> Bool,
                  (||) :: Bool -> Bool -> Bool,
                  not :: Bool -> Bool) |])
eq = $(p [| ((==) :: Int -> Int -> Bool, (/=) :: Int -> Int -> Bool,
   (==) :: Char -> Char -> Bool, (/=) :: Char -> Char -> Bool,
   (==) :: Bool -> Bool -> Bool, (/=) :: Bool -> Bool -> Bool,
   (==) :: [Int] -> [Int] -> Bool, (/=) :: [Int] -> [Int] -> Bool,
   (==) :: [Char] -> [Char] -> Bool, (/=) :: [Char] -> [Char] -> Bool,
   (==) :: [Bool] -> [Bool] -> Bool, (/=) :: [Bool] -> [Bool] -> Bool) |])
lists = $(p [| (map       :: (a -> b) -> (->) [a] [b],
                (++)      :: [a] -> [a] -> [a],
                filter    :: (a -> Bool) -> [a] -> [a],
                concat    :: [[a]] -> [a],
                concatMap :: (a -> [b]) -> (->) [a] [b],
                length    :: (->) [a] Int,
                replicate :: Int -> a -> [a],
                take      :: Int -> [a] -> [a],
                drop      :: Int -> [a] -> [a],
                takeWhile :: (a -> Bool) -> [a] -> [a],
                dropWhile :: (a -> Bool) -> [a] -> [a],
                lines     :: [Char] -> [[Char]],
                words     :: [Char] -> [[Char]],
                unlines   :: [[Char]] -> [Char],
                unwords   :: [[Char]] -> [Char],
                reverse   :: [a] -> [a],
                and       :: [Bool] -> Bool,
                or        :: [Bool] -> Bool,
                any       :: (a -> Bool) -> (->) [a] Bool,
                all       :: (a -> Bool) -> (->) [a] Bool,
                zipWith   :: (a -> b -> c) -> (->) [a] ((->) [b] [c])) |])
reallyall :: ProgramGenerator pg => pg
reallyall = mkPG (list ++ bool ++ boolean ++ eq ++ lists)
```

Table 2. The simplest example. From the actual output, qualifications like `GHC.Types.`, `MagicHaskeller.LibTH.` are removed for avoiding clutter.

```
Prelude> :set +s
Prelude> :m +MagicHaskeller.LibTH
Prelude MagicHaskeller.LibTH> init075
(0.02 secs, 4438028 bytes)
Prelude MagicHaskeller.LibTH> printOne (\f -> f "abc" == "abcba")
\a -> list_para a (\b c -> c) (\b c d e f -> b : d (b : e) e) [] a
(14.61 secs, 6331014756 bytes)
Prelude MagicHaskeller.LibTH> printAny (\f -> f "abc" == "abcba")
\a -> list_para a (\b c -> c) (\b c d e f -> b : d (b : e) e) [] a
\a -> list_para a (\b c -> c) (\b c d e f -> b : d (b : e) e) [] []
\a -> list_para a (\b c -> b) (\b c d e f -> b : d f (b : f)) a []
\a -> list_para a (\b c -> b) (\b c d e f -> b : d f (b : f)) [] []
^CInterrupted.
Prelude MagicHaskeller.LibTH> (\a -> list_para a (\b c -> c) (\b c d e f ->
  b : d (b : e) e) [] a) "abcd"
"abcdcba"
(0.00 secs, 538152 bytes)
Prelude MagicHaskeller.LibTH> xss <- filterFirst (\f -> f "abc" == "abcba")
(0.00 secs, 536428 bytes)
Prelude MagicHaskeller.LibTH> let (e,f):_ = concat xss
(0.00 secs, 618488 bytes)
Prelude MagicHaskeller.LibTH> pprint e
"\\a -> list_para a (\\b c -> c) (\\b c d e f -> b : d (b : e) e) [] a"
(6.75 secs, 2712408304 bytes)
Prelude MagicHaskeller.LibTH> f "abcd"
"abcdcba"
(0.00 secs, 0 bytes)
```

1. When expressions with the same type as or more general type than $\forall a_1 \ldots a_k.A_1 \to \cdots \to A_m \to B$ are requested, it replaces a_1, ..., a_k with new type constructors G_1, ... , G_k to obtain the monomorphic type $M = (A_1 \to \cdots \to A_m \to B)[G_1/a_1, \ldots, G_k/a_k]$. Then, find expressions whose types unify with M, by calling 2.
2. When expressions whose types unify with $A_1 \to \cdots \to A_m \to B$ are requested, it first adds $A_1 \ldots A_m$ to the list of available types, and try to generate expressions whose types unify with B.
3. In order to generate expressions whose types unify with B (where B is not a functional type), it does the following for each T of the list of available types:
   - Let $X_1 \to \cdots \to X_n \to Y = T$ (where n can be 0). However, if Y is just a type variable, replace it with b, $X_{n+1} \to b$, $X_{n+1} \to X_{n+2} \to b$, ... and try all of them, where b, X_{n+1}, X_{n+2}, ... are fresh type variables.[1]

[1] Because there are infinite number of alternatives, depth-first search is not adequate here.

Table 3. Finding recursive definitions from closed-form solution. Again, qualifications like `GHC.Num.`, `MagicHaskeller.LibTH.` are removed.

```
Prelude> :set +s
Prelude> :m +MagicHaskeller.LibTH
Prelude MagicHaskeller.LibTH> init075
(0.02 secs, 4433280 bytes)
Prelude MagicHaskeller.LibTH> let phi = (1 + sqrt 5) / 2
(0.00 secs, 1891844 bytes)
Prelude MagicHaskeller.LibTH> let pred f n = (f :: Int->Int) n == round
((phi^n - (1-phi)^n) / sqrt 5)
(0.00 secs, 1065584 bytes)
Prelude MagicHaskeller.LibTH> printOne (\f -> all (pred f) [0..9])
\a -> nat_para a (\b c -> c) (\b c d e -> c e (d + e)) (succ 0) 0
(14.96 secs, 5997624872 bytes)
Prelude MagicHaskeller.LibTH> printAny (\f -> all (pred f) [0..9])
\a -> nat_para a (\b c -> c) (\b c d e -> c e (d + e)) (succ 0) 0
\a -> nat_para a (\b c -> c) (\b c d e -> c e (e + d)) (succ 0) 0
\a -> nat_para a (\b c -> c) (\b c d e -> c (d + e) d) (succ 0) 0
\a -> nat_para a (\b c -> c) (\b c d e -> c (e + d) d) (succ 0) 0
\a -> nat_para a (\b c -> b) (\b c d e -> c e (e + d)) 0 (succ 0)
\a -> nat_para a (\b c -> b) (\b c d e -> c e (d + e)) 0 (succ 0)
\a -> nat_para a (\b c -> b) (\b c d e -> c (d + e) d) 0 (succ 0)
\a -> nat_para a (\b c -> b) (\b c d e -> c (e + d) d) 0 (succ 0)
\a -> nat_para a (\b c -> c) (\b c d e -> c (d + e) (succ d)) 0 0
\a -> nat_para a (\b c -> c) (\b c d e -> c (e + d) (succ d)) 0 0
\a -> nat_para a (\b c -> b) (\b c d e -> c (succ e) (e + d)) 0 0
\a -> nat_para a (\b c -> b) (\b c d e -> c (succ e) (d + e)) 0 0
^CInterrupted.
Prelude MagicHaskeller.LibTH> map (\a -> nat_para a (\b c -> c) (\b c d e ->
 c e (d + e)) (succ 0) 0) [0..20]
[0,1,1,2,3,5,8,13,21,34,55,89,144,233,377,610,987,1597,2584,4181,6765]
(0.00 secs, 2212352 bytes)
Prelude MagicHaskeller.LibTH> xss <- filterFirst (\f -> all (pred f) [0..9])
(0.04 secs, 14194704 bytes)
Prelude MagicHaskeller.LibTH> let (e,f):_ = concat xss
(0.00 secs, 0 bytes)
Prelude MagicHaskeller.LibTH> pprint e
"\\a -> nat_para a (\\b c -> c) (\\b c d e -> c e (d + e)) (succ 0) 0"
(10.34 secs, 3651214948 bytes)
Prelude MagicHaskeller.LibTH> map f [0..20]
[0,1,1,2,3,5,8,13,21,34,55,89,144,233,377,610,987,1597,2584,4181,6765]
(0.00 secs, 542668 bytes)
```

– Try to unify Y and B; if they do not, the search (of the current branch) fails and *mzero*, or the empty set, is returned; if they do unify, their most general unifier substitution is computed.
– Then the algorithm has to generate subexpressions; if $X_1 \dots X_n$ did not include type variables it could just recursively call 2, but they usually do, so it has to apply the current substitution to X_1, recursively call 2 to obtain the resulting substitution, then apply it to X_2, recursively

Table 4. Limiting the search space by replacing the primitive component library

```
Prelude> :set +s
Prelude> :m MagicHaskeller.LibTH
Prelude MagicHaskeller.LibTH> init075
(0.02 secs, 4438024 bytes)
Prelude MagicHaskeller.LibTH> setPG  $ mkMemo075 (nat ++ $(p [| (+) ::
Int -> Int -> Int |]))
(0.08 secs, 19774144 bytes)
Prelude MagicHaskeller.LibTH>  let phi = (1 + sqrt 5) / 2
(0.01 secs, 1845520 bytes)
Prelude MagicHaskeller.LibTH> let pred f n = (f :: Int->Int) n == round
 ((phi^n - (1-phi)^n) / sqrt 5)
(0.01 secs, 1817232 bytes)
Prelude MagicHaskeller.LibTH>  printOne (\f -> all (pred f) [0..9])
\a -> nat_para a (\b c -> c) (\b c d e -> c e (d + e)) (succ 0) 0
(9.25 secs, 3454396104 bytes)
```

Table 5. Interpretation of alternatives and combinations, &c. $S \supset T$ means the prioritized set T is a subset of S. The last rule is enough to explain all the rest, though they are provided for pedagogical purposes.

rules	interpretations
$\dfrac{B_1}{A} \quad \cdots \quad \dfrac{B_n}{A}$	$\Vert A\Vert = \bigoplus_{i=1}^{n} \Vert B_i\Vert = \Vert B_1\Vert \oplus \cdots \oplus \Vert B_n\Vert$
$\dfrac{x_1 :: B_1 \quad \cdots \quad x_n :: B_n}{x_1 \otimes ... \otimes x_n :: A}$	$\Vert A\Vert \supset \Vert B_1 \ldots B_n\Vert = \Vert B_1\Vert \langle\otimes\rangle \ldots \langle\otimes\rangle \Vert B_n\Vert$
$\dfrac{x :: B}{f\ x :: A}$	$\Vert A\Vert \supset fmap\ f\ \Vert B\Vert = liftM_1\ f\ \Vert B\Vert$
$\dfrac{}{x :: A}$	$\Vert A\Vert \supset return\ x = liftM_0\ x$
$\dfrac{x_{11} :: B_{11} \quad \cdots \quad x_{1n_1} :: B_{1n_1}}{f x_{11} ... x_{1n_1} :: A}$ $\vdots$ $\dfrac{x_{n1} :: B_{m1} \quad \cdots \quad x_{mn_m} :: B_{mn_m}}{f x_{m1} ... x_{mn_m} :: A}$	$\Vert A\Vert = \bigoplus_{i=1}^{m} liftM_{n_i}\ f\ \Vert B_{i1}\Vert \ldots \Vert B_{in_i}\Vert$

call 2 ... until X_n. We have to pass the current substitution to traverse $X_1 \ldots X_n$.

The above search is conducted in the breadth-first manner using a variant of Spivey's monad for breadth-first search[Spivey(2000)], though it can easily be replaced with another search strategy such as depth-first search and depth-bound search by just replacing the monad to be used. Also, the algorithm memoizes subexpression calls for efficiency. The function to be memoized takes the list of

Table 6. A simple rule set for generating λ expressions.

$$\frac{x :: A, \Gamma \vdash e :: B}{\Gamma \vdash \lambda x.e :: A \rightarrow B} \rightarrow\text{R}$$

where x does not appear as a label in Γ

$$\frac{\Gamma, f :: A_1 \rightarrow ... \rightarrow A_n \rightarrow B \vdash e_1 :: A_1 \quad ... \quad \Gamma, f :: A_1 \rightarrow ... \rightarrow A_n \rightarrow B \vdash e_n :: A_n}{\Gamma, f :: A_1 \rightarrow ... \rightarrow A_n \rightarrow B \vdash f e_1 ... e_n :: B} \text{Ax+}\rightarrow\text{L}$$

where B is not a function type

Table 7. Inference rules in question

$$\frac{}{\Gamma; x :: A \vdash x :: A} \text{Axiom}$$

where A is not a functional type

$$\frac{\Gamma; \vdash e_1 :: A \qquad \Gamma; y :: B \vdash e_2 :: C}{\Gamma; f :: A \rightarrow B \vdash e_2[f e_1/y] :: C} \rightarrow\text{L}$$

$$\frac{\Gamma, x :: A; x :: A \vdash e :: B}{\Gamma, x :: A; \vdash e :: B} \text{Cont}$$

where A is not a functional type

$$\frac{\Gamma, x :: A; \vdash e :: B}{\Gamma; \vdash \lambda x.e :: A \rightarrow B} \rightarrow\text{R}$$

where x does not appear as a label in Γ

available types and the requested type, and returns the monadic value representing breadth-first search, holding the lists of expressions, the required substitutions, and the fresh variable generator. In order for the memoization table to hit often, the type variable names are normalized and the same types in the list of available types are put together.

2.4 Reducing the Amount of Generated Expressions

Since the number of programs bloats exponentially as the program size increases, how to slow down such bloating is a key to making a useful generate-and-test approach. Because MagicHaskeller challenges this problem while sticking to exhaustive search, what it can do is quite limited: to minimize the double-counting of semantically equivalent but still syntactically different expressions.

There have been two approaches to this issue taken by MagicHaskeller:

- not generating expressions that are theoretically known to be equivalent to another one that are already generated, by not generating reducible

expressions (except that η-long expressions are generated) and optimizable expressions which can be detected by simple pattern match [Katayama(2005a)],
– detecting the redundancy by execution with random arguments [Katayama(2008)] — this is discussed in detail in Section 4.

2.5 Efficiency Comparisons

[Hofmann et al.(2009)Hofmann, Kitzelmann, and Schmid] worked on comparisons between recent inductive programming approaches including MagicHaskeller, and the work is specialized to inductive functional programming and continued at the website of inductive-programming.org. One interesting point they show is that the efficiency of MagicHaskeller competes well against other approaches, although it does not use any heuristics. For example, according to [Hofmann et al.(2009)Hofmann, Kitzelmann, and Schmid], MagicHaskeller outperforms ADATE, FFOIL, and FLIP on most problems, though it falls behind Igor 2 and GOLEM. Also, according to the website, the old stand-alone version (which means the version with all optimizations) of MagicHaskeller behaves the best of the four major IFP systems, namely, ADATE, Igor 1, Igor 2, and MagicHaskeller, for about one-third of the benchmarks against which it was evaluated, and outperforms ADATE for more than half of them. Considering that Igor and GOLEM require many examples while MagicHaskeller as a generate-and-test approach requires much less — usually one or some — examples, we could say MagicHaskeller does well enough.

Of course, it is true that an exhaustive search approach should be sensitive to exponential bloat. However, actually this sensitivity also applies to heuristic approaches unless the heuristics successfully exploit the problem structure for guiding search, because there is no free lunch. Until someone finds some useful heuristics for searching for interesting programs, the systematic approach that try hard to avoid double-counting can be the best generate-and-test approach for general purposes, though for a specific purpose another method can be the best.

3 Exhaustive Program Generation by Interpretation of Herbelin's LJT Variant

3.1 Introduction

In TFP2005 symposium we presented an algorithm to generate a stream of all the possible expressions with a given type from a given set of expressions by using breadth-first search [Katayama(2005a)], and since then the algorithm has been released and updated as a generate-and-test style inductive functional programming system, called MagicHaskeller. The research, started as an antithesis to heuristic approaches that tends to ignore systematic search, has attracted some positive-minded scientists, while its lack in enough formalization has been a source of difficulty in understanding and theoretically manipulating the algorithm.

In the same year of 2005 Augustsson released Djinn, that generates one or some functional programs with the given type, based on theorem proving by Roy Dyckhoff's LJT [Dyckhoff(1992)] (a.k.a. G4ip by Hudelmaier [Hudelmaier(1992)]). That has driven us to work on formalization of our exhaustive search algorithm, though Dyckhoff's LJT cannot straightforwardly be applied to exhaustive program/proof generation because it replaces equivalent expressions for making its $\supset\Rightarrow_4$ rule efficient, but actually replacing equivalent expressions corresponds to several proofs, and thus should multiply the number of proofs.

As the matter of fact, there is also a correspondence between automatic proof and the algorithm behind MagicHaskeller. This on-going research starts with monadic interpretation of each rule of a variant of Herbelin's LJT[Herbelin(1995)] in combination of Spivey's algebraic framework for combinatorial search [Spivey(2006)], and aims at associating our algorithm presented at [Katayama(2005a)] with generation of the stream of all the proofs for the given proposition.

3.2 Basic Ideas

It is well known that there is a correspondence, called Curry-Howard correspondence, between values in a type and proofs of a proposition. Automatic proof systems such as Coq and Agda take advantage of this correspondence, and (usually with human helps) they can generate a program that satisfies a given specification specified as a type by generating a proof tree, just in the same way as they generate a proof of a given proposition.

What MagicHaskeller does for generating programs is essentially the same thing, except that it only supports Hindley-Milter type system, and it generates an infinite stream of expressions exhaustively, from small ones to large ones. The algorithm behind MagicHaskeller, as specified in [Katayama(2005a)], can be viewed as interpretation of the rule set of Herbelin's LJT, i.e., it interprets a sequent as a monadic proof search or a prioritized infinite set of its proofs, and an inference rule as set inclusion of its premise by its conclusion.

We use Spivey's monad for combinatorial search[Spivey(2006)]. By using his algebraic interface, we can easily implement combinatorial search using the bind operator $\triangleright$ for combinations or set comprehension and plus operator $\oplus$ for alternative selectionsor direct sum. Also, search failure or the empty set is denoted with *zero*, and a unit set with the primary priority can be created with *return* function. Hence, when generating proofs of some proposition, if the proposition matches conclusions of plural inference rules, we only need to generate proofs of premises of such rules and compute the direct sum of such processes (which means backtracking when generating a single proof), and if the proposition matches the conclusion of an inference rule which has plural premises, we only need to generate proofs of the premises and compute the direct product of such processes. In general, such alternation and combination of proof tree generation can be interpreted in the way shown in Table 5, where $[\![X]\!]$ denotes the monadic value holding the infinite stream of proofs of X, and $\langle\otimes\rangle$ denotes a multiplication, whose definition is dependent on how to construct a pair of proofs. $\langle\otimes\rangle$ can be defined in Haskell as follows using monadic operators defined in [Spivey(2006)]:

$$x\langle\otimes\rangle y = x \triangleright \lambda a \rightarrow y \triangleright \lambda b \rightarrow \mathit{return}\ (a \otimes b)$$

i.e.

$$x\langle\otimes\rangle y = \mathit{liftM2}\ (\otimes)\ x\ y$$

3.3 A Simple, But More Concrete Example

Let us consider a more concrete and more interesting inference rule set, with which we can indeed generate an infinite set of λ-expressions. Consider the inference rule set shown in Table 6.

We assume that each premise is not a list but a set.

The rule set can be used to infer the types of λ-expressions. Also, it can be used to mechanically generate a proof of a proposition by matching from the bottom to the top, and we are interested in generating the infinite set of all the proofs.

The proviso for Ax+→L rule is added in order to permit only η-long normal form and identify η-equivalent proofs. This limitation does not only limit the unnecessary search space expansion by η-equivalent program generations when generating programs (proofs) from the bottom to the top, but also make implementation simpler and more efficient by preventing the proposition to be proved from matching plural conclusions of inference rules.

In order to show the implementations, we first define a datatype of λ-expressions:

```
data Expr = Expr :$Expr     -- function application
          | Lambda Var Expr  -- lambda abstraction
          | V Var            -- variable
```

Then, the rule set can be interpreted as follows.

$$[\![\Gamma \vdash A \rightarrow B]\!] = \langle \lambda x. \rangle ([\![x :: A, \Gamma \vdash B]\!]) \qquad (1)$$

$$[\![\Gamma \vdash B]\!] = \bigoplus_{f::T \in \Gamma} [\![\Gamma; f :: T \vdash B]\!], \qquad \text{if } B \text{ is not a function type.} \qquad (2)$$

$$[\![\Gamma; f :: A_1 \rightarrow ... \rightarrow A_n \rightarrow B \vdash B]\!] = \mathit{wrap}^n\ (\mathit{return}(V f)\ \langle :\$ \rangle\ [\![\Gamma \vdash A_1]\!]\ \langle :\$ \rangle\ ...\ \langle :\$ \rangle\ [\![\Gamma \vdash A_n]\!] \ ) \qquad (3)$$

$$[\![\Gamma; f :: T \vdash B]\!] = \mathit{zero}, \qquad \text{if } T \text{ does not return } B. \qquad (4)$$

We assume $\langle :\$ \rangle$ is left associative. *zero* means the empty set. $\langle \lambda u. \rangle (m)$ means mapping λ-abstraction by u of each element of m, i.e.

$$\langle \lambda u. \rangle\ (m) = \mathit{fmap}\ (\mathit{Lambda}\ u)\ m$$

or

$$\langle \lambda u. \rangle\ (m) = m \triangleright (\mathit{return} \circ \mathit{Lambda}\ u)$$

Rule →R is straightforwardly interpreted to Equation 1. As for the non-functional case corresponding to Ax+→L, the interpretation should be the ⊕ sum of all the possible choices of $f \in \Gamma$ as in Equation 2, that return the same type as the requested one.

We silently insert the *wrap* operation from [Spivey(2006)], that pushes the search process deeper in the search tree, into the product operation, which corresponds to function application. This is done because we regard the search depth as the program (proof) size, measured by the number of function applications.[2]

3.4 A Variant of of Cut-Free LJT for Program Generation

The rule set shown in Table 6 can equivalently be translated to the rule set shown in Table 7. This rule set is Herbelin's cut-free LJT[Herbelin(1995)], except that there are provisos that prevent η-equivalent expressions from being generated.

Herbelin's LJT is a variant of the intuitionistic sequent calculus LJ that only permits one proof that correspond to one λ-expression. In Herbelin's LJT some kind of duplicate proofs that correspond to the same λ-expressions are disabled by preparing a special place for the current assumption called *stoup*. (A stoup is placed between ; and $\vdash$ in the inference rules shown in Table 7.)

Also we use cut-free calculus for this research, because we do not like to expand the search space, i.e., we do not introduce local variables by let expressions. This should not be a problem for now, because we cannot generate large programs anyway.

In addition, as mentioned in the previous section, we stick to η-long expressions, which is forced by the provisos for the Axiom rule and Cont rule.

Finally, we omit rules for $\vee$, $\wedge$, $\perp$, and $\exists$. As for $\forall$L and $\forall$R, we start with the rule set without them and then extend it.

Figure 1 an example of how the rule set generates an expression having the given type, and how it infers the type of a λ expression.

3.5 Interpretation of the Rule Set

In this section we assign an interpretation to each inference rule and the whole rule set. Compared to other rule sets, interpretation of LJT is somewhat easier because the conclusion of each rule is exclusive each other and matches only one pattern. (except that there are alternative choices for $x :: A$ in the Cont rule).

Table 8 shows the interpretation of each inference rule in Table 7, based on the interpretation policy specified in Table 5. The Axiom rule does not have any premise, thus the variable name in the stoup is just returned. The →L rule branches the proof tree, hence we recursively generate proof trees and combine them using $liftM_2$. The Cont rule has exactly one premise and hence interpretation with *fmap* applies, but the function to be mapped in this case is the identity.

[2] The *wrap* operation can be included in $\langle : \$ \rangle$, though for efficiency it should be applied as soon as the arity is known.

$$
\dfrac{\dfrac{\dfrac{\dfrac{\dfrac{\dfrac{\dfrac{\dfrac{}{\Gamma; z :: A \vdash z :: A}\text{Axiom}}{\Gamma; \vdash z :: A}\text{Cont} \quad \dfrac{\dfrac{\dfrac{}{\Gamma; y :: B \vdash y :: B}\text{Axiom}}{\Gamma; \vdash y :: B}\text{Cont} \quad \dfrac{}{\Gamma; v :: C \vdash v :: C}\text{Axiom}}{\Gamma; w :: B \to C \vdash wy :: C}\to\text{L}}{\Gamma; x :: A \to B \to C \vdash xzy :: C}\to\text{L}}{\Gamma; \vdash xzy :: C}\text{Cont}}{x :: A \to B \to C, y :: B, z :: A; \vdash xzy :: C}\text{definition of } \Gamma}{x :: A \to B \to C, y :: B; \vdash \lambda z.xzy :: A \to C}\to\text{R}}{x :: A \to B \to C; \vdash \lambda yz.xzy :: B \to A \to C}\to\text{R}}{; \vdash \lambda xyz.xzy :: (A \to B \to C) \to B \to A \to C}\to\text{R}
$$

where $\Gamma = x :: A \to B \to C, y :: B, z :: A$

Fig. 1. An example of how the rule set without quantification works

Table 8. Interpretation of each rule

rules	interpretations
Axiom	$\llbracket\Gamma; x :: A \vdash A\rrbracket \supset return(Vx)$
$\to$L	$\llbracket\Gamma; A\to B\vdash C\rrbracket \supset liftM_2(\lambda e_2 e_1.e_2[fe_1/y])\ \llbracket\Gamma; B\vdash C\rrbracket\ \llbracket\Gamma;\vdash A\rrbracket$
Cont	$\llbracket\Gamma, x :: A; \vdash B\rrbracket \supset \llbracket\Gamma, x :: A; x :: A \vdash B\rrbracket$
$\to$R	$\llbracket\Gamma; \vdash A \to B\rrbracket \supset \langle\lambda u.\rangle(\llbracket u :: A, \Gamma; \vdash B\rrbracket)$
	where u does not appear in Γ

The $\to$R rule also has exactly one premise, and the resulting interpretation *fmaps* λ-abstraction to the interpretation of the premise.

Then, we collect each alternative that can result in each possible sequent pattern. Firstly, if its stoup is filled with a non-functional type, only the Axiom rule may be used for the current sequent. It can be applied only when the type of the conclusion and the stoup are the same, thus we have the following equations:

$$\llbracket\Gamma; x :: A\vdash A\rrbracket = return(Vx), \text{ unless } A \text{ is a functional type} \tag{5}$$

$$\llbracket\Gamma; x :: A\vdash B\rrbracket = zero, \text{ unless } A \text{ is a functional type or } A = B \tag{6}$$

If the stoup is filled with a functional type, only the $\to$L rule applies, and it always applies.

$$\llbracket\Gamma; f :: A\to B\vdash C\rrbracket = liftM_2(\lambda e_2 e_1.e_2[fe_1/y])\ \llbracket\Gamma; y :: B\vdash C\rrbracket\ \llbracket\Gamma;\vdash A\rrbracket \tag{7}$$

If the stoup is empty and the succedent is not a functional type, only the Cont rule applies. However, because the Cont rule has options in which antecedent to choose, this type of sequent is interpreted as the union of those alternatives.

$$\llbracket\Gamma; \vdash B\rrbracket = \bigoplus_{(x::A)\in\Gamma} \llbracket\Gamma; x :: A \vdash B\rrbracket, \text{ unless } B \text{ is a functional type} \tag{8}$$

Finally, if the stoup is empty and the succedent is a functional type, only the $\to$R rule applies. Thus,

$$\llbracket\Gamma; \vdash A \to B\rrbracket = \langle\lambda x.\rangle\llbracket x :: A, \Gamma; \vdash B\rrbracket$$

where x does not appear in Γ.

The interpretation $[\![\Gamma; \vdash X]\!]$ given here does not exactly correspond to $[\![\Gamma \vdash X]\!]$ defined by Equations 1–2, because when generating subexpressions the former generates the first argument last and the last argument first, but the latter generates the first argument first and the last argument last. Those interpretations are equivalent if the search monad is implemented as a stream of bags rather than a stream of lists, but still they are different in efficiency — for example, if we are using assumption $Int \to Char \to Bool$ and expression with type $Char$ cannot actually be generated, the last-argument-first order is more efficient because it can prune unnecessary branches earlier, but if the assumption is $Char \to Int \to Bool$ the first-argument-first order is more efficient. The actual implementation of MagicHaskeller uses the first-argument-first order.

3.6 Interpretation of Rule Sets with ∀s

In this section, we augment the rule set with ∀ rules in order to support parametric polymorphism. Table 9 shows the Curry-style variant of the ∀ rules of LJT. [Katayama(2005a)] generates expressions in Curry-style rather than in Church-style, and we follow the policy also in this paper.

Table 9. ∀ rules in Curry style

$$\frac{\Gamma; x :: A(a) \vdash E :: B}{\Gamma; x :: \forall s.A(s) \vdash E :: B}\ \forall\text{L}$$

$$\frac{\Gamma; \vdash x :: A(T)}{\Gamma; \vdash x :: \forall s.A(s)}\ \forall\text{R}$$

where T does not appear in Γ.

One problem in generating programs from rule sets with quantification is to which type to instantiate existential variables, and that happens exactly when applying the ∀L rule. [Katayama(2005a)] decides the type by the unification algorithm. This can be viewed as an intuitionistic version of SLD resolution, and [Kiselyov(2005)] also does similar thing for generating single expression having a given type.

Unification algorithm is stateful in that it updates and passes current substitution over recursive calls and that such substitution backtracks the branches. For this reason, in order to adopt the ∀L rule we have to change the type of $[\![\cdot]\!]$ accordingly, or wrap the monad for search with the state monad transformer [Liang et al.(1995)Liang, Hudak, and Jones] that implicitly carries the current substitution. The actual implementation adopted by [Katayama(2005a)] is the latter, carrying the fresh variable ID at the same time. Given the type of the search monad m and that of the state, i.e., the current substitution $Subst$, the state-holding version of the search monad $STS\ m$ can be defined as follows:

$$\begin{aligned}
STS\ m\ a &= StateT\ Subst\ m\ a \\
&= Subst \rightarrow m(a \times Subst) \\
return_{(STS\ m)}\ x\ \sigma &= return_m(x, \sigma) \\
(f \triangleright_{(STS\ m)} g)\ \sigma &= f\sigma \triangleright_m uncurry\ g \\
zero_{(STS\ m)}\ \sigma &= zero_m \\
(f \oplus_{(STS\ m)} g)\ \sigma &= f\sigma \oplus_m g\sigma
\end{aligned}$$

Also, we introduce two kinds of type variables: existential ones denoted by $a, b, ... \in \mathcal{V}$ to which type expressions can be assigned as a result of unification, and universal ones denoted by $T, U, ... \in \mathcal{U}$ which behaves as constants during unification. Those variables are introduced during ∀L and ∀R rules:

$$\begin{aligned}
\llbracket \Gamma; x :: \forall s.A(s) \vdash y :: B \rrbracket &= \llbracket \Gamma; x :: A(a) \vdash y :: B \rrbracket \\
\llbracket \Gamma; \vdash x :: \forall s.A(s) \rrbracket &= \llbracket \Gamma; \vdash x :: A(T) \rrbracket
\end{aligned}$$

where a is a fresh existential variable not appearing in Γ, and T is a fresh universal variable not appearing in Γ.

In addition, we have to modify the interpretation rules accordingly to the introduction of unification. Firstly, if the stoup is filled by something which is neither a function nor an existential variable, only the Axiom rule can apply. Then, whether it applies or not depends on whether unification succeeds or fails.

$$\begin{aligned}
\llbracket \Gamma; x :: A \vdash B \rrbracket &= zero, \\
&\qquad \text{unless } A \text{ is a functional type or an existential variable,} \\
&\qquad \text{nor do } A \text{ and } B \text{ unify;} \\
\llbracket \Gamma; x :: A \vdash B \rrbracket \sigma &= return_m(x, \tau \circ \sigma), \\
&\qquad \text{if } A \text{ is neither a functional type nor an existential variable,} \\
&\qquad \text{and if } \tau \text{ is the MGU of } A \text{ and } B
\end{aligned}$$

If there is a function in the stoup, only →L rule applies, but because the proof tree branches at →L rules, we have to apply the substitution from one branch to the conclusion type of the other branch. Also note that we should compute the second premise first and then the first one, thus we can prune search failures earlier because the second premise often fails.

$$\llbracket \Gamma; f :: A \rightarrow B \vdash C \rrbracket = liftM_2(\lambda e_2 e_1.e_2[fe_1/y])\llbracket \Gamma; y :: B \vdash C \rrbracket\ (\lambda\sigma.\llbracket \Gamma; \vdash \sigma A \rrbracket \sigma)$$

Things become a little complicated if an existential type variable is in the stoup, because it can become functional and non-functional. In this case we try both cases and connect them with $\oplus$. Thus,

$$\begin{aligned}
\llbracket \Gamma; x :: a \vdash B \rrbracket \sigma = return_m(x, \tau \circ \sigma) \oplus \llbracket \Gamma; x :: b \rightarrow c \vdash B \rrbracket (\{a \mapsto b \rightarrow c\} \circ \sigma), \\
\text{if } a \in \mathcal{V} \text{ and } \tau \text{ is the MGU of } a \text{ and } B
\end{aligned}$$

where b and c are fresh existential type variables not appearing in Γ or B.

Finally, other two rules can be used without changes. Therefore,

$$\|\Gamma; \vdash B\| = \bigoplus_{(x::A)\in\Gamma} \|\Gamma; x :: A \vdash B\|, \text{ unless } B \text{ is a functional type;}$$

$$\|\Gamma; \vdash A \to B\| = \langle \lambda x. \rangle \|x :: A, \Gamma; \vdash B\|$$

where x does not appear in Γ.

3.7 Summary

The algorithm behind MagicHaskeller is described in a new proof theoretic way. The new description sheds a clearer light on the algorithm, and should make the algorithm easier to manipulate. In fact, the type system is extended from Hindley-Milner system to enable arbitrary-rank polymorphism, though we do not have empirical experience under higher-rank situations. Yet, we have not presented the structural rules for bundling the variables with the same type, which are useful for efficient implementation, especially in combination with memoization.

Our recent work on removing semantically equivalent expressions [Katayama(2008)] requires more complicated implementation, and we have not proved the exhaustiveness under such circumstances. We hope that further formalization will reinforce this line of research.

4 Quick Filtration of Semantically Equivalent Expressions in Program Search Results

4.1 Introduction

In [Katayama(2008)] we have proposed a Las Vegas algorithm for removing all the semantically equivalent programs except one by Monte-Carlo search within the program space, for the purposes of

- speeding up exhaustive search by bootstrapping,
- improving the readability of search results (like search engines such as Google which bundle "similar pages")
- providing guesses on how quickly the search space bloats

The results of applying the proposed filtration algorithm to MagicHaskeller were impressing – the algorithm's estimation of the number of functions with type $\forall\, a.\, [a] \to [a]$ which consist of nil, cons, and foldr, and is constructed with λ-abstractions and 10 or less function applications was below a hundred. Moreover, even when we used a set of tens of library functions as the primitive set, there were only hundreds of functions with type $\forall\, a.\, [a] \to [a]$, which is constructed with λ-abstractions and 7 or less function applications. Those interesting results suggest a new possibility of search-based non-heuristic inductive functional programming.

On the other hand, the filtration algorithm requires more computational cost than that is expected from the fewness of the final result, because it is dependent on execution of huge amount of expressions generated. Especially to our regret, if the set of programs to be filtered is not very redundant, i.e., if it does not include a lot of semantically equivalent expressions (e.g. when using the primitive set with only constructors and induction functions), program generation with such filtration costs more time than that without it. Hence we improve the efficiency of the filtration algorithm.

4.2 The Old Algorithm

Monte-Carlo algorithms are randomized algorithms whose final results may be inaccurate, while Las Vegas algorithms always yield the correct answers if they halt, though their computational costs are random and unknown before execution. It is often the case that a Monte-Carlo algorithm can be converted into a Las Vegas algorithm by repetition until the correct answer is obtained, especially when we can tell if the obtained result is correct or not.

Our algorithm presented in [Katayama(2008)] is based on a similar idea, though we cannot exactly decide if the obtained infinite stream exhaustively include semantically different expressions. Here is the rough sketch of the filtration algorithm presented in [Katayama(2008)]:

- let S_d the search result until depth d; define equivalence by a random point set r: $f \sim_r g \overset{def}{\Leftrightarrow} \forall p \in r. f(p) = g(p)$;
- generate a stream of random point sets $\{r_d\}_{d=0,1,\ldots}$;
- compute the quotient set $S_d \,/ \sim_{r_d}$ and the complete set of representatives; expressions without uniqueness proof will simply be dropped;
- use iterative deepening, and refine $\sim_{r_d}$ at each iteration by letting $r_d \subset r_{d+1}$; thanks to the deepening, dropped but distinct expression will resurrect.

The above algorithm requires at least nb times of executions when filtering n expressions for computing the depth b, because each expression has to be executed for b or more random points. Obviously this is inefficient and rather deteriorates the efficiency, because the number of expressions exponentially increases as the iteration goes deeper. For this reason, when applying this filter to subexpressions during program generation for efficiency, [Katayama(2008)] uses a more efficient filter which permits minor redundancy that uses only a small fixed number of random points per expression, and then apply the above inefficient but not redundancy-permitting filter to the final result. Its idea is that the set of expressions is already thinned up by the efficient filter when the inefficient filter is applied, and thus the usage of the inefficient filter is not the bottleneck any longer.

By using this two-staged filtration, the total computational cost using a rich primitive set have reduced from the original algorithm not using such filtration and the one using only the above inefficient filter. However, when using minimal primitive sets that consist of constructors and induction functions, the algorithm using the two-staged filtration is still slower than the original algorithm without filtration. In this research we seek more efficient filtration process.

4.3 The Improved Algorithm

We focus on improving the execution time of filtration (which includes that of the generated (sub)expressions) rather than that of program synthesis, because the time profiling reports show that most of the total computation time is comprised of that part. Two-staged filtration is dependent on iterative deepening, and when new expressions are generated, expressions at the shallower nodes in the search tree are re-executed with a different random point set as the argument, and re-categorized into new equivalence classes based on it, along with the newly generated expressions. The new improved algorithm omits the re-execution.

Given the set of expressions before filtration at depth d as x_d, the resulting set y_d of expressions at depth d after the first filtration of the two-staged filtration was

$$y_0 = pick(S_0 \ / \sim_{r_0})$$
$$y_d = pick((S_d \ / \sim_{r_d})\backslash_{\sim_{r_{d-1}}}(S_{d-1} \ / \sim_{r_{d-1}}))$$

where $pick$ is a function that collects representatives from equivalence classes, $\backslash_r$ is an operator for set subtraction by using the equivalence defined by the point set r, and $S_d = \bigcup_{i=0}^{d} x_i$.

The new algorithm computes y_d as

$$y_d = pick \left(\bigcup_{i=0}^{d}((x_{d-i} \ / \sim_{r_i})\backslash_{\sim_{r_i}}(S_{d-i-1} \ / \sim_{r_i})) \cup x_0 \ / \sim_{r_d}\right)$$

The ideas are:

- the computation of $S_d \ / \sim_{r_d}$ costs $|S_d||r_d|$ because r_d includes all the points in $r_i|_{i<d}$; thus we want to use r_0 instead of r_d for computing x_d;
- Because $r_i|_{i>0}$ is a refinement of r_0, representatives of $x_{d-i} \ / \sim_{r_0}|_{i>0}$ should fall into different equivalence classes of $x_{d-i} \ / \sim_{r_i}|_{i>0}$, and in order to avoid duplicates we subtract $S_{d-1} \ / \sim_{r_0}$.

Also, by starting with small number of random points, we can keep the random values small at first, by which we can expect edge and corner cases to be checked often.

4.4 Experimental Results

Table 10 shows some results on the *mnat* primitive set and the *reallyall* primitive set defined in Table 1. *mnat* consists only of 0, successor function, and addition and paramorphism for natural numbers. *reallyall* is rather a large primitive set consisting of 5 boolean operations, 12 instances of (in)equality predicates, and 24 list operations taken from the Standard Prelude. All the experiments are conducted using the same parameters as [Katayama(2008)] on Intel Pentium D 2.8.GHz machine running Linux 2.6.24.

The proposed filter requires less time for generating more programs than the old filter.

Table 10. Experimental results. (o.m. means out of memory, and ∞ means no result in an hour.)

	time (sec)	number of programs at each depth									
generating $Int \to Int$ from the *mnat* primitive set until depth 10.											
not filtered (redundant)	3.5	2	2	6	22	78	326	1506	7910	44806	283014
with old Filter 2	∞	2	2	3	4	12	27	62	146	448	N/A
with old Filter 1 + Filter 2	24	2	2	3	4	12	27	28	107	282	842
with the new filter	11	2	2	3	4	12	27	52	109	321	1009
generating $[Char] \to [Char]$ from the *reallyall* primitive set until depth 9.											
not filtered (redundant)	o.m.	2	5	42	225	1755	12228	98034	771730	N/A	
with old Filter 2	o.m.	2	1	3	13	21	113	299	1082	N/A	
with old Filter 1 + Filter 2	72	2	1	3	12	21	98	264	981	3692	
with the new filter	51	2	1	5	18	35	160	422	1611	6256	

4.5 Related Work

Evaluating semantical equivalence of syntactically different expressions by supplying random arguments is not a new idea. [Martin(1971)] discussed a method that guesses the equivalence of two algebraic expressions by evaluating them using finite field arithmetic.

Monte-Carlo search for program errors is called random testing in the field of software engineering, and forms a lively research field. Especially, QuickCheck [Claessen and Hughes(2000)] is an outstandingly famous random testing library for Haskell, and our filtration algorithm borrows their idea on how to generate functions randomly.

5 Conclusions

This paper introduced MagicHaskeller, our inductive functional programming library based on systematic search, and two recent improvements. The first one was proof theoretic re-interpretation of the algorithm behind MagicHaskeller, as an exhaustive algorithm for generating all the proofs of the given proposition under a variant of Herbelin's LJT. As a result of the first work, the algorithm has become clearer and easier to manipulate, and extended to the type system supporting arbitrary-rank polymorphism. The second improvement has been brought to efficiency of its filtration algorithm that removes redundancy in the search results.

Acknowledgements

This work was supported by JSPS KAKENHI 21650032.

References

[Claessen and Hughes(2000)] Claessen, K., Hughes, J.: QuickCheck: a lightweight tool for random testing of Haskell programs. In: ICFP 2000: Proceedings of the 5th ACM SIGPLAN International Conference on Functional Programming, pp. 268–279. ACM, New York (2000)

[Dyckhoff(1992)] Dyckhoff, R.: Contraction-free sequent calculi for intuitionistic logic. Journal of Symbolic Logic 57, 795–807 (1992)

[Herbelin(1995)] Herbelin, H.: A lambda-calculus structure isomorphic to Gentzen-style sequent calculus structure. In: Pacholski, L., Tiuryn, J. (eds.) CSL 1994. LNCS, vol. 933, pp. 61–75. Springer, Heidelberg (1995)

[Hofmann et al.(2009)Hofmann, Kitzelmann, and Schmid] Hofmann, M., Kitzelmann, E., Schmid, U.: A unifying framework for analysis and evaluation of inductive programming systems. In: Proceedings of the Second Conference on Artificial General Intelligence (2009)

[Hudelmaier(1992)] Hudelmaier, J.: Bounds on cut-elimination in intuitionistic propositional logic. Archive for Mathematical Logic 31, 331–354 (1992)

[Katayama(2006)] Katayama, S.: Library for systematic search for expressions and its efficiency evaluation. WSEAS Transactions on Computers 12(5), 3146–3153 (2006)

[Katayama(2005a)] Katayama, S.: Systematic search for lambda expressions. In: Sixth Symposium on Trends in Functional Programming, pp. 195–205 (2005)

[Katayama(2008)] Katayama, S.: Efficient exhaustive generation of functional programs using monte-carlo search with iterative deepening. In: Ho, T.-B., Zhou, Z.-H. (eds.) PRICAI 2008. LNCS (LNAI), vol. 5351, pp. 199–210. Springer, Heidelberg (2008)

[Katayama(2005b)] Katayama, S.: MagicHaskeller (2005b), `http://nautilus.cs.miyazaki-u.ac.jp/~skata/MagicHaskeller.html`

[Katayama(2007)] Katayama, S.: Systematic search for lambda expressions. In: Trends in Functional Programming, vol. 6, pp. 111–126, Intellect (2007)

[Kiselyov(2005)] Kiselyov, O.: Reversing haskell typechecker: converting from undefined to defined (2005), `http://okmij.org/ftp/Haskell/types.html#de-typechecker`

[Kitzelmann(2007)] Kitzelmann, E.: Data-driven induction of recursive functions from input/output-examples. In: AAIP 2007: Proceedings of the Workshop on Approaches and Applications of Inductive Programming, pp. 15–26 (2007)

[Liang et al.(1995)Liang, Hudak, and Jones] Liang, S., Hudak, P., Jones, M.P.: Monad transformers and modular interpreters. In: POPL 1995: 22nd ACM SIGPLAN-SIGACT Symposium on Principles of Programming Languages (1995)

[Martin(1971)] Martin, W.A.: Determining the equivalence of algebraic expressions by hash coding. Journal of the Association for Computing Machinery 18(4), 549–558 (1971)

[Olsson(1995)] Olsson, R.: Inductive functional programming using incremental program transformation. Artificial Intelligence 74(1), 55–81 (1995)

[Spivey(2000)] Spivey, M.: Combinators for breadth-first search. Journal of Functional Programming 10(4), 397–408 (2000)

[Spivey(2006)] Spivey, M.: Algebras for combinatorial search. In: Workshop on Mathematically Structured Functional Programming (2006)

[illegible] (20[illegible]) [illegible] [illegible] (20[illegible])

[illegible] (20[illegible]) [illegible] [illegible] [illegible] [illegible] [illegible] (20[illegible])

[illegible] (20[illegible]) [illegible] [illegible] (20[illegible])

[illegible] [illegible] [illegible]

Author Index